Lecture Notes of the Institute for Computer Sciences, Social Informatics and Telecommunications Engineering 298

More information about this series at http://www.springer.com/series/8197

Phan Cong Vinh · Abdur Rakib (Eds.)

Context-Aware Systems and Applications, and Nature of Computation and Communication

8th EAI International Conference, ICCASA 2019
and 5th EAI International Conference, ICTCC 2019
My Tho City, Vietnam, November 28–29, 2019
Proceedings

 Springer

Editors
Phan Cong Vinh 🆔
Nguyen Tat Thanh University
Ho Chi Minh City, Vietnam

Abdur Rakib 🆔
The University of the West of England
Bristol, UK

ISSN 1867-8211   ISSN 1867-822X   (electronic)
Lecture Notes of the Institute for Computer Sciences, Social Informatics
and Telecommunications Engineering
ISBN 978-3-030-34364-4   ISBN 978-3-030-34365-1   (eBook)
https://doi.org/10.1007/978-3-030-34365-1

This Springer imprint is published by the registered company Springer Nature Switzerland AG
The registered company address is: Gewerbestrasse 11, 6330 Cham, Switzerland

Preface

The 8th EAI International Conference on Context-Aware Systems and Applications (ICCASA 2019) and the 5th EAI International Conference on Nature of Computation and Communication (ICTCC 2019) are international scientific events for research in the field of smart computing and communication. These two conferences were jointly held during November 28–29, 2019, in My Tho City, Vietnam. The aim, for both conferences, is to provide an internationally respected forum for scientific research in the technologies and applications of smart computing and communication. These conferences provide an excellent opportunity for researchers to discuss modern approaches and techniques for smart computing systems and their applications. The proceedings of ICCASA 2019 and ICTCC 2019 are published by Springer in the *Lecture Notes of the Institute for Computer Sciences, Social Informatics and Telecommunications Engineering* series (LNICST; indexed by DBLP, EI, Google Scholar, Scopus, Thomson ISI).

For this eighth edition of ICCASA and fifth edition of ICTCC, repeating the success of the previous years, the Program Committee received submissions from 12 countries and each paper was reviewed by at least three expert reviewers. We chose 20 papers after intensive discussions held among the Program Committee members. We appreciate the excellent reviews and lively discussions of the Program Committee members and external reviewers in the review process. This year we had three prominent invited speakers, Prof. Herwig Unger from Fern Universität in Hagen, Germany, Prof. Phayung Meesad from King Mongkut's University of Technology North Bangkok (KMUTNB) in Thailand, and Prof. Waralak V. Siricharoen from Silpakorn University in Thailand.

ICCASA 2019 and ICTCC 2019 were jointly organized by The European Alliance for Innovation (EAI), Tien Giang University (TGU), and Nguyen Tat Thanh University (NTTU). These conferences could not have been organized without the strong support of the staff members of these three organizations. We would especially like to thank Prof. Imrich Chlamtac (University of Trento), Lukas Skolek (EAI), and Martin Karbovanec (EAI) for their great help in organizing the conferences. We also appreciate the gentle guidance and help from Prof. Nguyen Manh Hung, Chairman and Rector of NTTU, and Prof. Vo Ngoc Ha, Rector of TGU.

November 2019

Phan Cong Vinh
Abdur Rakib

Organization

Steering Committee

Imrich Chlamtac (Chair)	University of Trento, Italy
Phan Cong Vinh	Nguyen Tat Thanh University, Vietnam
Thanos Vasilakos	Kuwait University, Kuwait

Organizing Committee

Honorary General Chairs

Vo Ngoc Ha	Tien Giang University, Vietnam
Nguyen Manh Hung	Nguyen Tat Thanh University, Vietnam

General Chair

Phan Cong Vinh	Nguyen Tat Thanh University, Vietnam

Program Chairs

Abdur Rakib	The University of the West of England, UK
Vangalur Alagar	Concordia University, Canada

Publications Chair

Phan Cong Vinh	Nguyen Tat Thanh University, Vietnam

Publicity and Social Media Chair

Cao Nguyen Thi	Tien Giang University, Vietnam

Workshop Chair

Nguyen Ngoc Long	Tien Giang University, Vietnam

Sponsorship and Exhibits Chair

Bach Long Giang	Nguyen Tat Thanh University, Vietnam

Local Chair

Duong Van Hieu	Tien Giang University, Vietnam

Web Chair

Do Nguyen Anh Thu	Nguyen Tat Thanh University, Vietnam

Technical Program Committee

Chernyi Sergei	Admiral Makarov State University of Maritime and Inland Shipping, Russia
Chien-Chih Yu	National ChengChi University, Taiwan
David Sundaram	The University of Auckland, New Zealand
Duong Van Hieu	Tien Giang University, Vietnam
François Siewe	De Montfort University, UK
Gabrielle Peko	The University of Auckland, New Zealand
Giacomo Cabri	University of Modena and Reggio Emilia, Italy
Hafiz Mahfooz Ul Haque	University of Lahore, Pakistan
Huynh Trung Hieu	Industrial University of Ho Chi Minh City, Vietnam
Huynh Xuan Hiep	Can Tho University, Vietnam
Ijaz Uddin	The University of Nottingham, UK
Iqbal Sarker	Swinburne University of Technology, Australia
Issam Damaj	The American University of Kuwait, Kuwait
Krishna Asawa	Jaypee Institute of Information Technology, India
Kurt Geihs	University of Kassel, Germany
Le Hong Anh	University of Mining and Geology, Vietnam
Le Nguyen Quoc Khanh	Nanyang Technological University, Singapore
Manisha Chawla	Google, India
Muhammad Athar Javed Sethi	University of Engineering and Technology (UET) Peshawar, Pakistan
Nguyen Duc Cuong	Ho Chi Minh City University of Foreign Languages – Information Technology, Vietnam
Nguyen Hoang Thuan	Can Tho University of Technology, Vietnam
Nguyen Manh Duc	University of Ulsan, South Korea
Nguyen Thanh Binh	Ho Chi Minh City University of Technology, Vietnam
Ondrej Krejcar	University of Hradec Kralove, Czech Republic
Pham Quoc Cuong	Ho Chi Minh City University of Technology, Vietnam
Prashant Vats	Fairfield Institute of Management & Technology in Delhi, India
Rana Mukherji	The ICFAI University Jaipur, India
Tran Huu Tam	University of Kassel, Germany
Tran Vinh Phuoc	Ho Chi Minh City Open University, Vietnam
Vijayakumar Ponnusamy	SRM IST, India
Waralak V. Siricharoen	Silpakorn University, Thailand
Zhu Huibiao	East China Normal University, China

Contents

ICCASA 2019

Declarative Approach to Model Checking for Context-Aware Applications

Ammar Alsaig[✉], Vangalur Alagar, and Nematollaah Shiri

Concordia University, Montreal, QC, Canada
{A_alsaig,alagar,shiri}@encs.concordia.ca

Abstract. Systems need to be formally verified to ensure that their claimed properties hold at all times of system operation. Deterministic Finite State Machines (FSM) are widely used as model checkers to verify system properties. However, for context-aware systems that have regular inputs and contextual inputs, FSM models become more complex and less intuitive, and do not precisely represent the system behavior. In this paper we use simple examples to introduce the declarative reasoning framework *Contelog* , a theoretically and practically well grounded work in progress, as a complementary approach that can be used to represent, reason, verify data-centric and contextual properties of context-aware systems.

Keywords: Formal verification · Context-aware modeling · Model checking · Context-based knowledge base systems

1 Background

As technologies progress, their dependence on pervasive, ubiquitous, and Knowledge base system features is increasing in order to meet application demands in different fields. In many of these application domains safety-criticality plays a crucial role in decision making. Some examples are (1) rule-based medical diagnosis systems [8,10], (2) rule-based access control [7] systems to enforce security/privacy, and (3) rule-based expert systems [6] for prediction. Due to this criticality, formal verification is necessary on the modeled system to ensure that safety, security, and privacy properties hold at all times throughout the operation of the system. One method of formal verification is through model checking [9]. Many model checkers that are available for hardware/software checking are also being used to model check context-aware system properties. However, it is pointed out [13] that traditional checking models are insufficient, inefficient, and non-intuitive for verifying properties of context-aware systems. The dynamism, and the rapid change of the behaviour of context-aware systems make them prone to adaptation-faults and unexpected behaviours [12]. This makes context-aware verification a challenging process. It is in this context that we propose *Contelog* reasoner for model checking context-aware systems.

© ICST Institute for Computer Sciences, Social Informatics and Telecommunications Engineering 2019
Published by Springer Nature Switzerland AG 2019. All Rights Reserved
P. C. Vinh and A. Rakib (Eds.): ICCASA 2019/ICTCC 2019, LNICST 298, pp. 3–10, 2019.
https://doi.org/10.1007/978-3-030-34365-1_1

Example in Fig. 1 is to motivate where and how contexts arise and how they can be brought into FSM modeling. The illustrated scenario is that of entry to an emergency room in a hospital. Based on access control model, both patients and doctors are authenticated to enter the room. Whereas a doctor is allowed to enter using the authorized barcode at any time, patients and other staff are allowed to access the room only at specific time periods using their authorized barcodes. Because there might exist many emergency rooms, a person may require to use the same or different bar code to enter many rooms subject to time constraints for entry, the pairs "⟨ times, emergency room locations ⟩" become the set of contexts at which barcode authentication should be certified for valid entry. Because any combination logic can be represented as a deterministic Finite State Machine (FSM) [16], the above example can be represented as an FSM as shown in Fig. 2. However, the FSM representation in Fig. 2B in complicated scenarios becomes complicated and non-intuitive. This is because it is less descriptive as it reduces most of the details to context. Although there is a rich volume of literature [4,14] dedicated to increasing the expressiveness of FSMs, their representation, understandability, and verification become more challenging when a variety of contexts, that are multi-dimensional objects, need to be represented. As observed in [11,12], standard FSM can have states, input, and outputs, but adding context can only be in terms of inputs which does not represent the actual conceptual relevance of context to the system. Thus, we are motivated to introduce our framework *Contelog* to model context-aware systems. *Contelog* is a Datalog program [1] in which context is integrated as a first class citizen in order to enable contextual reasoning. The declarative semantics of *Contelog* can prove theoretically that certain property holds for the entire world of inputs and contexts embedded in it.

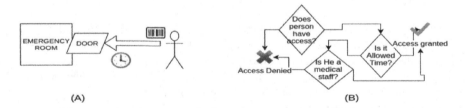

Fig. 1. Illustration (A) gives general overview of the example, illustration (B) gives the scenario in if-statement diagram

1.1 Outline

In Sect. 2 we briefly introduce the theoretical foundation of *Contelog* . In Sect. 3 we discuss the reasoning tool and comment on the Book of Examples [2] that we have implemented using the reasoning tool. In Sect. 4 we describe *Contelog* programs for the Microwave Example, the most often cited first example in model checking, and the access control example Fig. 2. We conclude the paper in Sect. 5 with a brief description of our work in progress.

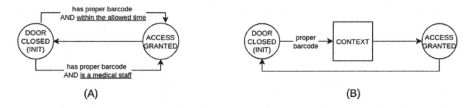

Fig. 2. Illustration (A) represents Fig. 1 in FSM (B) provides an equivalent diagram using context

2   Formalization of Context, and *Contelog*

In this section we briefly summarize our results on context formalization [3] and the work completed so far on *Contelog* creation. Context is a multi-disciplinary concept that has diverse conceptualizations. However, it has been commonly perceived as the "settings of a system" and "a surrounding environment" [5,15]. Our context theory is conceptualized in three layers, in order to allow maximum flexibility for system designers to choose meaningful contexts and at the same time provide sufficient formalism for building a context calculus on which contexts can be manipulated at system level. The layers are respectively Context Schema(CS) layer, Typed Context Schema(TCS) layer, and Context Instances(CI) layer. Contexts are viewed as multi-dimensional objects where a dimension represent a type of the settings being described, and attributes associated with each dimension give the detailed description for a particular dimension.

Definition 1. *Let D be a finite, non-empty set of dimensions, A be a set of attributes, and V^T is a set of values of type T. A context Schema $\mathscr{C}$ is a set of pairs defined as follows:*

$$CS = \mathscr{C} = \{< d, A_d > \mid d \in D \wedge A_d \subseteq A\}$$

$$TCS = \mathscr{C}^T = \{< d, A_d > \mid d \in D \wedge A_d \subseteq A^T\}$$

$$CI = I_i(\mathscr{C}^T) = \{< d, V_d > \mid d \in D \wedge V_d \subseteq V^T\} \quad \blacksquare$$

As described in [3], context operations are Join ($\oplus$) and Meet ($\odot$). The definitions of operations on context schemas lead to a closed lattice structure, thus making our context calculus a complete universe. Datalog also considers closed world under Herbrand structures. Consequently, when we integrate it with the declarative semantics of Datalog we achieve "closed world assumption" for context reasoning. Thus, *Contelog* is a logic-based framework that uses "context" as a first class citizen, extends Datalog's syntax and semantics to reason with contextual knowledge in a declarative fashion. *Contelog* syntax is formally presented as follows:

Definition 2. *A Contelog program P ($\mathscr{C}$-program) is a four-tuple $\langle T, S_{\mathscr{C}^*},$ $F, R \rangle$ whose components are defined as follows:*

1. T is the set of truth values $\{True, False\}$
2. $S_{\mathscr{C}*}$ is a set of instantiated contexts partially ordered by $\sqsubseteq$. We assume that $< S_{\mathscr{C}*}, \sqsubseteq, \oplus, \odot >$ is a complete lattice. The least upper bound is denoted by $C_\top$, and the greatest lower bound by $C_\perp$.
3. F is a finite set of annotated ground atoms, each of which is in the form q@c, where q is a ground atom, and c is a context name in $S_{\mathscr{C}*}$.
4. R is a finite set of rules, each of which is in the form:

$$r : \quad H : - B_1, B_2, \ldots, B_n$$

where $H, B_1, \ldots, B_n$ are annotated atoms. Standard datalog predicates may be annotated with context C where C is a context variable, e.g., $q(\bar{X})@C$.

As in datalog, we use uppercase letters for variables and lower case letters for constants in the universe. As is customary in database and logic programming frameworks, we restrict the semantics of ($\mathscr{C}$-program) to Herbrand structures. We have developed the declarative semantics for ($\mathscr{C}$-program) P to be the least model of P, defined by the intersection of all the Herbrand models of P. We also developed a bottom-up, fixpoint semantics of ($\mathscr{C}$-program) and show that the fixpoint model of any ($\mathscr{C}$-program) P coincides with the least model of P. We have built a running prototype of the Contelog framework which computes the fixpoint semantics of ($\mathscr{C}$-program) . The prototype system has been tested with a number of examples and is available for evaluation at the link [2].

3   *Contelog* System

Contelog system is a tool that implements both context calculus and *Contelog* reasoner. This prototype tool is a playground for *Contelog* programs to be able to implement simple and small-sized *Contelog* programs. The system can be accessed online through this link [2]. The system allows input in two modes. These are respectively context and code input modes. The rationale is to allow context calculus to be tried independently from executing a *Contelog* program. In context input mode, context representation, as formalized by us, should be used. The user interface guides the user to input syntactically correct input with correct typed values. In code input mode the syntax of *Contelog* is used to guide the user to create the program. The syntax checker will ensure that only those contexts that have already been constructed are used in the program rules. This is to avoid any inconsistency in reasoning. The reasoning is currently operating using the naive reasoning method. The complexity is polynomial, as for Datalog programs, yet it is an exhaustive approach and not efficient for large-sized applications. The current running version is just a proof of concept, just to demonstrate the different kinds of examples that we have implemented, and give users a forum to use the system and give us feedback.

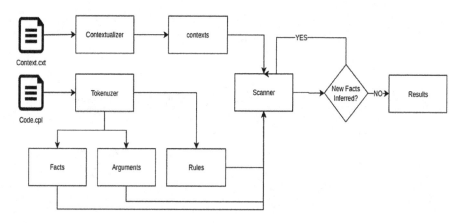

Fig. 3. *Contelog* structure

4 Reasoning with *Contelog* : Access Control and Microwave Examples

We claim that a FSM for context-aware systems can be represented using *Contelog* in three steps. In Step 1, each non-contextual input/edge is represented as a ground predicate (fact) in *Contelog* . For instance, the barcode input in Fig. 1 is represented as *input(barcode)* in *Contelog* . In Step 2, each contextual input or any input that is dynamic in nature is represented as context using our notation. For instance, staff context is represented as $C_{staff} = \{time\_constraint : [none], type : [staff]\}$, where *time_constraint* and *type* are dimensions. Each state is represented as a rule, while the edge (condition) to move from one state to another is represented in the rule body. For instance, to represent the event of moving from "init state" to "open state" we write *state*(open-door)@C : -*input*(barcode), *type*(staff)@C. Finally, the initial state is given as a ground fact. Following this transformation rule we get the two contexts $\mathscr{C}_s = \{time : [no], type : [staff]\}$, and patient context $\mathscr{C}_p = \{time : [yes], type : [patient]\}$ for medical staff and patient categories. Inputs, states, and events are represented in terms of facts and rules. The resulting *Contelog* program and its execution in our *Contelog* system are shown below:

Contelog representation for the motivating example

```
1  input(1,barcode)@cs.
2  input(2,barcode)@cp.
3  state(X,open)@C:-input(X,Z)@C,time(no)@C,type(staff)@C.
4  state(X,open)@C:-input(X,Z)@C,time(yes)@C.
5  state(X,closed)@C:-state(X,open)@C.
6  ***** RESULTS *****
7  {input(1,barcode)@cs, input(2,barcode)@cp, **state(1,open)@cs,
8  **state(2,open)@cp, **state(1,closed)@cs, **state(2,closed)@cp.}
```

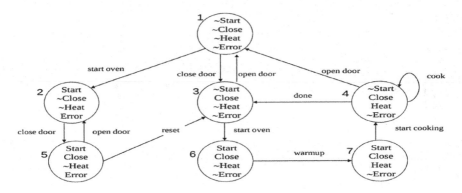

Fig. 4. *Contelog* structure

In the commonly known Microwave example contexts are used to model "from-to relationship" between states in the FSM shown in Fig. 4. Inputs are regular facts, while first state is the initial state. The program recursively fires the rules and generates all output, given the correct set of input. If system is not given the input "startoven" it will not generate any of the other answers as they are all chained together through contexts. The *Contelog* representation for Microwave example is shown below. In order to verify a feature or a property such as "heat does not start with door opened", a query like $features(heat)@c1*c2*c3$ can be used. The idea is to identify all contexts where door is open and use it in the query. Basically, can heat feature be present in all three contexts at the same time? If the answer to the query is an empty set (no answer) then heat is not present in all the three contexts at the same time, which means that heat while door is closed is satisfied.

Contelog representation for the Microwave example

```
1   Note: context 4, 41, 42 are edges coming out of the same state.
2   ## CONTEXT ##
3   c1={'to':['startoven','c2'],
4       'features':['~start','~close','~heat','~error']}
5   c2={'to':['closedoor','c5']},
6       'features':['start','~close','~heat','error']}
7   c5={'to':['opendoor','c2']},
8       'features':['start','close','~heat','error']}
9   c51={'from':['c5'],'to':['reset','c3']},
10      'features':['start','close','~heat','error']}
11  c3={'to':['startoven','c6']},
12      'features':['~start','close','~heat','~error']}
13  c31={'from':['c3'],'to':['opendoor','c1']},
14      'features':['~start','close','~heat','~error']}
15  c6={'to':['warmup','c7']},
16      'features':['start','close','~heat','~error']}
17  c7={'to':['startcooking','c4']},
18      'features':['start','close','heat','~error']}
19  c4={'to':['cook','c4']},
20      'features':['~start','close','heat','~error']}
21  c41={'from':['c4'],'to':['done','c3']},
22      'features':['~start','close','heat','~error']}
23  c42={'from':['c4'],'to':['opendoor','c1']},
24      'features':['~start','close','heat','~error']}
```

```
25  ## CODE ##
26  input(startoven).
27  input(closedoor).
28  input(opendoor).
29  input(reset).
30  input(warmup).
31  input(startcooking).
32  input(done).
33  input(cook).
34  state(1)@c1.
35  state(X)@C:−state(X)@W,input(M),to(M,C)@W.
36  state(X)@C:−state(X)@W,from(W)@C.
37  ### RESULTS ###
38  { input(startoven), input(closedoor), input(opendoor), input(reset),
39  input(warmup),input(startcooking),input(done),input(cook),state(1)@c1,
40  **state(1)@c2,**state(1)@c5,**state(1)@c51,**state(1)@c3,**state(1)@c6,
41  **state(1)@c31,**state(1)@c7,**state(1)@c4,**state(1)@c41,**state(1)@c42 }
```

5 Conclusion

In this paper we have proposed *Contelog* as an approach to model check context-aware system properties through examples. Our study on *Contelog* was originally motivated from the need to provide a formal framework for representing and reasoning about contextual knowledge. With that goal we have completed a context formalism, *Contelog* semantics, and constructed a prototype implementation as a proof concept of what we have achieved. We believe that our approach needs to be fine-tuned with query optimization techniques to deal with the reasoning of large context-aware systems. We are undertaking a deeper study of model checking methods, especially for protocol and contract specifications, investigate how contextual reasoning may be necessary in ubiquitous applications, and find ways to improve our current approach to handle such larger real life practical problems.

References

1. Abiteboul, S., Hull, R., Vianu, V.: Foundations of Databases: the Logical Level. Addison-Wesley, Boston (1995)
2. Alsaig, A.: Book of examples: a prototype environment for reasoning with contexts (2017). http://www.contelog.com
3. Alsaig, A., Alagar, V., Shiri, N.: Formal context representation and calculus for context-aware computing. In: Cong Vinh, P., Alagar, V. (eds.) ICCASA/ICTCC -2018. LNICST, vol. 266, pp. 3–13. Springer, Cham (2019). https://doi.org/10.1007/978-3-030-06152-4_1
4. Bresolin, D., El-Fakih, K., Villa, T., Yevtushenko, N.: Deterministic timed finite state machines: equivalence checking and expressive power. arXiv preprint arXiv:1408.5967 (2014)
5. Brézillon, P.: Context in problem solving: a survey. Knowl. Eng. Rev. **14**(1), 47–80 (1999)
6. Buchanan, B.G., Shortliffe, E.H., et al.: Rule-Based Expert Systems, vol. 3. Addison Wesley, Reading (1984)

7. Carminati, B., Ferrari, E., Perego, A.: Rule-based access control for social networks. In: Meersman, R., Tari, Z., Herrero, P. (eds.) OTM 2006. LNCS, vol. 4278, pp. 1734–1744. Springer, Heidelberg (2006). https://doi.org/10.1007/11915072_80

8. Clancey, W.J.: The epistemology of a rule-based expert system–a framework for explanation. Artif. Intell. **20**(3), 215–251 (1983)

9. Clarke, E.M., Henzinger, T.A., Veith, H., Bloem, R.: Handbook of Model Checking. Springer, Heidelberg (2018)

10. Lamperti, G., Zanella, M.: Rule-Based Diagnosis, pp. 193–233. Springer, Dordrecht (2003)

11. Le, H.A.: Formal modeling and verification of context-aware systems using event-b. EAI Endorsed Trans. Context-Aware Syst. Appl. **1**, e4 (2014). https://doi.org/10.4108/casa.1.2.e4

12. Liu, Y., Xu, C., Cheung, S.: Afchecker: effective model checking for context-aware adaptive applications. J. Syst. Soft. **86**(3), 854–867 (2013)

13. Schmidtke, H.R., Woo, W.: Towards ontology-based formal verification methods for context aware systems. In: Tokuda, H., Beigl, M., Friday, A., Brush, A.J.B., Tobe, Y. (eds.) Pervasive 2009. LNCS, vol. 5538, pp. 309–326. Springer, Heidelberg (2009). https://doi.org/10.1007/978-3-642-01516-8_21

14. Skelin, M., Wognsen, E.R., Olesen, M.C., Hansen, R.R., Larsen, K.G.: Model checking of finite-state machine-based scenario-aware dataflow using timed automata. In: 10th IEEE International Symposium on Industrial Embedded Systems (SIES), pp. 1–10. IEEE (2015)

15. Strang, T., Linnhoff-Popien, C.: A context modeling survey. In: Workshop Proceedings (2004)

16. Wagner, F., Schmuki, R., Wagner, T., Wolstenholme, P.: Modeling Software with Finite State Machines: A Practical Approach. Auerbach Publications (2006)

Planquarium: A Context-Aware Rule-Based Indoor Kitchen Garden

Rahat Khan[1], Altaf Uddin[2], Ijaz Uddin[3(✉)], Rashid Naseem[3], and Arshad Ahmad[4]

[1] UET, Peshawar, Pakistan
[2] AWKUM, Mardan, Pakistan
[3] City University of Science and Information Technology, Peshawar, Pakistan
ijazktk@gmail.com
[4] University of Sawabi, Anbar, Sawabi, Pakistan

Abstract. Planquarium is a context-aware indoor kitchen garden system, where a user can grow fresh plants and vegetables without prior knowledge. Further, the Planquarium will take care of the plants that are inside it using a Rule-Based Context-Aware environment, that is capable to monitor different aspects of the plant and can provide an ideal environment for the plant inside. Different plants have different requirements therefore, we have integrated profiling systems so that a person can select a plant and the Planquarium will adjust itself accordingly. Initially, we have deployed temperature, humidity, moisture, water and light(Artificial sunlight full spectrum) sensors to monitor the plants. In the future, we can further add soil quality monitors to optimum growth. Planquarium is suitable for congested smart cities, smart homes and for people who care for organic food.

Keywords: Context-aware · Rule-base · Indoor kitchen garden

1 Introduction

Context-aware systems are based on the notion that a device is capable to perceive its environment and then react to the changes. These changes can be in different form e.g, reaction to emergency scenario [1] or collection of a different scenario to provide an assisted living for elder people [2]. The context-aware systems are widely used in smart cities, where different devices are connected with each other and provides a smart space for a user in different locations and scenarios. In smart cities, all included domains are supposed to be smart e.g., hospital, office and market to name some. Where a user is assisted in his daily life with the help of technology. Smart homes are emerging from concept towards implementation where the lights, electronic equipments are connected with a user and act on behalf of a user according to some rules specified by the user or on a self-learning technology. Rules are favourable in the case where

© ICST Institute for Computer Sciences, Social Informatics and Telecommunications Engineering 2019
Published by Springer Nature Switzerland AG 2019. All Rights Reserved
P. C. Vinh and A. Rakib (Eds.): ICCASA 2019/ICTCC 2019, LNICST 298, pp. 11–19, 2019.
https://doi.org/10.1007/978-3-030-34365-1_2

expert knowledge is required to be encoded into a computer system. A minute amount of knowledge can be represented in a single rule, and the collection of such rule is called a knowledge base. In the context of smart cities and smart homes, one ignored domain is smart gardening, considering the limitation of land in congested cities, people are living in technologically equipped small and smart homes. This paper addresses the issue of planting plants and vegetables in a controlled context-aware rule-based device, which will not be able to grow without sunlight and outdoor environment otherwise. Planquarium, on one hand, will provide fresh vegetables to a user without any expert knowledge, while it will also provide fresh and clean air to a user by recycling the indoor air and produce Oxygen. Initially, this concept will be implemented on a small scale with few and essential sensors attached to check the quality of vegetables grown inside. Further, it can be used to grow more plants or fruits, with soil checking capability to fully automate the system. This paper is distributed as follow Sect. 2 provides the motivation which drive us to carry out this research work. Section 3 define the preliminaries in detail from very basic. Related work is discussed in Sect. 4 followed by our proposed model. Section 5 is about the conclusion and future work.

2   Motivation and Preliminaries

The motivation for this paper comes from the technologically complex world of smart cities and connected technologies where the aspect of natural living is demising slowly. The concept of green living is kept in mind in this research work. In smart cities, we have observed the technology has overcome different life aspect, for example, smart laundry management system in congested buildings, smart parking systems, smart environment, smart elder care but unfortunately, when we think of smart gardening we find that the existing systems are not automated as discussed in the Section Related Work. This motivates us to develop a conceptual model and a prototype to assist the user in promoting indoor gardening for keeping the air clean and have fresh vegetables. With the help of having a smart indoor garden, the concept of a smart home will be completed. In order to make it perceive its environment, the system has to be designed on the paradigm of context-aware systems, where the context will monitored using sensors. When enough is gathered, it is understood that the context will be processed by some mechanism and must produce some output or deduce some output. The output can be in terms of controlling sensor e.g., temperature adjustment or deducting new context. The deduction or the reasoning capacity is generated using a rule-engine. A rule engine will have set of rules and it will match the context in terms of facts with the rules and if a rule match is found it will process it accordingly. In order to completely understand the rule-engine working mechanism in context of context-aware system, the following study is recommended [3].

3   Related Work

In this section, we discuss the latest technology that is related to smart gardening. We tried to study the latest literature to find out the latest trends in indoor smart gardening. The article [4] discusses smart gardening with IoT perspective. However, the paper has not discussed any technical infrastructure. The author has connected all the sensors in a manner so that it can send the sensor values to the user and the user has to take some action. By implementing such a system the automation is not achieved as it is merely sending the details to the application that a user should have, and then the user has to decide the matter. The concept of smart technology is not purely implemented. In article [5] shares our argument that lack of space for gardening and apartment lifestyle have an impact on indoor gardening techniques. The system although looks quite mature in terms of technology but still it lacks the context-awareness and no such technique is there to automate the growth of the plant. In this system, sensors are attached near the plant to measure different aspects such as temperature, humidity and soil moisture to name some. This data is then sent to the user mobile application which can then make changes accordingly. In both [4,5] the problem is that if the user does not check the data on time or ignore it for a while, it can be damaging for the plant. Some automation can be seen in the research work [6]. In this system, the base on the soil moisture the watering of soil is carried out. It can check if the soil is under moisture or overmoisture and then it can start or stop watering of the soil. The system is mainly used for the garden purpose and does not entertain many sensors, instead, it only has light and moisture sensor. The same concept is discussed in the [7], for terrace gardening. It also has the only temperature and moisture sensor installed. Apart from these, there are commercially available indoor gardens (*CLICK and GROW, OGarden Smart, TreGren, Postscapes* which also claim to be fully automatic, however, there is no research work behind these models to support their claims. After the study of recent literature work and to the best of our knowledge, there is no such system available which is fully automatic, context-aware and is rule-based that can make the indoor gardening a really automatic without user intervention at all in terms of maintaining the environment.

4   Proposed Model

In this section, we define in detail the working mechanism of the Planquarium, its different components and how profiling can be used effectively. In this paper, we are combing the power or RBS with the CA computing paradigm. By fusing both, we can actually make a system that can act like a human expert. The CA system will provide context relative to a plant in a raw form, which will be transformed into a high-level context and made ready to be processed by the RBS as a fact. The context related to a plant can be temperature around the plant, humidity, light, moisture, water level to name some. These contexts can be utilized by the RBS to provide an ideal plant growing environment indoor.

4.1   Physical Properties and Sensors Used

The modal is made of transparent box shape which contains the plant and soil. Different sensors are attached for monitoring the plant. A water tank is externally attached to the box, which contains water. The water tank is used to water the plant whenever required. Another external device is the regulator, which is the brain of the whole system and programmed in a way to perform the reasoning on the available context and accordingly regulate the plant environment. The sensors and controller used are briefly defined in the next section.

Arduino Uno. It is an open-source, Microchip ATmega328P microcontroller based microcontroller board. Arduino Uno and its variants are developed by Arduino.cc. It has both digital (14 pins) and analogue (6 pins) I/O pins, which can be connected with different sensors and shield or even boards. The programming is carried out in Arduino IDE and uses type B USB cable for connectivity. It can be powered with a USB cable or a 9-V adapter. Arduino Uno can accommodate a variety of sensors, but we will discuss sensors which are relevant to our research work.

Water Level Sensor. The water level sensor (ICSG001A)[1] indicates the level of liquid. It can be deployed in the water tank which is attached externally to the plant box. This will monitor the water level and inform the user in case the water level drop beyond a certain threshold. The sensor is shown in the Fig. 1. It needs an initial calibration to fetch values, after which it can detect values from the container and programmed accordingly.

Fig. 1. Water level sensor

---

[1] https://www.instructables.com/id/How-to-use-a-Water-Level-Sensor-Arduino-Tutorial/.

Humidity Sensor

Humidity and Temperature Sensor. The humidity and temperature sensors (DHT11 or DHT22) are available as a single unit which can be connected to the Arduino board to get values. The sensor DHT11 and DHT22 both have the same function but with more reliable results with DHT22. Both are considered sluggish as it cannot provide data more than once a second. The image of the sensor is provided in Fig. 2.

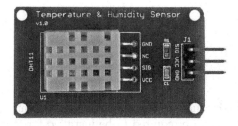

Fig. 2. Temperature and humidity sensor

Moisture Sensor. Moisture sensor (SEN-13322) is installed in the soil to detect and regulate the moisture level of the soil. The sensor must be installed near the roots for optimum results. The image sensor is provided in Fig. 3. Since all of these sensors can check on most of the vital requirements of the plant which needs to be controlled for better growth of the plant. The most important factor for the growth of any plant is sunlight. The natural sunlight has its own properties for plant growth. However, since the proposed model is based on the concept of an indoor kitchen garden, it is always possible that the natural light may not be available. Therefore, artificial sunlight has to be maintained in order to make the system a complete working prototype. The artificial sung-light is discussed in the next section.

4.2 Artificial Sunlight

Sunlight is a universal and balanced source of wavelengths necessary for plant growth. However, artificial light can also provide the necessary light requirements. Depending upon the nature of plants, different light wavelengths are necessary e.g., according to the author [8] Foliage growth requires blue wavelength light. Flowering and fruiting plants require red wavelength light. The green wavelength lights are used less and therefore the wavelengths are reflected which gives the leaves green colour. There are various types of artificial lights, some require to be near the plants as they emit cool light such as fluorescent lights. Fluorescent lights are more economical, and release blue wavelengths, and are good for foliage growth. However, they do not provide a full spectrum

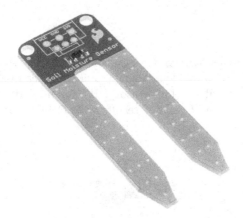

Fig. 3. Moisture sensor

of wavelengths. Normally they are mixed with Incandescent lights. Incandescent lights emit more heat and are required to be installed far from plants, but they release more of the red wavelengths. Depending on the plant nature, the lights can be combined together to provide well-balanced lights. LED lights are customizable and some people prefer to install customized LED bulbs, LED lights are economical and very cheap to maintain. For the full spectrum light, Halogen lights can be used. The drawback of halogen lights is that they produce a lot of heat and less energy efficient. Especially designed horticultural grow lights are available now for indoor use. They provide a full spectrum of wavelengths and are widely used in research and growing of hybrid plants.

4.3   Sensors Integration and Working Mechanism

In Fig. 4 the sensors mentioned earlier are installed. Each sensor has to be installed at a specific position to provide optimum results. In our system, Water level sensor is submerged in the water tank. The water sensor checks the level of the water and it can provide two mechanisms. If the tank is connected with a water source, it can pump water to the tank and fill itself. Alternative, if the water source is not connected with the tank and the water level drops, then it can alert the user to fill the tank. The moisture sensor is installed within the soil near the roots if a single plant is intended to grow. It checks the soil moisture and detects if the plant needs more water or not. If the water is required, the regulator release water according to the requirements. The humidity sensor is installed to check for the humid air, if the air is too humid the regulator turns the fan on to let the humidity reduce. The temperature sensors also utilize the fan to control the temperature. The integration of all the sensors with the controller ensures that the plant has all the requirements within the ideal growing environment. The artificial sunlight is also controlled with the regulator and it can mimic the pattern of sunlight intensity according to the time of the day.

Since the planquarium is designed in a fashion that it can change according to the plant inside. This adaption is carried out by the profiling system. Profiling system has data for different plants. A user just needs to change the plant type in case if he changed the plant inside. The profile management then regulates the regulator according to the new type. We intend to host the database of different plants so that user can simply update their planquarium and the newly available profile will be available for usage. The profile for one simple plant is provided in the next section.

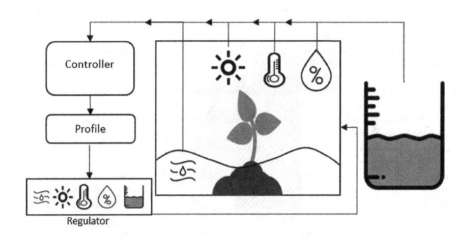

Fig. 4. Planquarium architecture

4.4 Sample Profile

In Table 1, we have defined in the first column, the rule. The rule has variables that are replaced with the facts when received from the sensors. The second column shows the consequent or the actions that will be taken based on the rules defined in the first column. The third column shows which plant the rule belongs to. As different plants have different requirements so we can not generalize the rules instead we have to define rules for every plant that we want to grow inside the planquarium and then differentiate them from each other based on the profile system. In this Table, which is a sample from a big table, we have P2, P3, P4 and P5. This shows that within that sample different rules are shows when we want to grow P2. We will enable the P2 rules, which will apply all the rules on planquarium which belong to Plant 2 or P2. To demonstrate let us assume the following statements separated by commas to make it as close to the rule

we have planquarium named ?p, there is a water tank ?wt, plaquarium ?p has water tank ?wt, water sensor has id ?id, planquarium has water sensor id ?id, water level is ?wl, if planquarium has water level less then 11 then refill the water tank ?wt.

The resultant rule will be as shown below

Planq(?P), watertank(?wt), haswatertank(?p,?wt), wsensorID(?id), hasWSensorId(?p,?id), waterlevel(?wl), hasWaterLevelLessThen(?p,11) with action to take refill(?wt)

Table 1. Profiling rules for different plants

Rule	Consequent	Profile
Planq(?P), watertank(?wt), haswatertank(?p,?wt), wsensorID(?id), hasWSensorId(?p,?id), waterlevel(?wl), hasWaterLevelLessThen(?p,11)	refill(?wt)	P3
Planq(?P), watertank(?wt), haswatertank(?p,?wt), wsensorID(?id), hasWSensorId(?p,?id), waterlevel(?wl), hasWaterLevelGreaterThen(?p,90)	Stoprefill(?wt)	P3
Planq(?P), TemperatureSensor(?id), hasTempSensor(?p,?id), temp(?temp), hasTempGreaterThen(?p,45)	StartFan(?fan)	P5
Planq(?P), TemperatureSensor(?id), hasTempSensor(?p,?id), temp(?temp), hasTempLessThen(?p,30)	StopFan(?fan)	P5
Planq(?P), HumiditySensor(?id), hasHumiditySensor(?p,?id), humidity(?h), hasHumidityLessThen(?p,60)	StartSpray(?spray)	P3
Planq(?P), HumiditySensor(?id), hasHumiditySensor(?p,?id), humidity(?h), hasHumiditygreaterThen(?p,90)	StopSpray(?spray)	P4
Planq(?P), MoistureSensor(?id), hasMoistureSensor(?p,?id), Moisture(?m), hasMoisturegreaterThen(?p,55)	StopWater(?wtr)	P2
Planq(?P), MoistureSensor(?id), hasMoistureSensor(?p,?id), Moisture(?m), hasMoistureLessThen(?p,25)	StartWater(?wtr)	P2

5   Conclusion and Future Work

In this paper, we have demonstrated the concept and early experiment of our Planquarium, which is an intelligent context-aware rule-based indoor kitchen garden growing system. All the user need is to plug in the planquarium and let the plants grow inside by selecting the profile of the plant from the controller menu. The Planquarium is in line with the smart cities concept, and we have tried to connect a simple plant with the smart cities. It is equally beneficial for users who have limited space and they want to grow fresh plants inside their homes. In the future, we will further add a mechanism for effective profiling, as in the future we see the size of the rule-base might be huge due to many profiles stored in single rule-base. Furthermore, the soil quality tester sensor will be deployed which will check if the soil the Planquairum is suited for the plant inside or not. If not then how do we restore the soil to match the quality requirements of the soil. Moreover, we also want to take the experiment to the level of small fruit trees. In this way, we can develop a big Planquarium with more sensors and larger space and an effective cooling/heating mechanism to grow a plant of approximately 2 meters in length so that indoor fruit garden can also be deployed.

References

1. Uddin, I., Ul Haque, H.M., Rakib, A., Segi Rahmat, M.R.: Resource-bounded context-aware applications: a survey and early experiment. In: Vinh, P.C., Barolli, L. (eds.) ICTCC 2016. LNICST, vol. 168, pp. 153–164. Springer, Cham (2016). https://doi.org/10.1007/978-3-319-46909-6_15
2. Uddin, I., Rakib, A., Haque, H.M.U., Vinh, P.C.: Modeling and reasoning about preference-based context-aware agents over heterogeneous knowledge sources. Mob. Netw. Appl. **23**, 13–26 (2017)
3. Uddin, I.: A rule-based framework for developing context-aware systems for smart spaces, July 2019
4. Thamaraimanalan, T., Vivekk, S., Satheeshkumar, G., Saravanan, P.: Smart garden monitoring system using IoT (2018)
5. Min, B., Park, S.J.: A smart indoor gardening system using IoT technology. In: Park, J.J., Loia, V., Yi, G., Sung, Y. (eds.) CUTE/CSA -2017. LNEE, vol. 474, pp. 683–687. Springer, Singapore (2018). https://doi.org/10.1007/978-981-10-7605-3_110
6. Al-Omary, A., AlSabbagh, H.M., Al-Rizzo, H.: Cloud based IoT for smart garden watering system using Arduino Uno (2018)
7. Parmar, B., Chokhalia, J., Desarda, S.: Terrace garden monitoring system using wireless sensor networks. Res. J. Eng. Technol. Manage. **2**(01) (2019)
8. Lipford, D.: How to grow houseplants in artificial light (2012)

Text to Code: Pseudo Code Generation

Altaf U. Din[1(✉)] and Awais Adnan[2]

[1] AWKUM, Mardan, Pakistan
`altafkhattak@gmail.com`
[2] IMSciences, Peshawar, Pakistan
`awaisadnan@gmail.com`

Abstract. The evolutions in programming from machine language to these days programming software have made it easy, to some extent, to develop software but it is not as easy as programming in natural language. In order to transfer natural language text to any programming language code, it felt necessary to first transform natural language text into pseudo code algorithm then with the help of right API library, such algorithms can be transform into any programming language code. The main aim of this research work is to produce pseudo code from text however this work is very loosely bound to natural language processing. Main components of this proposed work is text analyser that utilizes language tools (spelling check, grammar check) to remove type errors and then eliminate different ambiguities. For this step of ambiguity removal, an adaptive solution is proposed that learning from manual assistance. Once the text is cleared, pattern matching techniques is applied to it and later on parsed into a pseudo code. The concept model is tested with user scenario approach and also practically implemented by developing a prototype. This model is examined using 100 examples of different categories and achieved 73.

Keywords: Pseudo code generation · NL to programming code · Intelligent system · Code extraction from text

1 Introduction

How fascinating it would be if a person, who is not a programmer or coder, in need of certain specific application or program and all he does is to tell the computer about his requirements. The computer then creates the program according to his needs. The question that arises that is it possible to build such intelligent system? In couples of decades ago the answers were either no or quite vague for generating programming language code from natural language. However these days, with the advancement of technology, there is possibility that in near future people might come across such system that will facilitate them to produce software by using their natural language. The programming techniques are very tough for general users and, in today technology most of users of computer and smartphone are aware of customized software. It requires a lot

© ICST Institute for Computer Sciences, Social Informatics and Telecommunications Engineering 2019
Published by Springer Nature Switzerland AG 2019. All Rights Reserved
P. C. Vinh and A. Rakib (Eds.): ICCASA 2019/ICTCC 2019, LNICST 298, pp. 20–37, 2019.
https://doi.org/10.1007/978-3-030-34365-1_3

of tools and effort to write a program, but it needs a user to understand the programming concepts. Moreover the programmers must be able to know more than one programming language styles where their libraries, structure and syntax might vary. Since the beginning of computing era, it is always in focus of researchers to make programming easier. Assembly language was introduced to use mnemonics and other prompts in order to get over with machine language programming. But still it was not enough, high level languages were introduced that could adjust most of the programming parts with words from English language. The High Level languages did provide ease and comfy to programmers, not only just making their code writing easy but it was also easy to learn as well. However the issue that still exist is that a novice programmer still has a long route to polish his skills in programming. An expert coder must have to keep himself up to date with the advancement in technologies as well as updates in programming languages. Moreover a layman is still paying huge sum of amount in order to develop certain software or program that somehow reflects upon his requirements. On the other hand the implementation style of different available programming language is also different from each other. On the other hand the implementation style of different available programming language is also different from each other. [1] There is need to provide users with a conventional way where they can state their requirement in natural language (i.e. English language) and the system is able to process the text and provide output is some form of pseudo code. Pseudo code can be transformed into any programming language code with the help of appropriate libraries or API. From the current advancement in other fields of computer science and enhanced techniques (for instance machine learning techniques, data and text mining techniques, natural language techniques etc.) it is assumed that generating code from natural language is possible now with so much development [2]. In this research work a conceptual modal has been proposed that fulfills the purpose of collecting requirement text, in natural language, from user and aims to provide a pseudo code that could easily be transformed to any programming language. The model is composed of four layers that are *"Application Layer"*, *"Text Formalization Layer"*, *"Translation Layer"* and *"Code Generation Layer"*. The application layer is the interface where user will input text as requirement of a particular program. The text formalization layer is where the text is refined down for easily transferred to pseudo code. The translation layer is where pseudo code will be generated and code generation layer is where programming language code from pseudo will be generated. This research work is a small contributory step into long term vision of programming in natural language. The following is exploring the model in detail and implementing the model in order to observe the result.

2   Literature

The concept of bringing down the technology, to the level, where a layman can easily communicate with computer systems is not new. Since 1960 researches are working to create more natural language adaptable systems and applications.

SHRDLU [3] is considered as one of the earliest interface that could answer the questions of a user by manipulating the objects known as blocksworld. However that was an application to step into understanding the natural language. The intended work is more inclined toward programming with natural language. People have proposed their work time to time that requires input in natural language and transform into something that can be meaningful for programming or software development for instance Deeptimahanti and Sanyal [4] have proposed a semi-automatic technique in their work that helps developers to generate UML machine from normalize natural language requirements. Abirami et al. [5] have conducted their study on a classifier that is supposed to separate Functional Requirements (FR) from Non Functional Requirements (NFR), from text that is written in natural language. Siasar djahantighi et al. [6] has worked with same the theme of exploring natural language to produce SQL queries. Their technique is mainly based on a parse tree that is able to identify verb, noun and entities in a statement and generate SQL query. Moreover it is worthy to mention the Natural Language Interface to a Database (NLIDB) [7]. That is among one of the earliest concept mentioned for the ease of general mass to use database application. As the user uses an interface with which they would communicate in their own language with the database application. There is very little related or similar work available where code is generated from plain text in natural language. Price et al. [8] introduced naturaljava. The purpose of naturaljava is to provide such interface for users where they are able to type a command in natural language without any worry about the syntax and the output will be produced in java code. The architecture of naturaljava is shown in Fig. 1. NaturalJava is composed of three main components that are sundance, PRISM and TreeFace. Sundance grabs the input in natural language and generate case frames. PRISM is the case frame interpreter that gathers operations from case frames and Treeface is Abstract Syntax Tree (AST) manager. PRISM uses Treeface to manage the syntax tree of currently java program in progress. Vadas and Curran [9] have mentioned few problems related to naturaljava in their work. According to them Naturaljava can process the accomplishment of

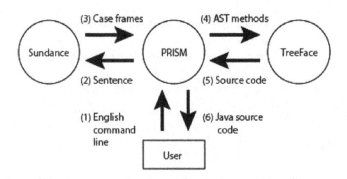

Fig. 1. Architecture of NaturalJava

one sentence at a time and it can only produce code in java language and cannot be adopted to any other language. Their proposed system architecture is given below in Fig. 2. The input text will be parsed by Combinatory Categorical Grammar (CCG) parser [10] and the output of CCG parser will be transformed into more generic representation of text. Afterward a python code output will be generated. There is a dialog session with user in every step as to handle ambiguity but there is no mechanism that will record the dialog session for future reference so that the system should not repeat the same dialog session for any similar scenario. Nadkarni et al. [11] have introduced a conceptual model that has approach of writing an algorithm in natural language and it will be converted to c language code. The input should not be in absolute natural language as they tend to force semi natural language algorithms to be converted into c language code. The challenges for code generation from algorithm typed in semi natural language are the polysemy of algorithms is hard to process, different structure of different programming languages and flexibility. After the user provides input through user module then next stage is to apply standard or basic language processing steps in which each line is explored as well as each word of each line. Then the interpreter section is divided into two steps the first step is to spot the

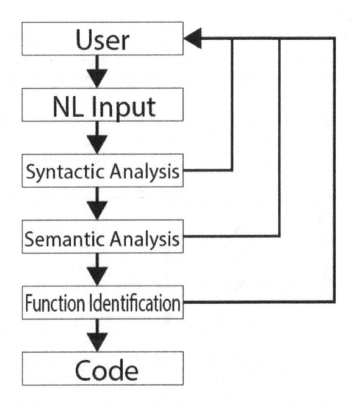

Fig. 2. System architecture

keywords while in next step, if it is identified properly, then it will transformed into code. Meanwhile the synonyms of the words will also be checked and on top of that it will also facilitate users to mould the system according to their algorithm writing style. They did their implementation through user scenario example and in the end they concluded with showing how flexible their modal is but the issue is that input should be provided that is projecting syntax in natural language style hence the input mechanism is not flexible toward as ease of using natural language. Thomas et al. [12] proposed a model of a compiler that will convert natural language into source code of any programming language. They have used the pipeline architecture that will utilize three different databases in order to produce output. Their compiler works in three phases and each phase will overcome the following three issues. proposed model showing natural language compiler interaction. The first phase is named as "Find Meaning" where an array will be created of the text and words will be checked against their available commands and variables. The next phase name is "solve commands" that will check for commands that may or may not need input or output. The last phase is labelled as "Convert intermediate code" that is basically parsing according to each pattern matched in above phases.

- Variations of word
- Context of word
- Generation code in any language

According to their work the NLP compiler has pipeline architecture hence it can be modified a little and transform into a compiler that will convert natural lan-

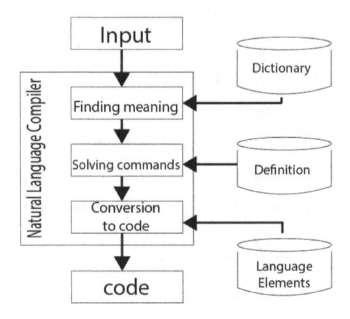

Fig. 3. NL compiler interactions

guage into programming code. The Fig. 3 is the After going through the study of previous work, it has been found that either the input method is not entirely into natural language or the output generated is in a specific programming language. The proposed method will tackle with the mentioned limitations of previous work by accepting input as in pure natural language and output should be in some form of vague code that could be translated to any other language easily. On the other hand there is no mechanism that should explicitly handle the ambiguity. Anjali and Babu Anto [13] argues that solution for ambiguities is very complex task however different methods of NLP (such as machine learning techniques, machine translation or methods of information retrieval) may provide a good resolution in future.

3 Proposed Model

The conceptual model for generating code from plain text, written in natural language, is composed of four different layers.

- Application Layer
- Text Formalization Layer
- Translation Layer
- Code Generation Layer

Figure 4 shows the model of proposed solution in next sub section.

3.1 Application Layer

The application layer is actually the interface for the user. The UI should be user friendly. Moreover the view of interface should have capacity for the following basic points. **"Input Space":** An input area for the user to type in their program requirements in natural language. **"Trigger":** Once a user is done with the input, a trigger (a button for example) should be provided to grab user text from input space and send it to processing. **"Result display space":** After processing text to mock code there should be space provided to display the pseudo code. **"Assistant wizard":** If the system is unable to generate pseudo code then it should initiate Wizard for the user. The wizard will guide the user through dialog session in order to figure out any issue. **"Code generation trigger":** After successfully generating pseudo code a trigger should be provided for users to generate any specific programming language application. A trigger here can be a dropdown list of different programming languages options (i.e. c++, java, php etc.)

3.2 Text Formalization Layer

From text formalization it means to bring down the informal/usual form of text into a standardized form. The reason for putting text into a proper format is that it will make way easy for pseudo code generation. **"Spelling and grammatical** mistakes removal" is quite easy these days with the advanced technique how-ever **"ambiguity removal"** is still a challenge. There are some mechanisms available to remove certain types of ambiguities but these techniques are not enough and more work requires as it is complex area of field [14]. In this model ambiguity removal have been placed explicitly as with the passage of time new techniques can be added to the system in order to make it more robust. The process of ambiguity removal is shown in Fig. 5. **"Text refining"**: The purpose of text refining is to put the sentences in order as well as replace the "typical words" with associated "programming word". The term typical words are used here to expresses bunch of words regarding any keyword that is usually used in programming. For example Table 1 shows keywords and the typical words regarding keyword. The process of text refining stage is highlighted with the help of Fig. 6.

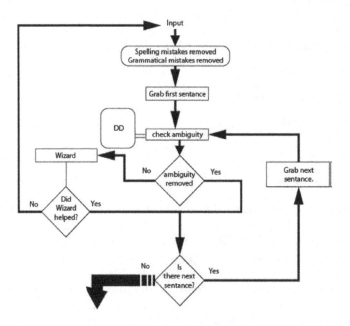

Fig. 4. Ambiguity removal

Table 1. Programming word and its matches

Programming word	Typical words
if	Condition, whether ... etc.
else	Otherwise, if not, ... etc.
loop	Iterate, repeat, recur ... etc

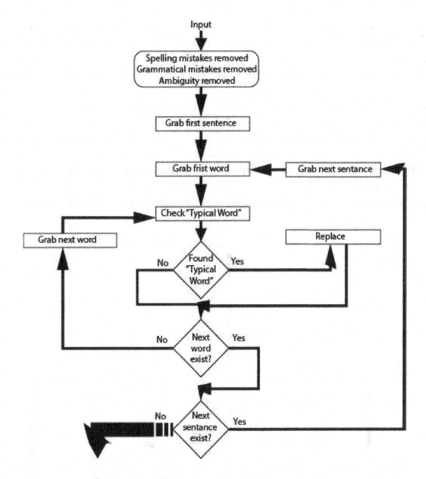

Fig. 5. Text refining

3.3 Translation Layer

The translation layer is divided in two different phases that are pseudo code generation phase 1 and phase 2. In "Pseudo code generation phase 1" the "word patterns" will be matched and replaced. Word pattern is actually occurrence of certain words in such an order that will comply with syntax of a programming style. Considering the example of if-else statement. The syntax of if-else statement is

If(condition)
-do something-
Else
-do something else-

Now processing the statement "if answer is 1 then print Earth else print rest of the Universe." The pattern here is, anything between word "if" and "then" is usually condition. Anything between word "then" and "else" has to happen when condition is true. Anything between "else" and full stop has to happen if condition does not meet as expected. So looking at the word patterns in the above statement, the pseudo code it will generate as

if(answer is 1) **Print** Earth **else Print** rest of the Universe

Figure 7 shows the process of phase 1.

In the "**pseudo code generation phase 2**" the generated pseudo code so far will be checked if each line is in arrangement of a programming code style. If there is any line that does not confirm the style then wizard will be invoked to get the issue out of that line. Figure 8 shows the process of phase 2.

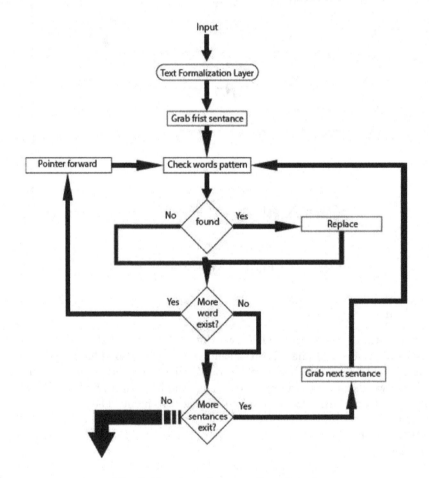

Fig. 6. Pseudo code generation phase 1

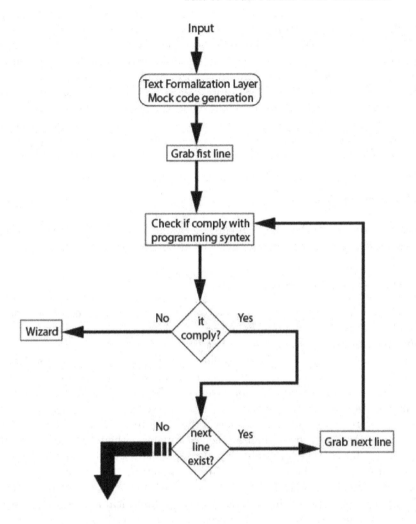

Fig. 7. Pseudo code generation phase 2

3.4   Code Generation Layer

The code generation is subjected to be completed in future as the main aim of this work is to deliver pseudo code from natural language input. Because if a system is able to convert requirement provided in natural language into algorithm then, with the aid of right API and library, it will not be difficult to generate any programming code from algorithm. Apart from the layers there are three main components to the system that are data dictionary, variable check points and assistant wizard. **Data Dictionary** The data dictionary is actually the database of the system. **Variable checkpoints** Variable checkpoints are the way to handle variable declaration. First check point for variable declaration will be after text refining stage. At this point all the noun words will be declared as variable. The next variable checkpoint is after pseudo code generation phase 2. At the stage the system will discard all the noun variables that are not used. Meanwhile it will declare some more variables that are in use but not declared. **Assistant Wizard** Assistant Wizard is a dialogue session with the user. Assistant Wizard will be initiated when the system is unable to process the text provided. It will guide the user as well as collect information from the user and with the successful completion of session it will record the scenario for future reference.

4   Implementation

A user scenario approach of implementation should be carry out before practical implementation in order to understand the mechanism thoroughly.

4.1   User Scenario Approach

The following text should be processed out through each layer of the model manually. *"A user is enter marks. Check for marks if it is great than 49 then disply pass otherwise it should disply fail."*

The spelling and grammatical mistakes are deliberately left there for demonstration purpose. The first layer is "application layer". A user will be able to provide the text through application layer. Next is the text formalization layer. The first section of text formalization is to remove the spelling mistakes. The underlined words have spelling mistakes in the input text. "A user is enter marks. Check for marks if it is great than 49 then disply pass otherwise it should disply fail." After removing spelling mistakes the statement will be converted to: "A user is enter marks. Check for marks if it is great than 49 then display pass otherwise it should display fail." Then grammatical mistakes will be removed as the underlined parts in the statement have grammatical mistakes. "A user is enter marks. Check for marks if it is great than 49 then display pass otherwise it should display fail." After removing grammatical mistakes the statement will be converted to "A user will enter marks. Check for marks if it is greater than 49 then display pass otherwise it should display fail." After getting rid of grammatical and spelling mistakes, the ambiguity will be checked. Looking at the statement the ambiguity lies where it says "it should display fail." The system will not be able to decide where "it" directs to. So removing the ambiguity the statement will take the face as:

"A user will enter marks. Check if marks is greater than 49 then display pass otherwise display fail." The next stage is "Text Refining" where the typical words is spotted and replaced. The underlined words in the statement includes typical words. "A user will enter marks. Check if marks is greater than 49 then display pass otherwise display fail." The typical words can be replaced as enter to input, is greater than to >, display to print, if remains as if and otherwise to else. The text will be converted to: "A user will input marks. Check if marks

> 49 then print pass else print fail" The variable checkpoint will declare words user and marks as variable as they are noun and proceed to translation layer. In the first phase of pseudo code generation the system will check for the words pattern and replace it with the vague code accordingly. For instance in the above statement the word phrase of first sentence that says "A user will input marks." The word input indicated there should be variable around where value should be stored. At the left side of word input is "will" which is a modal verb that is kind of base for the verb and not noun while on the right side "marks" is noun and there is no preposition etc. between the word input and marks hence marks should be a variable. As the word "input" indicates someone will enter the input through keyboard because if there was word phrase "stores", "have value", "keeping number" and so on that would meant to store some value in marks variable. So the pseudo code for it will be "input marks= from keyboard". The full stop indicates to jump to new line. And the word phrase in next sentence is "if marks > 49 then" the word "if" indicates there is conditional statement of if-else. Usually anything between if and then is considered as condition and should be put in small brackets e.g. if(marks > 49). Anything between then and else is body of the if statement section when condition is true and it should be kept between and . So getting the phrase of then to else and put it in order it will be displayed as print pass. There is else word included then the word phrase is anything between else and full stop is body of else. This in this example is print fail. Putting it all together, after adding start and end to the algorithm generated, the output of the pseudo code generation phase 1 will be

Start
Input marks=from keyboard
if(marks > 49)
{
Print pass
}
else
{
Print fail
}
End

The next phase of pseudo code generation it will be checked if it complies with programming code style.

After successfully passing through phase 2 the variable checkpoint will discard "user" variable as it is not used (Table 2).

4.2 Practical Implementation

For practically implementing the proposed model, an initial prototype application was developed using mySql and netBeans IDE. Around 20 people were asked to provide at least 10 different statements regarding four simple mathematical functions (addition, subtraction, multiplication and division) between two values. About 200 statements were collected and placed in their respective group of

Table 2. Generated pseudo code to programming code

Generated pseudo code	Programming code style
Start	Start of the program
Input marks=from keyboard	Input by user
if(marks > 49)	if(condition)
{ Print pass }	{ Do something }
Else	Else
{ Print fail	{ Do something else }
}	}
End	End of the program

addition, subtraction, multiplication and division. Most of the statements were almost similar but there were few statements that actually helped in building up small data dictionary of typical words regarding the four basic mathematical operations. A simple statement of "deduct var2 from var1 and show result to user" was processed through it and the resulting algorithm was successfully generated by the prototype application. Figure 9 shows the resulting pseudo code generated for the above mentioned statement. Likewise "twinkle twinkle little stars." was provided as input and Fig. 10 shows the result of invoking assistant wizard. Later on the database was updated more in order to process natural language text including conditional statements of if-else and "if student1 is greater than student2 then display student1 has gotten high marks." was provided as input to the prototype. Figure 11 shows it successfully processed the text.

5   Analysis

The system was able to produce output for different natural language text input against different programming statements. Although it did call upon wizard in order to resolve some issues that is due to the lack of mature data dictionary at this stage as well as no proper ambiguity resolution mechanism attached to the system, as the prototype is in initial phases.

100 different basic statements are tested on the proposed system out of which 73% are understood correctly and for the rest of 27% wizard was prompted. Details about the statement and corresponding result are illustrated in the Table 3 below.

Following are a few results observed from the above cases. Words like display, Print, Show, Get, Input, Output, subtract are identified with 100 Some words, which initially were considered simple, showed high level of error. One such word is times, which confuses multiplication and loop. Another such example is dividing. Initially it was considered simple words but experimental results shoes that system was confused between multiplication (e.g. divide 10 apples among 5 student 10/5 identified correctly, divide 2 cakes in to 10 pieces each, identified as

Fig. 8. Result for subtraction algorithm

Table 3. Results with and without wizard prompts

Type of statements	Statements tested	Result without wizard	Wizard prompted
Input statements	10	10	0
Output statements	10	9	1
Addition	10	9	1
Subtraction	10	9	1
Multiplication	10	7	3
Division	10	8	2
If statements	10	8	2
If-else	10	6	4
For loop	5	3	2
While loop	5	2	3
Do-while loop	5	1	4
Switch statements	5	1	4
Total	100	73	27

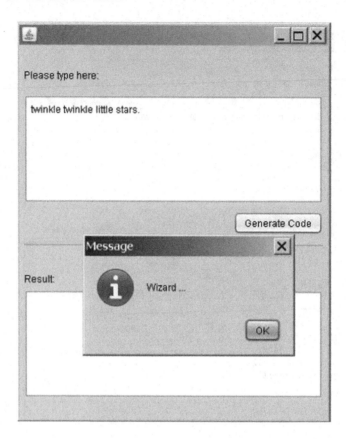

Fig. 9. Assistant wizard invoke

2/10, where is actual formula should be 2 * 10). Similarly the word do, which means do something whereas in computers sciences this word is used for loop. Most of the errors were observed in conditional statements especially in multi branching (switch statement). It is worth to mention that the proper data dictionary development and ambiguity are the core obstacle in programming with natural language in general. After implementation it can be said that there are three different situational cases can occur with the system that are:

Best Case

When the system produces output smoothly for provided input.

Average Case When the system initiate assistant wizard for provided input.

Worst Case

When the assistant wizard is not able to help user and directs him to application layer to provide more clear input. Figures 12, 13 and 14 shows best, average and worst case scenario respectively.

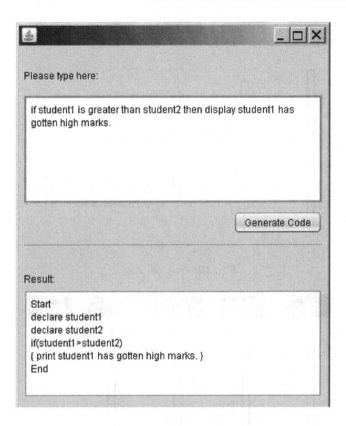

Fig. 10. Conditional statement result

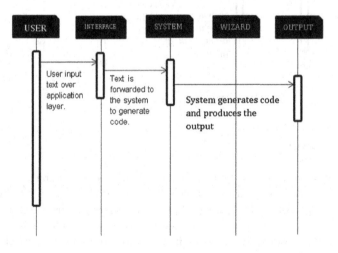

Fig. 11. Best case

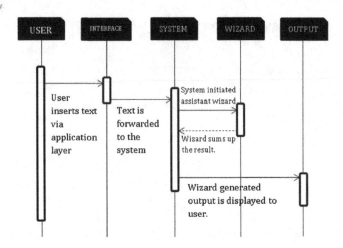

Fig. 12. Average case

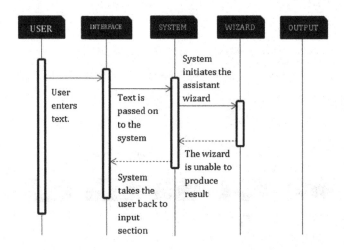

Fig. 13. Worst case

6 Conclusion

Code generation from natural language text should be considered as big system. This research work is a small contribution toward making such big system possible. The initial prototype test provided promising results at minute level however it is not claimed that the proposed model is absolute solution. It is intended to put more efforts in future in order to make it more reliable system. Moreover in future, more work need to tackle down ambiguity issue; proper assistant wizard and programming language code generation from pseudo code is recommended.

References

1. Stefik, A., Siebert, S.: An empirical investigation into programming language syntax. ACM Trans. Comput. Educ. (TOCE) **13**(4), 19 (2013)
2. Lieberman, H., Liu, H.: Feasibility studies for programming in natural language. In: Lieberman, H., Paternò, F., Wulf, V. (eds.) End User Development, vol. 9, pp. 459–473. Springer, Heidelberg (2006). https://doi.org/10.1007/1-4020-5386-X_20
3. Winograd, T.: Understanding natural language. Cogn. Psychol. **3**(1), 1–191 (1972)
4. Deeptimahanti, D.K., Sanyal, R.: Semi-automatic generation of UML models from natural language requirements. In: Proceedings of the 4th India Software Engineering Conference, pp. 165–174. ACM (2011)
5. Abirami, S., Shankari, G., Akshaya, S., Sithika, M.: Conceptual modeling of non-functional requirements from natural language text. In: Jain, L.C., Behera, H.S., Mandal, J.K., Mohapatra, D.P. (eds.) Computational Intelligence in Data Mining - Volume 3. SIST, vol. 33, pp. 1–11. Springer, New Delhi (2015). https://doi.org/10.1007/978-81-322-2202-6_1
6. Norouzifard, M., Davarpanah, S., Shenassa, M., et al.: Using natural language processing in order to create SQL queries. In: 2008 International Conference on Computer and Communication Engineering, pp. 600–604. IEEE (2008)
7. Androutsopoulos, I., Ritchie, G.D., Thanisch, P.: Natural language interfaces to databases-an introduction. Nat. Lang. Eng. **1**(1), 29–81 (1995)
8. Price, D., Rilofff, E., Zachary, J., Harvey, B.: Naturaljava: a natural language interface for programming in Java. In: Proceedings of the 5th International Conference on Intelligent User Interfaces, pp. 207–211. ACM (2000)
9. Vadas, D., Curran, J.R.: Programming with unrestricted natural language. In: Proceedings of the Australasian Language Technology Workshop, pp. 191–199 (2005)
10. Steedman, M.: The Syntactic Process, vol. 24. MIT Press, Cambridge (2000)
11. Nadkarni, S., Panchmatia, P., Karwa, T., Kurhade, S.: Semi natural language algorithm to programming language interpreter. In: 2016 International Conference on Advances in Human Machine Interaction (HMI), pp. 1–4. IEEE (2016)
12. Thomas, J., Antony, P.J., Balapradeep, K.N., Mithun, K.D., Maiya, N.: Natural language compiler for English and Dravidian languages. In: Shetty, N.R., Prasad, N.H., Nalini, N. (eds.) Emerging Research in Computing, Information, Communication and Applications, pp. 313–323. Springer, New Delhi (2015). https://doi.org/10.1007/978-81-322-2550-8_31
13. Anjali, M.K., Anto, P.B.: Ambiguities in natural language processing. Int. J. Innov. Res. Comput. Commun. Eng. 392–394 (2014)
14. Sag, I.A., Baldwin, T., Bond, F., Copestake, A., Flickinger, D.: Multiword expressions: a pain in the neck for NLP. In: Gelbukh, A. (ed.) CICLing 2002. LNCS, vol. 2276, pp. 1–15. Springer, Heidelberg (2002). https://doi.org/10.1007/3-540-45715-1_1

Context-Aware Mobility Based on π-Calculus in Internet of Thing: A Survey

Vu Tuan Anh[1], Pham Quoc Cuong[2], and Phan Cong Vinh[3(✉)]

[1] Faculty of Electronics Technology, Industrial University of Ho Chi Minh City,
Ho Chi Minh City, Vietnam
vutuananh@iuh.edu.vn
[2] Faculty of Computer Science and Engineering,
Ho Chi Minh City University of Technology, Ho Chi Minh City, Vietnam
cuongpham@hcmut.edu.vn
[3] Faculty of Information Technology, Nguyen Tat Thanh University,
Ho Chi Minh City, Vietnam
pcvinh@ntt.edu.vn

Abstract. Nowadays, the computing is becoming faster and faster to support very other scientific areas. Internet of Thing (IoT) is taking much advantage from it. At the beginning of IoT, the static things joined in IoT such as: cameras, sensors, and vending machines. Due to the progress of computing science, IoT is expanding on mobile things such as cars, patients, cellphones and other mobile things for traffic controlling, health care, or getting information. The network of mobile things is called as Internet of Mobile Things (IoMT). There are some problems to be solved in IoMT as: Security and Privacy, Mobile Data Collection and Analysis. The data collected from the mobile things can help to improve the security and privacy better, or using for special purposes. To get the data of mobile things, moved from one cluster to another one, we need an algorithm to solve following things: mobility of mobile nodes, and changing in number of the mobile nodes. The pi-calculus is one solution for this problem. Pi-calculus is introduced by Milner as a formal language for modeling and verifying system requirements. In this paper, a survey is performed on pi-calculus for IoMT, and other related calculi.

Keywords: IoT · IoMT · Pi-calculus

1 Intoduction

At the first days of IoT, the static things are connected to Internet by sensors to collect data for specific purposes. The data is analysed to get information from it. This process is context-aware. The context-awareness, used for getting information of the things in IoT, uses to improve the authentication and privacy in IoT. Nowadays, not only the static things join in the internet, but also

P. C. Vinh and A. Rakib (Eds.): ICCASA 2019/ICTCC 2019, LNICST 298, pp. 38–46, 2019.
https://doi.org/10.1007/978-3-030-34365-1_4

the mobile things connect to IoT by sensor controlled by android system to send WiFi signal to the data centre [3–5, 7–9]. The problem of mobile things is moving from one cluster to another. The mobility in IoMT relates to some problems, needed to solve in IoMT, as mobile data collection, mobile data analysis, energy management, and security and privacy [1]. In the paper [1], the process of IoMT introduces in the detail. First, IoMT need a MobilityFirst framework with protocol to support the communication among mobile nodes. The mobile node is applied Ipv4 or updated to IPv6 with 128 bits or 16 bytes length size of address to routing in Wireless sensor networks (WSNs). Each static node has static IP to communicate together in WSNs, but the mobile node is not. The mobile nodes move from one cluster to another one. That means the IP address must be changed. The IP address must be cleaned for next users when it moves out of the cluster. Besides, the number of mobile nodes also change in WSNs. To solve this problem, Milner introduces pi-calculus as a formal language for modeling and verifying system requirements. This paper has three parts. The first section is The calculus for the IoT (CaIT). The second section is survey on pi-calculus with some research work for IoT. The last section is survey on other calculi that are applied in IoT and IoMT to solve dynamic mathematics.

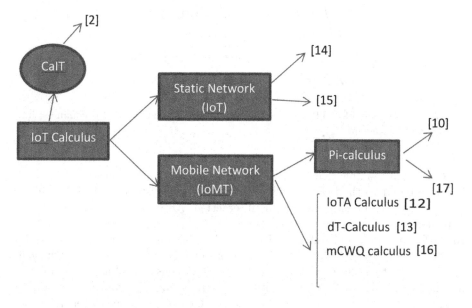

Fig. 1. The total view of calculi on survey

Figure 1 is total view of calculi on survey. The calculi are divided in two branches: Static Network (IoT) and Mobile Network (IoMT) with the papers listed in references section.

2   Calculus for IoT

The calculus for the IoT (CaIT) has two level structures: low level for processes, higher level for network of smart devices. Some example syntax of CaIT is showed in the Fig. 2

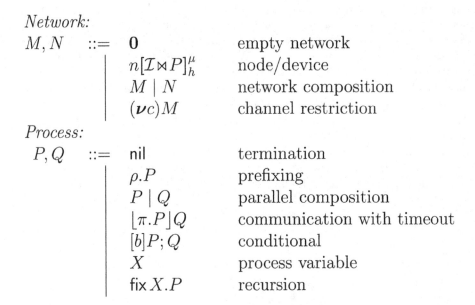

Network:

M, N	$::=$	$\mathbf{0}$	empty network
		$n[\mathcal{I} \bowtie P]_h^\mu$	node/device
		$M \mid N$	network composition
		$(\boldsymbol{\nu}c)M$	channel restriction

Process:

P, Q	$::=$	nil	termination
		$\rho.P$	prefixing
		$P \mid Q$	parallel composition
		$\lfloor \pi.P \rfloor Q$	communication with timeout
		$[b]P; Q$	conditional
		X	process variable
		fix $X.P$	recursion

Fig. 2. Some syntax of CaIT in [2] with n, m as nodes/devices; c,g for channels; h,k for (physical) locations.

CaIT is just simple reduction semantics to model the dynamics of systems in isolation based on the IoT paradigm. To interact IoT systems with the environment, it need to be emphasized this interaction. Authors in [2] have improved it to define a labelled bisimilarity. However, CaIT is only a calculus based on the IoT paradigm, and differs to IoT-calculus. In the paper [6], authors yield at the first process calculus for IoT systems to capture the interaction between sensors, actuators and computing processes. Both sensors and actuators in IoT are under the control of a single entity. This gives out the problem of security. Authors in the paper [14] proposed a calculus for wireless-based cyber- physical systems (CPS), allowed modeling and reasoning about cryptographic primitives, together with explicit notions of communication failure and unwanted communication. Main purpose of CPS is faithful representation denial-of-service. However, in the paper [15], X. Wu pointed out the calculus does not provide a notion of network topology, local broadcast and behavioural equivalence. The distinction between physical components (sensor and actuators) and logical ones (processes) is not clear. Finally, the paper in [15] (CWQ Calculus) introduce a static network topology and enrich the theory with a harmony theorem. The static network just only includes the static nodes. To more understanding on it, the smart house is an example. Everything is put sensors inside such as: television, lamp, air-controller, doors to control via smartphone, or to get information and save them in the data centre for other purposes. However, the mobile things are more difficult. They are mobile nodes, such as cars, patients, that move from one cluster to another one. When they drop out, the IP addresses are cleaned for next users. Besides, the mobile node need to be charged, or turned off (if it in inactive mode) to save the energy. This is dynamic mathematics in IoMT. We need another calculus to meet these standards as pi-calculus for example. The next section in this paper will review pi-calculus in more detail. The final section is other calculi on survey.

3   Pi-calculus for IoMT

In the paper [11], pi-calculus has two roles as modeling for networking and sending messages from site to side, or model of computation by Milner. Modeling for networking describes the networking to be how to synchronize and pass message between various activities. The model also describes the interaction inside. The pi-calculus has an advantage to solve the problems in concurrent and dynamic systems. The mobile nodes require a rapid identification authentication and privacy protection. They need a protocol to solve the problem: joining in a new cluster. In the paper [10], Jingjun Miao introduces a new protocol based on pi-calculus that can resist replay attack, eavesdropping attack, and tracking or location privacy attack. The protocol also confirms the ability to satisfy two privacy protection properties known as untraceability and forward privacy. The authors yield out the new calculus called the applied pi-calculus as language for describing concurrent processes and their interaction. Pi-calculus is extended by adding possibility to model cryptographic primitives through a signature and an equation theory. To understand it in more detail, the following Table 1 shows it.

In table, there are standard primitives from the pi-calculus together with ifthen-else and the possibility to output terms. This syntax is used to model the protocol. The plain processes and extended processes use for one side to execute a complete session when the protocol is running communication. In the paper, the security and privacy of the protocol is "no one knows content inside the data, and no one knows where it is sent to". This is called untraceability. There are a lot of authentication protocols with privacy but they are too heavy computation and communication, and are not suit for IoT. The authors introduce rapid authentication protocol in the applied pi-calculus. It is convenient protocol in the kind of environment of IoT. The mobile node is authenticated by the cluster node through this protocol. This protocol is not only simple authentication but also realize credible transmission of mobile node among clusters. In addition, the protocol can resist replay attack, eavesdropping attack and tracking or location privacy attack. However, the authors still do not have the solution for context-awareness (to improve the authentication and privacy, or use for specific

Table 1. The syntax of applied pi-calculus

Symbol	Meaning
P, Q, R ::=	Plain processes
0	Null processes
P|Q	Parallel composition
!P	Replication
vn.P	Restriction
If M = N then P else Q	Conditional
u(x).P	Message input
$\bar{u}$ <N>.P	Message output
A, B, C ::=	Extented processes
P	Plain processes
A|B	Parallel composition
vn.A	Name restriction
vx.A	Variable restriction
{M/x}	Active substitution

purposes), and mobility (moving of mobile nodes) in IoMT. In the below layers of mobile nodes network, the paper [17] yields out multi pi-calculus to modeling cognitive model for ad hoc network. The ad hoc network is a multi-hop temporary autonomous network system for mobile node system without fixed base station. It has no centre, and acts as self-organization, multi-hop routing and dynamic network topology structure. The multi pi-calculus work is used in many layers of the ad hoc network such as: access cognition layer, service agent cognition layer, service cognition layer. The multi pi-calculus provides powerful formal tool to contribute to accurately qualitative and quantitative analysis, and reasonable judgment basis for ad hoc network cognitive performance evaluation. In the same with the paper [10], the paper [17] still focuses on cognitive problem of the mobile nodes. Both of them need integrated more the solutions for the context-aware and mobility of the mobile nodes.

4   Other Calculi (Based on Pi-calculus)

In Wireless Sensor Network (WSNs), the important thing is node mobility that yields out abnormalities and decreasing the quality of service. In the paper [16], the authors give out the solution known as mCWQ calculus (CWQ calculus with mobility). The calculus shows how to capture the feature of node mobility and increase the quality of the communication. The calculus is based on Hoare Logic to describe the timing of observable actions. The mobility models are random motion of each entity node. The mCWQ calculus can be used for specifying the movement trajectory models of entity mobility of the nodes. The mCWQ updates the new nodes for mobility function. The mobility function changes at any time. We can refer to the syntax of mCWQ in the Fig. 3

Processes

$$P ::= nil \mid Act.P \mid [t_1 = t_2]P_1, P_2 \mid P_1 \parallel P_2 \mid P_1 + P_2 \mid$$
$$\text{case } e \text{ of some}(y) : P_1 \text{ else } P_2$$

$$Act ::= c!v \mid \sigma \mid b$$

$$b ::= c?x \mid \&_q(b_1, ..., b_n)$$

$$t ::= c \mid v \mid y$$

$$e ::= x \mid \text{some}(t) \mid \text{none}$$

Networks:

$$N ::= 0 \mid n[P]_T^f \mid N_1 \parallel N_2$$

Function:

$$F ::= D(\overrightarrow{l_1}, \overrightarrow{l_2})$$

Fig. 3. The syntax of mCWQ calculus

In the mCWQ calculus, the messages are passed between nodes. Channels are asynchronous, so the sender does not need to wait for the receiver, but send immediately. Result is the message to be able to be lost if there is no receiver, because of no buffering of message. The receiver still wait until message is available. The mCQW calculus not only has ability to capture the features of mobility, local broadcast, time delay and quality of WSNs, but also is provided a set of proof rules to verify the correctness of WSNs. The paper solves the mobility problem in IoMT, but still remains the context-aware problem in IoMT. Besides, in the paper [1], the mobility of IoMT needs to turn off the mobile node to save energy. That means the number of mobile nodes are changeable. The mCQW calculus is good in capturing the feature of node mobility and increasing the quality of the communication, but still does not have the solution for changing the number of mobile nodes. Other calculi, applied in IoT, are IoTA calculus [12] and dT-calculus [13]. IoTA is the first calculus for the domain of home automation. Home automation means being able to control the devices such as: lights, locks, refrigerators, televisions, and cameras. While as, dT-calculus is a formal method to specify distributed mobile real-time IoT system. In this paper, authors review more calculus as Time pi-calculus and d-Calculus. Time pi-calculus has capability to specify time properties, but lack of direct specifying both execution time of action and mobility of process itself such as: ready time, timeout, execution time, and deadline.

5   Summary and Development Direction

The progress of computing helps the sciences better. The IoT, especially IoMT, has taken advantage from the computing so much. In the paper [1], we make a survey on context-aware and mobility in IoT. The researches just focus on the protocols for security and privacy problem in IoT communication. It is need a calculus to solve the dynamic mathematics in IoMT in which there are moving of the mobile node from this cluster to another one, or changing of the number of mobile nodes. First, there is the calculus for IoT called CaIT. The CaIT is based on IoT paradigm to interact IoT systems with environment. The CaIT differs to IoT-calculus. The IoT-calculus branch divides in two branches. One is static network with the papers [14] and [15]. The other one is pi-calculus with the paper [10] and [17]. Besides, other calculi, based on pi-calculus, include IoTA calculus [12], dT-calculus [13], and mCWQ [16]. The static network is static nodes network without moving, so the researches on this field just focus on routing, communication between nodes, security, privacy and cognition. In the paper [14], authors have proposed applied quality calculus for wireless-based cyber-physical systems (CPS), allowed modeling and reasoning about cryptographic primitives. In the paper [15], CWQ calculus is used in static network topology. In IoMT, the nodes move from one cluster to another one, so it needs a new calculus to solve the mobility problem and changing number of mobile nodes. In the paper [10], authors introduce Applied Quality Calculus that focuses on modeling networking and sending messages from site to site to resist replay attack, eavesdropping attack, and tracking or location privacy attack. In the paper [17], authors yield out multi pi-calculus to modeling cognitive model for Ad hoc network. Both of them do not have any solution for the mobility of IoMT. That means the mobile node can be dropped when it move out of the cluster. Its IP address needs to be cleaned for next users. We need a calculus to capture the moving of the mobile nodes. The solution of this problem is yield out in the paper [16]. The mCQW in the paper [16] is a calculus with mobility that shows how to capture the feature of node mobility and increase the quality of the communication. However, there is a problem that needs to be solved is changing of the number of mobile nodes (inactive nodes turn off). Besides, there are some other calculi such as: IoTA (for domain of home automation), dT-calculus (specify distributed mobile real-time IoT system). As the survey of the paper [1], context-awareness is used to improve the security and privacy, or is used for specific purposes. So, the future researches are on combining of context-awareness and mobility (changing number of mobile nodes and moving of mobile nodes).

References

1. Anh, V.T., Cuong, P.Q., Vinh, P.C.: Context-aware mobility in internet of thing: a survey. EAI Endorsed Trans. Context-aware Syst. Appl. **6**(16), e3 (2019). https://doi.org/10.4108/eai.13-7-2018.158875
2. Castiglioni, V., Lanotte, R., Merro, M.: A semantic theory for the internet of things. CoRR abs/1510.04854 (2015). http://arxiv.org/abs/1510.04854

3. Cristescu, I., Hirschkoff, D.: Termination in a π-calculus with subtyping. Math. Struct. Comput. Sci. **26**(8), 1395–1432 (2016). https://doi.org/10.1017/S0960129514000620

4. Deng, P., Zhang, J., Rong, X., Chen, F.: A model of large-scale device collaboration system based on pi-calculus for green communication. Telecommun. Syst. **52**(2), 1313–1326 (2013). https://doi.org/10.1007/s11235-011-9643-9

5. Hildebrandt, T.T., Johansen, C., Normann, H.: A stable non-interleaving early operational semantics for the pi-calculus. J. Log. Algebr. Meth. Program. **104**, 227–253 (2019). https://doi.org/10.1016/j.jlamp.2019.02.006

6. Lanese, I., Bedogni, L., Felice, M.D.: Internet of things: a process calculus approach. In: Proceedings of the 28th Annual ACM Symposium on Applied Computing, SAC 2013, Coimbra, Portugal, 18–22 March 2013, pp. 1339–1346 (2013). https://doi.org/10.1145/2480362.2480615

7. Lekshmy, V.G., Bhaskar, J.: Programming smart environments using π-calculus. Procedia Comput. Sci. **46**, 884–891 (2015). https://doi.org/10.1016/j.procs.2015.02.158

8. Liu, Y., Jiang, J.: Analysis and modeling for interaction with mobility based on pi-calculus. In: 2016 IEEE 14th International Conference on Dependable, Autonomic and Secure Computing, 14th International Conference on Pervasive Intelligence and Computing, 2nd International Conference on Big Data Intelligence and Computing and Cyber Science and Technology Congress, DASC/PiCom/DataCom/CyberSciTech 2016, Auckland, New Zealand, 8–12 August 2016, pp. 141–146 (2016). https://doi.org/10.1109/DASC-PICom-DataCom-CyberSciTec.2016.42

9. Luca, G.D., Chen, Y.: Visual IoT/robotics programming language in Pi-calculus. In: 13th IEEE International Symposium on Autonomous Decentralized System, ISADS 2017, Bangkok, Thailand, 22–24 March 2017, pp. 23–30 (2017). https://doi.org/10.1109/ISADS.2017.32

10. Miao, J., Wang, L.: Rapid identification authentication protocol for mobile nodes in internet of things with privacy protection. JNW **7**(7), 1099–1105 (2012). https://doi.org/10.4304/jnw.7.7.1099-1105

11. Milner, R.: Communicating and Mobile Systems: The π-calculus. Cambridge University Press, New York (1999)

12. Newcomb, J.L., Chandra, S., Jeannin, J.B., Schlesinger, C., Sridharan, M.: Iota: a calculus for internet of things automation. In: Proceedings of the 2017 ACM SIGPLAN International Symposium on New Ideas, New Paradigms, and Reflections on Programming and Software, Onward! 2017, pp. 119–133. ACM, New York (2017). https://doi.org/10.1145/3133850.3133860

13. Sen, J., et al.: Internet of things: technology, applications and standardardization. CoRR abs/1808.09390 (2018). http://arxiv.org/abs/1808.09390

14. Vigo, R., Nielson, F., Nielson, H.R.: Broadcast, denial-of-service, and secure communication. In: Johnsen, E.B., Petre, L. (eds.) IFM 2013. LNCS, vol. 7940, pp. 412–427. Springer, Heidelberg (2013). https://doi.org/10.1007/978-3-642-38613-8_28

15. Wu, X., Zhu, H.: A calculus for wireless sensor networks from quality perspective. In: 16th IEEE International Symposium on High Assurance Systems Engineering, HASE 2015, Daytona Beach, FL, USA, 8–10 January 2015, pp. 223–231 (2015). https://doi.org/10.1109/HASE.2015.40

16. Xie, W., Zhu, H., Wu, X., Vinh, P.C.: Formal verification of mCWQ using extended hoare logic. MONET **24**(1), 134–144 (2019). https://doi.org/10.1007/s11036-018-1142-8
17. Zhao, G., Zhang, N., Sheng, L.: Study of cognitive model for ad hoc network based on high-order multi-type π-calculus modeling. In: IEEE International Conference on Intelligent Computing and Internet of Things, ICIT 2015, Harbin, China, 17–18 January 2015, pp. 141–144. IEEE (2015). https://doi.org/10.1109/ICAIOT.2015.7111556

High-Throughput Machine Learning Approaches for Network Attacks Detection on FPGA

Duc-Minh Ngo, Binh Tran-Thanh, Truong Dang, Tuan Tran,
Tran Ngoc Thinh, and Cuong Pham-Quoc$^{(\boxtimes)}$

Ho Chi Minh City University of Technology, VNU-HCM, Ho Chi Minh City, Vietnam
`cuongpham@hcmut.edu.vn`

Abstract. The popularity of applying Artificial Intelligence (AI) to perform prediction and automation tasks has become one of the most conspicuous trends in computer science. However, AI systems usually require heavy computational tasks and result in violating applications that need real-time interactions. In this work, we propose a system which is a combination of FPGA platform and AI to achieve a high-throughput network attacks detection. Our architecture consists of 2 well-known and powerful classification techniques, which are the Decision Tree and Neural Network. To prove the feasibility of the proposed approach, we implement a prototype on NetFPGA-10G board using Verilog-HDL. Moreover, the prototype is trained and tested with NSL-KDD dataset, the most popular dataset for network attack detection system. Our experimental results show that the Neural network core can detect attacks with speed at up to 9.86 Gbps for all packet sizes from 64B to 1500B, which is thoroughly 11x and 83x times faster than Geforce GTX 850M GPU and i5 8th generation CPU, respectively. The Neural Network classifier system can function at 104.091 MHz and achieve the accuracy at 87.3.

Keywords: Machine learning · FPGA platform · Network attacks

1 Introduction

In recent years, the capacity of a machine to imitate intelligent human behaviors called Artificial Intelligence (AI) [14] has become a prominent topic. AI has achieved several successes in practical applications such as visual perception, decision-making, speech recognition, and also object classification. Likewise, Machine learning (ML) [10] is well-known as a subset of AI with the ability to update, improve itself when exposed to more data; machine learning is flexible and does not require human intervention to make certain changes.

One of the most practical applications of ML is to solve classification problems. Many ML models such as Linear Classifiers, Logistic Regression, Naive Bayes Classifier, Support Vector Machines, Decision Trees, or Neural Networks can be used to make predictions for new data. For instance, an artificial neural

© ICST Institute for Computer Sciences, Social Informatics and Telecommunications Engineering 2019
Published by Springer Nature Switzerland AG 2019. All Rights Reserved
P. C. Vinh and A. Rakib (Eds.): ICCASA 2019/ICTCC 2019, LNICST 298, pp. 47–60, 2019.
https://doi.org/10.1007/978-3-030-34365-1_5

network (ANN) computation model which compose of multiple neuron layers, connections, and directions of data propagation has ability to learn features of data with multiple levels of abstraction by finding the suitable linear or non-linear mathematical manipulation to turn inputs into outputs. The learning processes, referred to as training phases, of a neural network are conducted to determine the value of parameters as well as hyperparameters (such as the number of neurons in the hidden layer, the weights apply to activation functions and the bias values) from training datasets. Based on results of these processes, each neuron will be assigned the most suitable weight value to form the trained neuron network. The entire network, then, can be used to compute corresponding outcomes for new data. This is referred to as the inference phase.

Real-time applications usually require heavy computational tasks; thus, general purpose processors (such as CPUs) are not efficient in system performance. Therefore, hardware accelerators such as Graphics Processing Units (GPUs), and Field Programmable Gate Arrays (FPGAs), have been employed to improve the throughput of ML algorithms in recent years. Although GPUs are mainly used for this purpose, they suffer from inflexibility in architecture due to hardwired configuration. Meanwhile, Field-Programmable Gate Arrays (FPGAs) play an important role in data sampling and processing industries due to its flexibility in custom hardware, high parallelism architecture, and energy-efficiency. While GPU is a good choice for the training phase of an ANN, FPGA is a promising candidate for processing inference phase [5,12].

In this work, we study on designing and implementing classification models for high-speed network attacks detection on FPGA platforms. In details, decision tree and neural network techniques are deployed into a NetFPGA-10G board to detect network attacks based on the NSL-KDD dataset [3]. The main contributions of this work are summarized as three folds.

- We design two classification models, the decision tree and neurons network, for detecting network attacks using the NSL-KDD dataset.
- We propose an architecture for implementing the models on FPGA platforms.
- We implement the first prototype version on the NetFPGA-10G board and validate the system with the NSL-KDD dataset. The experimental results shows that we can beat both Geforce GTX 850M GPU and Intel core i5 8th generation CPU in processing time.

The rest of this work is organized as follows. In Sect. 2, we discuss some relevant work and classification techniques used in this work. Section 3 presents our method to build and optimize machine learning models. Section 4 shows our implementation on the NetFPGA platform. We evaluate and analyze our system in Sect. 5. Finally, conclusion is discussed in Sect. 6.

2 Related Work and Background

2.1 Related Work

ID3 is a supervised learning algorithm which builds the tree based on attributes of a given set and the resulting model is used to predict the later samples. The more information it gains, the high precision the model is. However, researchers in [6] pointed out that its sensitivity on large value will yield low conditional values. C4.5 algorithm was proposed by the work in [1] to overcome the issues left by the ID3 algorithm by using information gain computation which produces measurable gain ratio. In order to increase its performance, researchers in [15] determined another alternative form of DT classification which is accelerated in the pipeline. The main idea is conducted on a binary decision tree in which input values going in the model are decided which subset will be executed instead of running through all the model at one time. After triggering the subset to execute, another input going in the model is calculated to choose the branch of the model while the previous subset is being executed.

In term of hardware-based, an implementation using FPGA approach is proposed in [15] for accelerating the decision tree algorithm. The architecture is constructed by various parallel processing nodes. In addition, the pipeline technique is applied to increase resource utilization as well as throughput. The proposed system is reported to be 3.5 times faster than the existing implementation. In recent years, classification and machine learning implementations are blockbuster research trends on FPGA platform. A hardware-based classification architecture named BV-TCAM, proposed in [16] aiming to implement a Network Intrusion Detection System (NIDS). The proposed architecture is a combination of the two algorithms, including Ternary Content Addressable Memory (TCAM) and Bit Vector (BV). This combination helps to represent data effectively as well as increasing system throughput.

There are various neural network implementations proposed on FPGA platform to take full advantages of the ability in reconfiguration, high performance and short developing time. The authors in [2] allows quickly prototyping different variants of neural networks. Other works focus on maximize resource utilization of FPGA hardware. Other works of James-Roxby [8] proposed an implementation of multi-layer perceptron (MLP) with fixed weights, which can be modified via dynamic reconfiguration with a short amount of time. A similar exploration is found in the work of [21]. On the one hand, in artificial neural networks (ANNs) FPGA-based implementations, weights are mostly represented in an integer format. Special algorithms are proposed in [9] represents weights by power-of-two integers. On the other hand, floating-point precision weights are also investigated in the work of [11]. However, there is rarely implement of floating-point weights on FPGA platform. In this paper, a MLP model is proposed with 32-bit floating-point precision weights for classification purposes on NetFPGA platform. In addition, a decision tree model is implemented for results comparison and evaluation.

2.2 Background

In this section, we introduce an overview of the two models, the decision tree and neurons network, that we use for building our high-throughput network attacks detection system. These models are used because they are efficient when implemented on FPGA.

Decision Tree. A decision tree [13] is a tree-like model for classifying data based on different parameters which are built as intermediate nodes. Each node functions as a test that provides possible answers for classifying data. The process is iterated until a leaf node is reached. The leaf nodes represent classifications of input data.

Artificial Neural Networks - ANN. ANNs [7] are computing systems that play an important role in variety of applications domain such as computer vision, speech recognition, or medical diagnosis. In ANNs, artificial neurons are connected through a directed and weighted connections and compute outputs based on the internal state and inputs (activation function). Compared to recurrent networks where neurons can be connected to other neurons in the same or previous layer, the feedforeword ones where neurons are formed a directed acyclic graph are mainly used in computing.

   Back Propagation has been dominated in the neural network as its efficiency as well as its stable error-minimizing for activation functions. Since the feed-forward is computed in the usual way, the back propagation depends on the output calculated from the activation function. In FPGA, the activation function will consume a huge amount of resources from hardware because of its complicated exponential equation, instead, a simulated activation which is simpler and implementable is applied in the model. To conduct the back propagation calculation, all the results of feed-forward computation from each node are cached so that it can compute the error of the function and narrow the weights to their most accurate values.

   Weights in a neural network can be treated as input going to a single node and fed to the network in feed-forward steps calculating the output of the single neuron. The main idea of back-propagation is using that output to calculate the error of the function and narrow the weights to their most accurate values. To handle the back-propagation computation, there are two values must be stored at each node:

- The output o of the node j in the feed-forward calculation
- The cumulative result of backward computation which is a back-propagated error, denote by δ

These two values are part of the gradient computation. The partial derivative of a function E respected to weight w is using the output of the neural network to calculate the impact of related weight inputs to the whole network can be express by Eq. 1.

$$\frac{\partial E}{\partial w_{ij}} = o_i \delta_j \tag{1}$$

We use Eq. 2 for calculating back-propagated errors, there are differences of finding at output layer and hidden layer. With the back-propagated error at output layer, the output target is required to compute using delta rule.

$$\delta = (target - output) * output * (1 - output) \tag{2}$$

With the back-propagated error at other layers, instead of finding difference between target activate value and actual output to calculate δ, they requires the total of multiplied back-propagated error of all nodes in the next layer and the respected weight since all single nodes of current layer connect to all node of the next layer.

$$\delta = \left(\sum \delta(nextlayer) * w\right) * output * (1 - output) \tag{3}$$

Once the gradient is computed in Eq. 3, the change of weight (Δw) can be calculated in Eq. 4 by multiplying it with the learning rate γ. Learning rate is a hyperparameter that controls how much weight it is adjusted in the network with respect to the loss gradient. The lower the learning rate, the slower travel on the slope of updating weight. It also means that it will take more time to get coverage.

$$\Delta w_{ij} = -\gamma o_i \delta_j \tag{4}$$

Finally, new weight are calculated by using current weight of j-th node adding the coverage of gradient respected to that weight in Eq. 5.

$$w_{new} = w_{old} + \Delta w_{ij} \tag{5}$$

3 Methodology

Our first prototype system on FPGA is developed to detect attacks on recorded network data. We choose NSL-KDD dataset [3] to construct and evaluate our design. Besides, the design of the FPGA-based approach which is parallel processing hardware is quite different from the software-based approach. With FPGA, hardware resources and tasks scheduling should be considered; thus, we try to optimize and find suitable machine learning models by using software-based before applying into FPGA. Furthermore, we can easily evaluate machine learning models which are built on software then using these results to compare with hardware in the same experiments (speed, accuracy test).

NLS-KDD [3] is chosen as the dataset for training and inference phases. For running with Weka tool [18], the dataset must be changed to the .arff format (ARFF stands for Attribute-Relation File Format). It is an ASCII text file that describes a list of instances sharing a set of attributes. There are 41 features

Table 1. The 6 features descriptions

Feature name	Description
duration	Length (number of seconds) of the connection
protocol_type	Type of the protocol, e.g. tcp, udp, etc.
src_bytes	Number of data bytes from source to destination
dst_bytes	Number of data bytes from destination to source
count	Number of connections to the same host as the current connection in the past two seconds
srv_count	Number of connections to the same service as the current connection in the past two seconds

in the data-set, however based on the hardware resource constraints, the 6 outstanding features [17] are selected due to their high impacts on the classification accuracy. The 6 features descriptions are shown in Table 1.

We have trained the system using 6 out of 41 features of NSL-KDD dataset as mentioned above to balance between accuracy and model size. The generated models are also tested with NSL-KDD dataset.

4   FPGA Implementation

In this section, we introduce our implementation of the proposed system, where a number of classification techniques are deployed on FPGA platform. Figure 1 illustrates the overview architecture of our system that can be partitioned into two layers, including CPU for running a software-based monitor tool and a device for deploying the FPGA-based architecture.

The CPU layer consists of monitor tools as interfaces for communication between administrators at the software level and the FPGA-based device. The FPGA-based device accommodates our proposed classification techniques in other to detect abnormal behaviors, including the following blocks:

1. The `Classifier` block is used to deploy classification techniques either decision tree or neural network. This block receives processed input features from the `Pre-processor` module to extract necessary features of incoming packets.
2. The `FIFO` memory buffers raw packets to increase the system throughput because of time-intensive of the Classifier block. This memory block is directly connected to Packet Pre-processor and Packet Controller.
3. The `Packet Controller` module receives results from Classifier and processes packets in the FIFO memory as well as sends alert signals based on decisions to administrators.

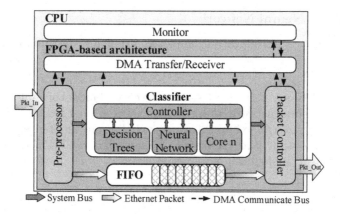

Fig. 1. First prototype system for applying classification techniques on FPFA

4.1 Decision Tree

The block diagram of the decision tree is represented in Fig. 2. There are 5 blocks in the architecture, including an input block, an output block, a recursive decision tree (sub-tree), a left-hand-side block, and a right-hand-side block. The input block is responsible for providing inputs to the recursive decision tree block while the output block gets the predictions from it. The recursive decision tree block decides which tree branch is enabled for making a prediction based on the combination of inputs. The left-hand-side tree branch is implemented as the LHS block while the right-hand-side tree branch is implemented as the RHS block.

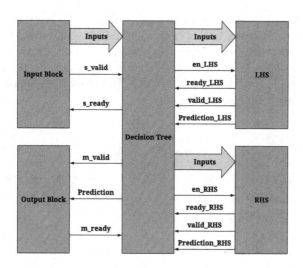

Fig. 2. Decision tree block diagram

4.2 Artificial Neural Network

In this section, we introduce our implementation for the proposed neuron-network core.

Feedforward Phase. Figure 3 illustrates the general model of a fully connected multiple layer neural network which is implemented on FPGA platform. The neural network is constructed from 4 layers, including one input layer, two hidden layers, and one output layer. Moreover, comparator and FIFO are added for outputs estimating and storing purposes.

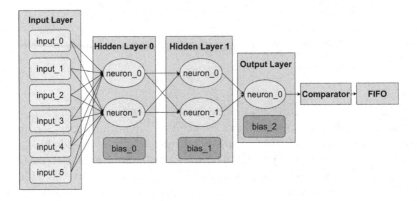

Fig. 3. Neuron network overview

There are 2 neurons in each hidden layer while only one neuron is implemented in the output layer. In addition, each hidden and output layer has dedicated configurable bias value for fitting different dataset. Furthermore, weight values in the two hidden and output layer are also adjustable for changing dataset or updating (neural network) model purposes. The block diagram of the multiple layer neural network is shown in Fig. 4.

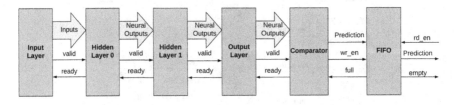

Fig. 4. Neuron network block diagram

For supporting asynchronous communication between modules, the handshaking mechanism is used in the neural network model. "Inputs" are passed through hidden layers and output layer for producing "Prediction" basing on weights and biases. These predictions are then written into a FIFO, waiting to be read. Moreover, the pipeline technique is used for increasing throughput of the system.

Update Weights Phase. As it can be seen in Fig. 5, there are two main elements in update weight implementation called delta calculator and weight calculator. The delta calculator must be executed in serial while the weight calculator can be started when the delta calculation is finished. The delta calculating flow top-down is ordered from the output layer back to the input layer.

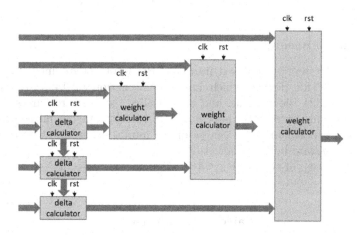

Fig. 5. Update weight block diagram

Delta calculator consists of three types. The delta calculator at output layer is the implementation of function in Eq. 2 while the other two is the implementation of function in Eq. 3. The weight calculator is the implementation of function in Eq. 5.

- Delta calculator at the output layer demands two inputs: result calculated from the output layer and the expected output from testing samples. This sub-module performs the back-propagated error calculation based on Eq. 2.
- Delta calculator at second hidden layer consists of the following inputs: the result calculated by the current neuron and all pairs of delta and coordinated weight of the right side layer that the neuron connects to. Because there are three neurons in the hidden layer so three instances of this module are required.
- Delta calculator at first hidden layer consists of the following inputs: the result calculated by the current neuron and all pairs of delta and coordinated weight of the right side layer that the neuron connects to. Because there are three neurons in the hidden layer so three instances of this module are required.

Weight calculator consists of three inputs which are the delta from the previous sub-module, the result from activation function and the weight respected to the output of activation function. The function of this module is that it will calculate the new weight based on the update function and the implementation is the same in all three layers.

5   Evaluation

In this section, we discuss the synthesis results, then present our experimental results for the proposed system. The classification cores are evaluated in two different experiments which are throughput and accuracy test.

5.1   Synthesis Results

Our proposed system is deployed into NetFPGA-10G board including Xilinx Virtex-5 xc5vtx240t device, which has a combination of 149,760 Registers, 149,760 LUTs, 324 BlockRAMs, and 37,440 Slice hardware resources in total. The system is synthesized with the Xilinx XPS 13.4 [20] and optimized using Xilinx PlanAhead toolchain [19]. Because of the limitation in hardware resources, we can not integrate both classification cores at the same time. Table 2 shows the resources usage of the system with either decision tree or Neural Network core.

Table 2. Resource usage

Resources	Decision tree	Neural network
Register	74,049 (49.45%)	117,078
LUT	67,552 (45.11%)	107,036 (71.47%)
BlockRAM	181 (55.86%)	181 (55.86%)
Maximum frequency	100.675 MHz	104.091 MHz

The results shows that the system with decision tree consumes nearly a haft hardware resources of xc5vtx240t device and the minimum frequency is 100.675 MHz. Meanwhile, the system with neural network consumes up to 78.18% Registers of this device with minimum frequency at 104.091 MHz. This result is one evidence that we have to separate decision tree from neural network in other to satisfy the availability of hardware resources.

5.2   Experimental Setup

The testing model in Fig. 6 is used to evaluate our system. The test uses two boards NetFPGA-10G with Xilinx xc5vtx240t device integrated into CPUs. Each board functions as a high-speed network transfer/receiver:

- One board NetFPGA-10G is installed OSNT (Open Source Network Tester) [4] which is responsible for sending packets at line-rate speed (up to 9.87 Gbps on each port) to our proposed system.
- Another board is our network attack detection system in which either the neural network or decision tree core is integrated The system is directly connected by network cable to the OSNT using SFP+ interface.

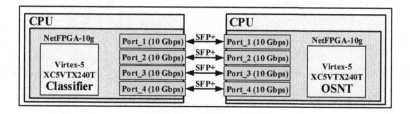

Fig. 6. Testing setup

Data using to test the system are attacking packets from NSL-KDD dataset with different lengths: 64B, 128B, 256B, 512B, 1024B and 1500B. To evaluate throughput of the system, we increase the sending rate of the OSNT board until it exceeds the maximum responding speed of the system.

5.3   Experimental Results

The throughput is recorded by the OSNT monitor tool with the setup in Fig. 6. Thank to the parallel architecture, decision tree on FPGA can achieve maximum throughput by up to 9.86 Gbps, as shown in Fig. 7. The throughput of the decision tree module is closed to throughput of incoming packets without any packet loss. Besides, the throughput of the neural network module gradually increases in the first three types of packet, from 1.28 to 3.40 and 6.96 Gbps with 64B, 128B, and 256B packets, respectively. With larger packets, 512B, 1024B, and 1500B, the processing throughput of both neural network and decision tree approximate to throughput of incoming packets without any packet loss.

For evaluating the accuracy of the neural network and decision tree core, we measure the percentage of correct predictions over total packets received. The testing set of NSL-KDD is used in this scenario. We also compare our cores on FPGA with the same models in different platforms which are GPU GeForce GTX 850M and CPU i5 8th generation with 16 GB RAM (Ubuntu 14.04). The results are shown in Table 3.

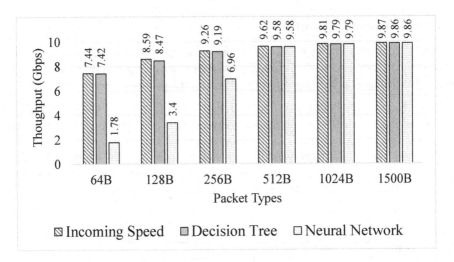

Fig. 7. Testing throughput

Table 3. Comparisons of three platforms in term of accuracy and processing time

Platform	Accuracy (%)		Processing time (s)	
	NN	DT	NN	DT
GPU GeForce GTX 850M	91.230	97.550	0.140	0.050
CPU i5 8300 with 16 GB RAM	87.300	95.102	1.007	0.405
FPGA with xc5vtx240t device	87.300	95.102	0.012	0.004

The accuracy values reported in Table 3 show that FPGA produces the same results as CPU does but faster than CPU for both cores. While GPU needs 0.14 s to finish the NN computation, the FPGA only need 0.012 s. In other words, speed-up of 11.6× is achieved when compared to GPU.

6   Conclusion

In this paper, we design and implement high-throughput machine learning techniques which are decision tree and neural network on FPGA platform to detect network attacks. The proposed system not only could examine network packets to detect various types of network attacks but also are flexible when different core can changed to adapt attacking types. We implement our proposal in Xilinx xc5vtx240t device with two detection cores: decision tree and neural network. The implemented neural network can detect attacks at 1.78 Gbps and up to 9.86 Gbps with packets size from 64B to 1500B, which thoroughly faster than Geforce GTX 850M GPU and i5 8th generation CPU 11x and 83x times, respectively. The neural network detection core can function at 104.091 MHz and achieve the accuracy at 87.3% while these numbers are 100.675 MHz and 95.1% for the decision tree core.

Acknowledgements. This research is funded by Ho Chi Minh City University of Technology - VNU-HCM, under Grant number T-KHMT-2018-25.

References

1. RuleQuest Research 2017: Is See5/C5.0 Better Than C4.5? https://rulequest.com/see5-comparison.html. Accessed 27 June 2019
2. Cox, C.E., Blanz, W.E.: GANGLION-a fast field-programmable gate array implementation of a connectionist classifier. IEEE J. Solid-State Circuits **27**(3), 288–299 (1992)
3. Canadian Institute for Cybersecurity: NSL-KDD dataset. https://www.unb.ca/cic/datasets/nsl.html. Accessed 27 June 2019
4. Github: OSNT 10G Home. https://github.com/NetFPGA/OSNT-Public/wiki/OSNT-10G-Home. Accessed 27 June 2019
5. Guo, K., Zeng, S., Yu, J., Wang, Y., Yang, H.: [DL] a survey of FPGA-based neural network inference accelerators. ACM Trans. Reconfigurable Technol. Syst. **12**(1), 21–226 (2019). https://doi.org/10.1145/3289185
6. Hssina, B., Merbouha, A., Ezzikouri, H., Erritali, M.: A comparative study of decision tree ID3 and C4.5. Int. J. Adv. Comput. Sci. Appl. **4**(2), 13–19 (2014)
7. Jain, A.K., Mao, J., Mohiuddin, K.: Artificial neural networks: a tutorial. Computer **3**, 31–44 (1996)
8. James-Roxby, P., Blodget, B.: Adapting constant multipliers in a neural network implementation. In: Proceedings 2000 IEEE Symposium on Field-Programmable Custom Computing Machines (Cat. No. PR00871), pp. 335–336. IEEE (2000)
9. Marchesi, M., Orlandi, G., Piazza, F., Uncini, A.: Fast neural networks without multipliers. IEEE Trans. Neural Netw. **4**(1), 53–62 (1993)
10. Mitchell, T.M.: Machine Learning, 1st edn. McGraw-Hill Inc., New York (1997)
11. Nichols, K.R., Moussa, M.A., Areibi, S.M.: Feasibility of floating-point arithmetic in FPGA based artificial neural networks. In: CAINE. Citeseer (2002)
12. Nurvitadhi, E., et al.: Can FPGAs beat GPUs in accelerating next-generation deep neural networks? In: Proceedings of the 2017 ACM/SIGDA International Symposium on Field-Programmable Gate Arrays, FPGA 2017, pp. 5–14. ACM, New York (2017). https://doi.org/10.1145/3020078.3021740
13. Quinlan, J.: Simplifying decision trees. Int. J. Man-Mach. Stud. **27**(3), 221–234 (1987). https://doi.org/10.1016/S0020-7373(87)80053-6. http://www.sciencedirect.com/science/article/pii/S0020737387800536
14. Russell, S., Norvig, P.: Artificial Intelligence: A Modern Approach, 3rd edn. Prentice Hall Press, Upper Saddle River (2009)
15. Saqib, F., Dutta, A., Plusquellic, J., Ortiz, P., Pattichis, M.S.: Pipelined decision tree classification accelerator implementation in FPGA (DT-CAIF). IEEE Trans. Comput. **64**(1), 280–285 (2013)
16. Song, H., Lockwood, J.W.: Efficient packet classification for network intrusion detection using FPGA. In: Proceedings of the 2005 ACM/SIGDA 13th International Symposium on Field-Programmable Gate Arrays, pp. 238–245. ACM (2005)

17. Tang, T.A., Mhamdi, L., McLernon, D., Zaidi, S.A.R., Ghogho, M.: Deep learning approach for network intrusion detection in software defined networking. In: 2016 International Conference on Wireless Networks and Mobile Communications (WINCOM), pp. 258–263. IEEE (2016)
18. T.U. of Waikato: Weka 3: Machine Learning Software in Java. https://www.cs.waikato.ac.nz/ml/weka/. Accessed 27 June 2019
19. Xilinx: PlanAhead Design and Analysis Tool. https://www.xilinx.com/products/design-tools/planahead.html. Accessed 02 Aug 2018
20. Xilinx: Xilinx Platform Studio (XPS). https://www.xilinx.com/products/design-tools/xps.html. Accessed 02 Aug 2018
21. Zhu, J., Milne, G.J., Gunther, B.: Towards an FPGA based reconfigurable computing environment for neural network implementations (1999)

IoT-Based Air-Pollution Hazard Maps Systems for Ho Chi Minh City

Phuc-Anh Nguyen, Tan-Ri Le, Phuc-Loc Nguyen, and Cuong Pham-Quoc[✉]

Ho Chi Minh City University of Technology, VNU-HCM, Ho Chi Minh City, Vietnam
cuongpham@hcmut.edu.vn

Abstract. Hazard map is one of the major parts in smart city model. It gives citizens an overview of a particular hazard in different areas within the city. In this paper, we research and implement an IoT-based air-pollution hazard map system for Ho Chi Minh City. The system consists of sensor and gateway nodes, a server, and maps. The collected sensor values include temperature, dust, carbon monoxide (CO), and carbon dioxide (CO_2). Data collected by sensors is transmitted to gateway nodes and forwarded to the server. The server saves received data to database and queries according to request from users. A web application have been built to display the data and give users an overview of air pollution state around them.

Keywords: Internet of Things · Hazard maps · LoRa

1 Introduction

The fourth industrial revolution (industry 4.0) has brought to our life technologies which take part in changing the world. One of the most significant factors of Industry 4.0 is Internet of Things (IoT). The appearance of IoT applications has led to the release of smart devices like smart TV, smart home, or even smart city. Among these innovations, smart city is the main target that Ho Chi Minh city has planned on its way heading to Industry 4.0.

The goals of smart city are to enhance living quality of life for citizens and improve service quality of the local government. A simple example of smart city is an air pollution monitoring system which helps citizens to easily get information about environment quality of their current location. Air pollution is one of biggest threats for the environment and affects everyone's health. The pollution is also the reason of climate change and global warming. In the past few years, Ho Chi Minh city's air pollution has reached an extremely high level. However, people living in this city do not have many channels to access the information of how polluted is the air. In this paper, we design and implement IoT-based air-pollution hazard maps systems for Ho Chi Minh city which is a part of building a smart city and also a contribution to citizens's quality of life improvement.

© ICST Institute for Computer Sciences, Social Informatics and Telecommunications Engineering 2019
Published by Springer Nature Switzerland AG 2019. All Rights Reserved
P. C. Vinh and A. Rakib (Eds.): ICCASA 2019/ICTCC 2019, LNICST 298, pp. 61–73, 2019.
https://doi.org/10.1007/978-3-030-34365-1_6

Components of our system include sensor and gateway nodes, a server, and maps. Sensor nodes collect 4 types of sensing data: temperature, dust, carbon monoxide (CO), and carbon dioxide (CO_2). Sensed data will then be transmitted to gateway in an AES-128 encrypted packet whose length is 13 bytes by using LoRa. Gateway is based on Raspberry Pi 3 Model B board running Android Things (AT) OS. When gateway receives the packet, it will validate data in it and create an AES-256 encrypted JSON string to send 4 sensing values to server through HTTP protocol. Server built by Nodejs is responsible for receiving and decrypting packets sent from gateways, interacting with MongoDB database, handling request from users, and displaying sensing data to web application. Users can view air pollution data on web application developed using ReactJS and OpenLayers library.

2   Background and Related Work

In this section, we introduce an overview of similar systems in other cities and discuss background knowledge used for our work.

2.1   Related Work

Deployed in the cities of Belgrade and Pancevo, EkoBus system has been developed in collaboration between Telekom Serbia, City of Pancevo, and Ericsson. Aim of the project is to monitor a set of environmental parameters over a large area by using public transportation vehicles. It uses instruments mounted onto existing public transportation vehicles in order to monitor temperature, relative humidity, CO, CO_2, NO_2, and vehicle location [1]. Sensor nodes make measurements and periodically send collected results to the server application with the help of GPRS data communication for further analysis and database storage.

The management of air quality in Canada's national capital region requires the identification of small-scale pockets of air pollutants in an area of over $5,000\,km^2$ and with a population of more than a million inhabitants. In order to cover this large area, AURA earth satellite observations, supported by local air quality sampling and modelling, were applied to provide comprehensive information about the spatial distribution and dispersion of air pollutants. A combination of information from fixed, mobile and portable air quality monitoring stations at ground level as well as the Aura instruments including the Ozone monitoring instrument from space was selected as the most effective approach for mapping local air quality. Hourly mapping of six pollutants was complemented by local information on transportation and stationary emission sources, land use, commuting patterns and meteorology. The end result was hourly displayed in the Canadian Geospatial Data Infrastructure with the following parameters: NO_2, NO, NOx, PM2.5, O_3, and CO [8].

2.2   Background

LoRa: LoRa (Long Range) is a wireless technology developed by Semtech. It has become the most popular LPWAN technology all over the world [4]. Advantages of LoRa are numerous: ability to transmit data in a long range (can reach kilometers), low power consumption, high reliability, Doppler robustness, etc. LoRa operates on an ISM band (Industrial, Scientific and Medical radio bands) which consists of free license radio bands reserved internationally for the use of industrial, scientific, and medical purposes. The frequencies of the band vary by region and data can be sent on 433, 868, or 915 MHz frequency band. Maximum payload length of a LoRa packet is allowed in the world varies from 51 to 222 bytes which depends on the data rate [3]. Despite having low data rate, LoRa is a reasonable solution for IoT applications that transmit small data packets between sensor nodes and a server/cloud.

Components of Sensor Nodes: For sensor nodes, we use Nucleo STM32L053R8 board to control operations. This board has an STM32L053R8 microcontroller whose core is ARM® Cortex® M0+ that has high performance and low power consumption. The chosen microcontroller has high-speed embedded memory with 64 Kbytes of Flash memory, 2 Kbytes of data EEPROM, and 8 Kbytes for RAM. Moreover, the microcontroller also supports traditional peripherals such as I2C, SPI, I2S, USART, LPUART, and crystal-less USB. In the operation mode, it consumes $88\,\mu A/MHz$ while also offering several sleep modes to reduce the power consumption.

Temperature sensor that we choose for the system is DS18B20. The sensor has digital output to achieve noise resistance ability and high precision. At the lowest resolution as 9-bit, DS18B20 only takes maximum 93.75 ms to convert temperature value. It can measure temperatures from $-55\,°C$ to $125\,°C$ with $\pm0.5\,°C$ accuracy within range from $-10\,°C$ to $85\,°C$.

CO sensors are MQ-7. This sensor can detect the presence of CO in the air with high sensitivity. Sensor's output supports both digital and analogue signals.

We choose SenseAir S8 LP as the CO_2 sensor. This sensor comes with miniature size and low power consumption. The sensor is based on non-disperive infrared (NDIR) technology to monitor CO_2. It is also built with self-correcting ABC algorithm. The algorithm constantly keeps track of the sensor's lowest reading over preconfigured time interval and slowly corrects for any long-term drift detected as compared to the expected fresh air value of 400ppm CO_2 [6].

Dust sensor which we choose for our sensor nodes is Sharp GP2Y1010AU0F. The sensor has low power consumption with 20 mA at max and 11 mA for average. It comes with an optical sensing system to detect dust in air and effectively detect fine particle. Output of the sensor is digital signal with typical sensitivity at $0.5\,V/0.1\,mg/m^3$.

We also integrate solar power in sensor nodes to extend life cycle of the nodes. Specifically, solar power management module DFR0559 is used to provide power for node's operation getting from LiPo battery and also to charge for the battery with power producing from solar panel. The module is controlled by CN3065 IC which has MPPT (Maximum Power Point Tracking) to maximize solar energy conversion efficiency under various sunlight. Battery can be charged by power from solar panel or through Micro USB port with maximum charge current at 900 mA. It also offers various features like Over charge/Reverse connection/Short circuit/Over current protections. Power output of the module is 5 V 1 A.

LoRa module Ra-02 is used for transmitting LoRa packets. It based on SX1278 chip from Semtech with receiving sensitivity as low as −141 dBm. The module has maximum transmit power at 18 dBm and 10 mW of output power.

Raspberry Pi 3 Model B: Pi is a mini computer which runs on operating systems with Linux core. Mainboard of Pi 3 already has components to make it like a normal computer such as CPU, GPU, RAM, MicroSD slot, Wi-Fi card, Bluetooth, 4 USB 2.0 ports, HDMI, etc. Raspberry Pi is developed by Raspberry Pi Foundation - a non-profit organization which targets to build multifunctional system that everyone can use for different purposes [5]. There are 3 OEMs responsible for manufacturing Raspberry Pi, including Sony, Qsida, and Egoman. Element14, RS Components, and Egoman are in charge of distribution. With a good specification and ability to be compatible with embedded operating systems, Raspberry Pi 3 is a suitable option for Gateway in a data collecting system.

Android Things: On May 7th, 2018, AT 1.0 was released at Google IO 2018. This is a OS that supports for IoT devices like smart speaker, CCTVs, etc with an Internet connection. Basically, AT was an update and renew version of Brillo - an OS based on Android for smart devices and IoT applications launched in the previous year. Similar to the original Android, AT was built as an open platform to support OEMs skipping the initial ecosystem development step and move straight to completing product process [2].

Below are some features of AT:

- Applications run on AT are coded with Java - one of the most popular object-oriented programming language in the present.
- The development process of an AT application is similar to mobile applications.
- Life cycle of an AT application is the same as an Android application.
- Similar to OTA (Over the air) updates on Android devices, developers can release updates for IoT devices in the same way with basic architecture that Google uses for their devices and services.
- Google Cloud Platform, Firebase, can easily be integrated into AT.
- AT is well compatible with Raspberry Pi 3 Model B. It provides APIs to use GPIO pins to communicate with other peripherals.

AES: AES (Advanced Encryption Standard) is an encryption algorithm which has been adopted by U.S Government. The algorithm is built based on the Rijndael Block Cipher developed by two Belgian cryptographers, Vincent Rijmen and Joan Daemen. AES works with a block size of 128 bits and cipher key with different lengths: 128, 192, and 256 bits. Expanded keys in AES are derived from the cipher key using Rijndael's key schedule. Most of operations in AES are performed with a finite field of bytes. Each 128 bits input block is divided into 16 bytes, arranged in 4 columns. Each column has 4 elements or a 4×4 matrix of bytes called state matrix. Depend on cipher key's length, the algorithm has different number of loops.

3 Proposed System

In this section, we introduce our proposed system with the aforementioned components. The system is suitable for deploying Ho Chi Minh City with reasonable cost.

3.1 Sensor and Gateway Nodes

Operations of our sensor node are controlled by STM32L053R8 microcontroller (as depicted in Fig. 1). The solar power management module DFR0559 is connected to a solar panel, a LiPo battery, and Nucleo board. The battery provides power for sensor node operations while solar panel produces power to charge the battery. These processes are managed by the solar power management module. Output of the module is provided for a Nucleo board which also supplies power for sensors. The flowchart of activities in sensor node is illustrated in Fig. 2.

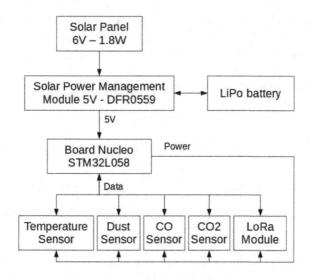

Fig. 1. Block diagram of sensor node

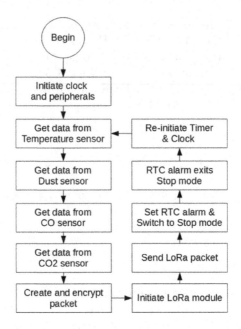

Fig. 2. Operation flowchart of sensor node

To optimize transmitting time of a LoRa packet, payload size should be minimized. Currently, Cayenne LPP [7] is applied by the Things Network for packaging information in payload. Cayenne LPP follows maximum payload size requirement and can be reduced to 11 bytes. As illustrated in Table 1, data is divided into 3 fields: Data channel, Type, and Value. Our version forked from Cayenne to follow the way value is encoded. We modify the packet structure to 13 bytes in length that contains 4 types of data including temperature, CO, CO_2, and dust concentration as shown in Table 2. The packets are encrypted with AES-128 and sent by LoRa to gateway.

Table 1. Example of Cayenne LPP payload in a device with 1 temperature sensor

Payload (HEX)	01 67 FF D7	
Data channel	Type	Value
$01 \Rightarrow 1$	$67 \Rightarrow$ Temperature	$FFD7 = -41 \Rightarrow -4.1\,°C$

The main responsibilities of gateway are to communicate with sensor nodes to gather environmental data and to forward to the server (as shown in Fig. 3). The major requirement for gateway is to have wireless communication within 100 m with sensor nodes. Furthermore, the main requirement for gateway is having ability to connect to the Internet by technologies like GSM or WiFi for sending

Table 2. Payload structure of packet from sensor node

1 byte	1 byte	2 byte	1 byte	2 byte	...
SensorID	Data1 Type	Data1	Data2 Type	Data2	...

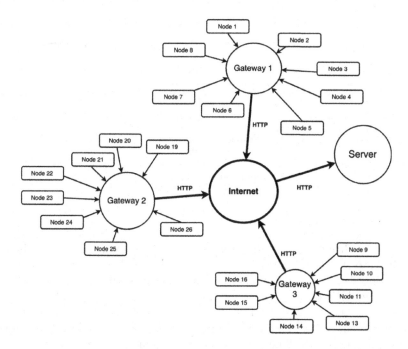

Fig. 3. Overview of gateway system

data to the cloud. In order to lower processing pressure on server, gateway is designed to filter received data. Only packets decrypted successfully and follow format will be sent to server.

Details of operations in gateway are illustrated in Fig. 4. At first, gateway registers to the server by sending a POST request that contains information about gateway (id, address, location, and name). Next, the initLoRa function is called to export necessary values to SPIdevices for setting LoRa module to running state. Most of the time LoRa module is in the sleep mode and will be woke up in 1 ms. The onReceive function is called to receive data. If there exists arriving data, the function sequentially saves data bytes until reaching 13 bytes of data as designed. In case received packets are shorter or longer than 13 bytes, gateway will skip these packets. When all 13 bytes of data received is valid, gateway will decrypt the packet and divide it into fields: sensorID, temperature, dust concentration, CO, and CO_2 concentration. Data will then be encoded to JSON string. Subsequently, gateway encrypts this string with AES-256 and sends to the server.

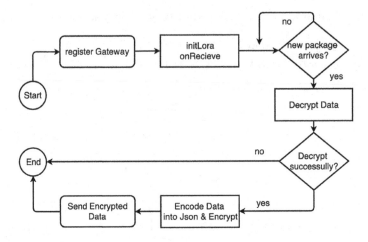

Fig. 4. Operation flowchar of gateway

3.2   Server and Maps

Data, collected from sensor nodes after being received by gateway, will then be transmitted to the server through the HTTP protocol. The server is responsible for gathering data from gateways, data decryption, saving them to database, and providing APIs to access data for clients.

The server architecture includes 3 modules (as shown in Fig. 5) with each module is in charge of distinctive function but can be combined to handle requests from client side. The three main modules in the server include:

- *Route module* defines API endpoints, pre-process attached data (decode, decrypt, ...), then call the Controller module to continue processing.
- *Controller module* interacts with database and accesses data based on inputs from the Route module.
- *Model module* is responsible for defining schemas in database. It combines with the Controller module to guarantee accessing right data from database.

To implement server as the above design, we use Nodejs to build the server and MongoDB for database that archives collected data. Using Nodejs helps the server to respond faster and gain better processing power. These advantages make Nodejs a right solution for frequently receiving data and supporting in real-time for client applications. Additionally, with collected data is discrete and does not have many relational constraints, the use of non-relational database like MongoDB speeds up queries and easily be expanded as the system grows.

After the implementation of the server and storing collected data, we next move to build a simple web application to display collected data as well as clarify development for the hazard map. ReactJS is used to build web application quickly and simply in combination with OpenLayers library to display a digital map. The application consists of 3 screens as follows.

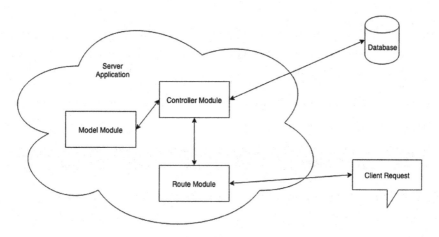

Fig. 5. Block diagram of server

Dashboard screen displays overview information extracted from gateways (as shown in Fig. 6). Information displayed includes average values of environmental parameters (based on 10 recent data collections), standard scale of health effects of parameters (will be showed when clicking on question mark ?ícon), 4 graphs corresponding to 4 parameters (temperature, dust - PM2.5, CO, CO_2 concentration). Besides, the bottom gives a view of the list of gateways and average values based on 20 recent data collections. This section allows users to quickly get information of any gateway.

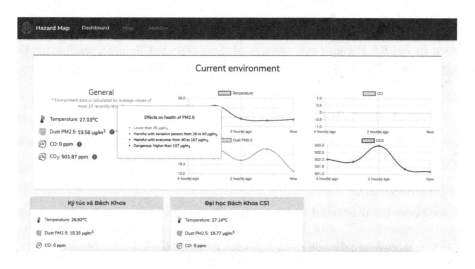

Fig. 6. Dashboard screen

Map screen displays a digital map by calling APIs of OpenLayers (as depicted in Fig. 7). The default location is set to the main campus of Ho Chi Minh city University of Technology. We use APIs supplied by the library to implement some features, including displaying gateway's location on the map or locating current location of user. With a digital map, web application will give users an intuitive view of the around environment status and easy access to parameters of nearby gateways.

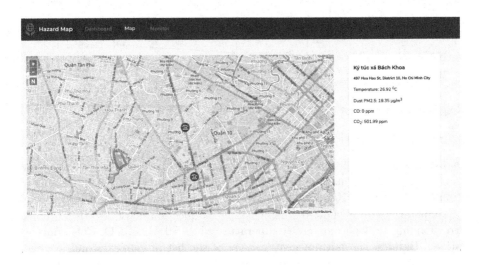

Fig. 7. Map screen

Monitoring screen displays collected data of each gateway in real-time (as shown in Fig. 8). Because the amount of data collected is huge, we limit this screen to show 20 recent data collections. The screen also shows 4 graphs corresponding to 4 parameters that enable user of monitoring instant change.

4   Deployment and Experiments

In this section, we describe our first prototype version deployed in Ho Chi Minh City.

4.1   Deployment

Sensor nodes (as illustrated in Fig. 9(a)) collects data of 4 sensors and sends to gateway through LoRa with AES-128 encryption. When gateway receives data, it will decrypt and validate data in the arrival packet. When data is valid, gateway creates a JSON string containing data of sensors and encrypts with AES-256. Gateway then sends the packet to server by HTTP protocol. Packets arrived at server will be decrypted and checked to store in database. New data arrived will be displayed on monitor screen on the web application as shown in Fig. 9(b).

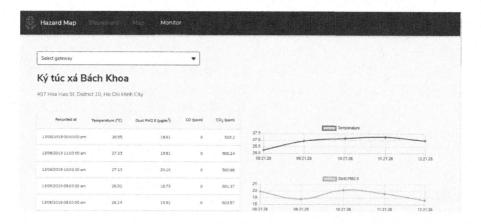

Fig. 8. Monitoring screen

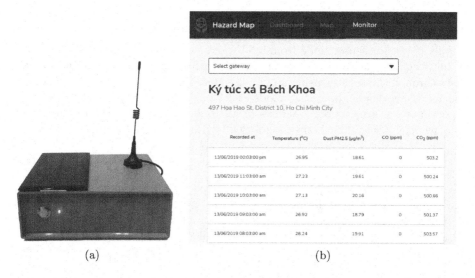

     (a)   (b)

Fig. 9. (a) Sensor node; (b) Data received at server and displayed on Web Application

4.2   Maximum Transmitting Range of Sensor Node

We have set up 2 scenarios to test the maximum range that sensor nodes can send LoRa packets successfully to the gateway. In the first scenario, data is transmitted in an environment with buildings around. Maximum transmitting range recorded in this scenario is 120.65 m (as shown in Fig. 10(a)). In the second scenario, data in transmitted in a clear environment without obstacles. Maximum transmitting range reached 181.89 m in this scenario (as illustrated in Fig. 10(b)).

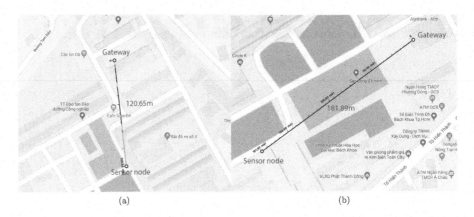

(a)   (b)

Fig. 10. (a) Experiment in environment with buildings around; (b) Experiments in clear environment

4.3 Power Consumption and Lifetime Estimation

Supply power for sensor node from a 5 V power source (V_{dd}) with a 1Ω resistor in between. We measure power consumption of the node by measuring power flows through the resistor using an Oscilloscope. Results are $V_T = 0.07485$ V for the average voltage in operation mode and $V_{sleep} = 0.04845$ V in sleep mode. In a period of 1 h, sensor node operates for 20.37 s and sleeps for the rest of time. The average voltage in 1-hour period (3600 s) is summarized in Eq. 1.

$$V_{\text{mean}} = \frac{V_T \times 20.37 + V_{\text{sleep}} \times (3600 - 20.37)}{3600} = 0.0486V \qquad (1)$$

where V_{mean} is the average voltage in 1-hour period. Applying the Ohm's law, the average current is 0.0486 A.

Capacity of sensor nodes (P_{node}) is calculated from capacity of the circuit (P_{circuit}) and capacity of resistors (P_R), as depicted in Eq. 2.

$$P_{\text{node}} = P_{\text{circuit}} - P_R = V_{dd} \times I - R \times I^2 = 0.24301 \text{ W} \qquad (2)$$

Let's call A is the battery capacity (Ah), T is total time using power from battery (hour), V is the battery voltage (V), η is the ratio of real battery capacity to capacity in specification (0.8 in normal). Life estimation of sensor node with power supply from a fully charged 1500 mAh 3.7V Li - Po battery is estimated in Eq. 3.

$$T = \frac{A \times V \times \eta}{P_{\text{node}}} = \frac{1.5 \times 3.7 \times 0.8}{0.24301} = 18.2707 \text{ h} \qquad (3)$$

Assume that a Li - Po battery may last 500 cycles, the total time that sensor nodes can normally operate using power supply from a Li - Po battery and solar panel before battery replacement needed is estimation in Eq. 4.

$$T_{\text{bat}} = \#\text{cycles} \times T = 500 \times 18.2707 = 9135.33 \text{ h} = 380.639 \text{ days} \qquad (4)$$

where T_{bat} is the battery life in hours.

5   Conclusion

Hazard maps systems have become a comprehensive analytical tool to provide information of vulnerability and risk for all users. From the government perspective, the system enables human operators to monitor the risk in a wide area that would help them on planning responses. As a citizen, hazard maps are the tool to actively deal with hazardous events. In this paper, we propose IoT-based Air-Pollution Hazard Maps Systems for Ho Chi Minh City to give people living in the city an overview of one of the biggest threats for health in urban areas. To achieve this aim, several design and techniques such as optimized payload structure or various screens for the web application have been used to complete the system design. By using LoRa to send packets between sensor and gateway nodes, sensor nodes do not need to be put in a close range with gateway like in systems using Wi-Fi or Bluetooth but still reach low power consumption.

Acknowledgment. This research is funded by Department of Science and Technology of Ho Chi Minh City under grant number 09/2018/HD-QKHCN.

References

1. Brković, M., Sretović, V.: Smart solutions for urban development: potential for application in Serbia. In: Proceedings of Regional Development, Spatial Planning and Strategic Governance (RESPAG) 2nd International Scientific Conference (2013)
2. Google Developers: Android things. https://developer.android.com/things/
3. LoRa Alliance: LoRaWAN^{TM} 1.1 Regional Parameters, January 2018
4. Mekki, K., Bajic, E., Chaxel, F., Meyer, F.: A comparative study of lpwan technologies for large-scale iot deployment. ICT Express **5**(1), 1–7 (2019). https://doi.org/10.1016/j.icte.2017.12.005
5. Raspberry Pi Foundation: What is a Raspberry PI? (2015). https://www.raspberrypi.org/help/what-is-a-raspberry-pi/
6. Senseair: Product Specification Senseair S8 LP Miniature CO2 sensor module width NDIR technique
7. The Things Network: Cayanne LPP. https://www.thethingsnetwork.org/
8. Urquizo, N., Spitzer, D., Pugsley, B., Robinson, M.: Mapping small scale air pollution distribution using satellite observations in a large Canadian city. In: 11th Conference on Atmospheric Chemistry of the Annual Conference of the American Meteorological Society, January 2009

Integrating Retinal Variables into Graph Visualizing Multivariate Data to Increase Visual Features

Hong Thi Nguyen[1], Lieu Thi Le[2], Cam Thi Ngoc Huynh[3],
Thuan Thi My Pham[4], Anh Thi Van Tran[5], Dang Van Pham[6,7],
and Phuoc Vinh Tran[4(✉)]

[1] University of Information Technology, Vietnam National University – HCMC,
Ho Chi Minh City, Vietnam
hongnguyen1611@gmail.com
[2] Thu Dau Mot University, Binhduong, Vietnam
lethilieu.qb@gmail.com
[3] Kiengiang Department of Education and Training, Kiengiang, Vietnam
camhuynhit@gmail.com
[4] Hochiminh City Open University, 35 Ho Hao Hon, Dist. 1,
Hochiminh City, Vietnam
{thuanptm.178i, phuoc.tvinh}@ou.edu.vn,
phuoc.gis@gmail.com
[5] Hochiminh College of Economics, Hochiminh City, Vietnam
anhttv@kthcm.edu.vn
[6] Nguyen Tat Thanh University, Ho Chi Minh City, Vietnam
pvdang@ntt.edu.vn
[7] Graduate University of Science and Technology, Hanoi, Vietnam

Abstract. The efficiency of a graph visualizing multivariate data is not only subjectively evaluated by human visual perception but also objectively estimated by visual features of graph. For a designed graph, it is necessary to improve visual features to enable human to extract better information from data. Integrating retinal variables into graph is an approach to increasing visual features of graph. In this study, the constituents of graph are grouped into classes of marks by qualitative and quantitative characteristics. The retinal variables are studied and structured to integrate into the classes of marks. A process of five steps is proposed to increase visual features by integrating retinal variables into graph. The process is illustrated with two case studies, increasing visual features of bus space-time map with qualitative mark classes and increasing visual features of the graph representing the data of hand-foot-mouth epidemic in Binhduong with qualitative and quantitative mark classes.

Keywords: Visual features · Retinal variable · Visual perception · Visualization · Multivariate data

P. C. Vinh and A. Rakib (Eds.): ICCASA 2019/ICTCC 2019, LNICST 298, pp. 74–89, 2019.
https://doi.org/10.1007/978-3-030-34365-1_7

1   Introduction

Information exists in various forms of data as sound, languages, words, signs, glyphs, graphs, pictures, and so on. The data shaped image contain much information than others and people can easily perceive information implicit in it [1]. Visualization refers to an approach to converting data of various forms to graphs to enable human to extract better information. In a visualization system, human is a component of the system and plays an important role in understanding the insights of graph [1]. Accordingly, the efficiency of a structure of graph is evaluated by human visual perception [2]. The challenge in increasing the efficiency of graph is that the improvement of visual features of graph is objectively evaluated while human perception of graph is subjectively evaluated. The problem to be solved is how to improve visual features of graph consistently with human perception.

The main idea is to integrate retinal variables into graph to improve its visual features. This study approaches the structure of graph to grouping its constituents into classes of structured marks by qualitative and quantitative characteristics consistent with human perception. Retinal variables are studied and suitably structured to integrate into the mark classes. This paper proposes a process integrating retinal variables into graph to increase visual features of the graph and simultaneously respond human capacity of visual perception.

This paper is structured as follows. The next section interprets related works together with the concepts as data variable, visual representation, visual features, structural marks, planar marks, and retinal variables. The third section proposes the process integrating retinal variables into multidimensional graph to increase its visual features. The fourth section applies this process for two case studies, improving visual features of bus space-time map and multidimensional graph representing the happenings of hand-foot-mouth epidemic in Binhduong province, Vietnam. The fifth section resumes the results of the paper.

2   Related Works and Conceptual Framework

2.1   Visual Representation of Multivariate Data

A dataset is considered as a combination of several subsets each of which is called a data variable depicting a unique attribute, i.e. each variable is a set of values. Visual representation of a set of multivariate data is a mapping of the set onto a multidimensional graph, called structural graph, where each data variable is converted to a structural variable shaped an axis of the graph, each data value or a data tuple is converted to a structural mark shaped a point, a line, or a polygon of the graph. Visual display is a mapping of structural graph onto planar graph on planar screen, where each structural mark is converted to a planar mark on planar screen. The integration of retinal variables into variables and marks of a graph, structural or planar, by visualization techniques converts the graph to visual graph.

2.2 Visual Features

The efficiency of a visual graph is subjectively evaluated by the levels of human perception. A visual graph is considered to be efficient if the duration to perceive necessary information is short, shorter and shorter [3]. An efficient graph enables human to extract significant information and discover valuable laws. A visual graph enables human to perceive the significance of data at the levels of structure of the graph according to associative, selective, ordered, quantitative characteristics, and length, which are also considered as visual features [3–5]. Accordingly, the efficiency of a visual graph can be objectively estimated by the levels of visual features.

Associative Feature. The associative feature refers to human perception on the similarity of marks, i.e. the associative feature enables human to group marks sharing one characteristic into a group.

Selective Feature. The selective feature refers to human perception on the selection of marks in accordance with given characteristic. In other words, the selective feature enables human to perceive the distinction between mark groups of different attributes or titles.

Ordered Feature. The ordered feature of a graph refers to human perception on the order of marks or mark groups representing data variables, such as one is bigger or smaller than another, one is higher or lower than another, one is nearer or farther than another, one is left or right from another, one is front or back from another, one is above or below from another.

Quantitative Feature. The quantitative feature refers to human perception on marks representing scale values or the ratio of two marks representing two real values.

Length. The length feature refers to the number of planar marks of a planar variable. This feature relates to the size and resolution of displayed screen, where the possible number of planar marks on a planar variable has to be more than the number of values of the data variable which it represents.

2.3 Visual Variables

A planar graph representing a set of multivariate data on 2-dimensional displaying environment is constituted by two types of visual variables, position variables and retinal variables [3, 5].

2.3.1 Position Variable

The position variable is a set of marks of points, lines, polygon, bar, pie, etc. positioned on structural graph. For visualization of a set of multivariate data, a mapping is applied to convert the constituents of the structural graph which is designed to represent data variables to position variables and marks on planar screen. In other words, a graph on displayed environment is the set of planar marks representing data values or data tuples.

2.3.2 Basic Retinal Variable

Basic retinal variables are composed of shape variable (S), size variable (Z), brightness variable (B), texture or symbol variable (L), color variable (C), and direction variable (D) [3, 5, 6] (Table 1).

Shape Variable, S. The *Shape* variable refers to geometrical planar marks. According to the concepts of geographic information science, the geometrical marks representing geographic objects comprises point, line, polygon or area, surface, and volume [7–10]. Point is indicated as a geometrical point positioned on planar screen. Line is traced as a curve or a polyline. Polygon or area refers to the area within a polygon of which vertices are on the same plane. Surface refers to a polygon of which vertices are not on the same plane. Volume refers to the space within a volume limited by planes. The *Shape* variable responds the associative and selective features. The *Shape* variable does not respond the ordered and quantitative features. The Shape variable can have numberless elements.

Size Variable, Z. The *Size* variable refers to the difference on size of marks. The *Size* variable responds associative, selective, and ordered features. The *Size* variable is hard perceived quantitative feature. The number of elements of *Size* variable is finite because of the resolution of human eyes and the size of planar screen.

Brightness Variable, B. The *Brightness* variable refers to human visual perception on the luminance of graphs. The *Brightness* variable is combined with the color variable for use. The *Brightness* variable responds associative, selective, and ordered features. The *Brightness* variable hard responds quantitative feature. The length of *Brightness* is finite because it depends on human's visual resolution.

Table 1. The table of basic retinal variables and their visual features.

Basic retinal variables	Elements of basic retinal variable (some illustrated examples)	Visual features				
		associa-tive	selec-tive	ordered	quanti-tative	Length (finite)
Shape *S*		✓	✓			
Size *Z*		✓	✓	✓	✓	✓
Brightness *B*		✓	✓	✓	✓	✓
Symbol *L*		✓	✓			
Color *C*		✓	✓			✓
Direction *D*		✓	✓	✓		✓

Symbol Variable, L. The *Symbol* variable refers to figures formed by points, line, curve, geometrical shape, star, cross, and so on which are arranged according to various types. The *Symbol* variable responds associative and selective features. The *Symbol* variable has not ordered feature. The *Symbol* variable does not limit the number of elements.

Color Variable, C. The *Color* refers to human visual perception by the discrimination of light waves reflecting from objects in real world. The *Color* variable refers to color spaces, where the usual space is RGB. In the RGB space, colors can be generated from three main colors, red, green, blue. Each generated color is defined by its coordinates on RGB space. The *Color* variable responds associative and selective features, but do not respond ordered and quantitative features. The number of colors which can be used depends on human color resolution.

Direction Variable, D. The *Direction* is generally indicated by the longitudes and latitudes of the Earth and presented on a plane. Each direction is indicated by the angle which is formed by the vector positioning object with the reference axis. The *Direction* variable responds associative, selective, and ordered features. The *Direction* variable does not respond quantitative feature. The number of directions is theoretically infinite but the demand of associative and selective features limits the number of directions.

3   The Integration of Retinal Variables into Graph

Visual representation of data refers to the conversion of various modes of data to image shaped graph of which significance is easily perceived by human. The level of human perception of graph depends on its visual features. The perception can be improved by integrating reasonably retinal variables into graph. The integration of retinal variables into a graph is a conversion of the multidimensional graph G' to the graph G of higher visual features. Technically, retinal variables can be integrated into structural or planar marks of structural or planar graph, respectively. The following is the process integrating retinal variables into graph.

3.1   Step 1. Grouping Marks of Graph into Mark Classes

A multidimensional graph G' displayed on planar screen is considered as set of planar marks $g_n | n = 1, 2, \ldots$. The planar marks are grouped into mark classes by qualitative or quantitative characteristics to meet the demand of problems extracting information or analyzing data. Each qualitative class is a set of marks of the same nominal characteristic or the same attribute, each quantitative class is a set of marks referring to values belonging to a defined segment.

Mathematically,

$$G' = \{g_n | n = 1, 2, \ldots\}$$
$$(G_m \cap G_{m'} = \varnothing) \vee (G_m \cap G_{m'} \neq \varnothing) | \forall (m \neq m')$$
$$(G_m \subset G' | \forall m) \wedge (G' = \bigcup_m G_m)$$

where $G_m | m = 1, 2, \ldots$ are mark classes which can be combined according to various modes G^k to restore multidimensional graph G':

$$G^k | k = 1, 2, \ldots \equiv G' = \{G_m | \bigcap_m G_m = \varnothing | m = 1, 2, \ldots\}$$

where modes $G^k | k = 1, 2, \ldots$ are restored from mark classes G_m with dimensional integrality [11].

3.1.1 Grouping Marks by Qualitative Characteristics

The constitution of mark classes by qualitative characteristics refers to the significance of constituents of graph and human perception. Mark classes are constituted by applying Gestalt principles [11–13], where the marks of the same nominal character-istic or the same attribute such as bus route, bus station, ground trajectory, the number of patients, humidity, rainfall, temperature, and so on are grouped into a mark class by qualitative characteristic, briefly called qualitative mark class. The mark classes may intersect one another or not, i.e. a mark may simultaneously belong to one or more classes, e.g. a bus station may be used for one or more bus routes, a ground trajectory belongs to both ground trajectory class and bus route class.

3.1.2 Grouping Marks by Quantitative Characteristics

The constitution of mark classes by quantitative characteristics, briefly called quanti-tative mark class, refers to values of data variables. The range of values of a variable can be divided into segments. The marks representing the values of a segment are grouped into a class, called a scale, where each scale is a subset of a class grouped by qualitative characteristics. The following are the ways to group the marks of a class into scales.

Number Table. Number table which refers to a data table of a data variable comprises two columns of which elements associate with one another on each line as a data tuple. As an example, wind speed is recorded in a table of two columns, one for wind speed in *m/s* and one for wind force scale in natural numbers. The wind speed table may be represented on a 2-dimensional orthogonal coordinates, where one coordinate indicates wind speed in *m/s*, another indicates wind force scale in natural numbers (see Fig. 1). In visualization, marks representing wind speed in real values are grouped into seg-ments each of which is a mark class, briefly called scale.

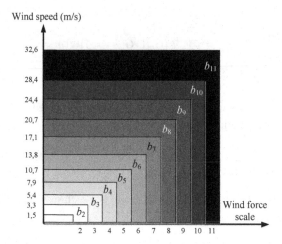

Fig. 1. Wind speed of real numbers mapped onto wind force scale of natural numbers.

Transfer Function. Mathematically, the relation between real values and scales is defined by a transfer function which is linear or nonlinear (see Fig. 2). Marks of a scale are grouped into a class, briefly called scale.

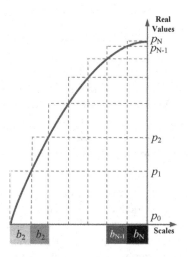

Fig. 2. The transfer function representing the relation between real values and scales of a data variable.

Local Maximum or Minimum. When marks representing local maxima or minima of a variable need to be dominated to evaluate the relation among variables, these marks and their neighbors are grouped into a class, briefly also called scale.

3.2 Step 2. Constituting Generated Retinal Variables

Generated retinal variables integrating into mark classes are constituted from basic retinal variables based on the number of mark classes, the characteristics of each class, and human capacity of visual perception. Each generated retinal variable is a subset of a basic retinal variable or a product of basic retinal variables. The number of mark classes, the characteristics of mark classes, the requests of visual features of classes are referred to form generated retinal variables.

3.2.1 Generated Retinal Variable for Qualitative Mark Classes

The integration of generated retinal variables into qualitative mark classes aims at dominating their qualitative characteristics. The generated retinal variables are designed as subsets of basic retinal variables. Each element of a generated retinal variable, called visual mark, which is used to integrate into a qualitative mark class has to be suitable for the characteristics and significance of the class, as well as the user's demands in extracting information. For example, the symbol of line is suitable for trajectories, the symbol of polygon for administrative units, the symbol of bar for the number of patients, the color is utilized to group or select the constituents of a qualitative mark class. The number of visual marks of a generated retinal variable is equal to the number of qualitative mark classes which they integrate into.

The problem to be solved to increase visual features of structural graphs is that the number of visual marks of a basic retinal variable can not respond all qualitative mark classes or that human visional resolution limits the number of visual marks of a generated retinal variable. Indeed, it is impossible to use all colors to increase visual features of graph because human is difficult to perceive the difference of two quite similar colors, human can not perceive the difference of two line marks of two different attributes.

Generated retinal variables are sets of visual marks extracted from basic retinal variables or from the product of two or more basic retinal variables. Mathematically, if let $R' = \{S, Z, B, L, C, D\}$ be the set of basic retinal variables, generated retinal variables are the subsets of the sets S, Z, B, L, C, D or the subsets of product sets SZ, ZB, BL, LC, CB, DS, and so on. The set of generated retinal variables is $R = \{R^S, R^Z, R^B, R^L, R^C, R^D, R^{SZ}, R^{ZB}, R^{BL}, R^{LC}, R^{CB}, \ldots\}$, where $R^S \subset S$, $R^Z \subset Z$, $R^B \subset B$, $R^L \subset L$, $R^C \subset C$, $R^D \subset D$, $R^{SZ} \subset SZ$, $R^{ZB} \subset ZB$, $R^{BL} \subset BL$, $R^{LC} \subset LC$, $R^{CB} \subset CB$, and so on.

The number of visual marks of a product set is equal to the product of the number of marks of individual sets. As an example, if the basic retinal variables $S = \{s_1, s_2, \ldots, s_M\}$ contains M visual marks, the basic retinal variables $Z = \{z_1, z_2, \ldots, z_N\}$ contains N visual marks, then the product set SZ has $M.N$ visual marks $SZ = \{s_1z_1, s_1z_2, \ldots, s_1z_N, s_2z_1, s_2z_2, \ldots, s_2z_N, \ldots, s_Mz_1, s_Mz_2, \ldots, s_Mz_N\}$. The increase of visual marks by the product of basic retinal variables results in the increase the number of mark classes which can be integrated visual marks.

3.2.2 Generated Retinal Variables for Scale Mark Classes

The integration of a generated retinal variable into mark classes of scales aims at dominating the quantitative characteristics of scale marks. In visualization, the values and scales of a data variable are simultaneously represented on graph, the marks representing real values are integrated by visual marks, the marks representing scales are also integrated by visual marks of generated retinal variable. Accordingly, each scale mark is integrated by two visual marks, one for characteristic of data variable and one for scale of data variable. In this case, the set of marks representing a data variable is visualized by two generated retinal variables, one retinal variable associates marks of the same characteristic or attribute of the data variable and another selects different scales of the data variable.

3.3   Step 3: Processing the Intersections of Mark Classes

Many marks of graph belong to two or more classes, such as some stations in bus space-time map simultaneously belong to two or more different classes of routes [14]. Mathematically, a mark belonging to many classes only shares one or few attributes or characteristics which it represents. Hence, a mark shared by different mark classes must represent common and individual attributes. In other words, a shared mark must satisfy all significances of the mark classes which it belongs to. For example, a station shared by several route represents a common attribute being station, and individual attributes being the names of bus routes to which it belongs as the bus station of routes 15. For displaying, a shared mark is structured as a combination of visual marks of the classes which it belongs to.

3.4   Step 4: Integrating Generated Retinal Variables into Mark Classes

The integration of generated retinal variables into mark classes converts graph G' to visual graph G. Mathematically, the integration of generated retinal variables into mark classes is a mapping of G' onto G by the Cartesian product of G' and the set of generated retinal variables R,

$$G = R \times G' = \{R^S, R^Z, \ldots\} \times \{G^1, G^2, \ldots\}$$
$$G = R \times G' = \{R^S \times G^1, R^Z \times G^2, \ldots\}$$

The products can be generally defined as follows.

$$R^S \times G^1 = \{s_1, s_2, \ldots\} \times \{G_1^1, G_2^1, \ldots\} = \{s_1 G_1^1, s_2 G_2^1, \ldots\}$$
$$R^Z \times G^2 = \{z_1, z_2, \ldots\} \times \{G_1^2, G_2^2, \ldots\} = \{z_1 G_1^2, z_2 G_2^2, \ldots\}$$
$$R^B \times G^3 = \{b_1, b_2, \ldots\} \times \{G_1^3, G_2^3, \ldots\} = \{b_1 G_1^3, b_2 G_2^3, \ldots\}$$
$$R^L \times G^4 = \{l_1, l_2, \ldots\} \times \{G_1^4, G_2^4, \ldots\} = \{l_1 G_1^4, l_2 G_2^4, \ldots\}$$
$$R^C \times G^5 = \{c_1, c_2, \ldots\} \times \{G_1^5, G_2^5, \ldots\} = \{c_1 G_1^5, c_2 G_2^5, \ldots\}$$
$$R^D \times G^6 = \{d_1, d_2, \ldots\} \times \{G_1^6, G_2^6, \ldots\} = \{d_1 G_1^6, d_2 G_2^6, \ldots\}$$

$\ldots$

where $G_m^k | k = 1, 2, \ldots$ is a mode combining mark classes G_m.

$$G = R \times G' = (R^S \times G^1) \cup (R^Z \times G^2) \cup (R^B \times G^3) \cup \ldots$$

The classes of marks representing data of real values and scales may be integrated by a generated retinal variable which is a product of two basic retinal variables. For example,

$$R^{BC} \times G^7 = \{b_1c_1, b_2c_1, \ldots\} \times \{G_1^7, G_2^7, \ldots\} = \{b_1c_1G_1^7, b_2c_1G_2^7, \ldots\}$$

where:

$$R^B = \{b_1, b_2, \ldots\} \subset B$$
$$R^C = \{c_1, c_2, \ldots\} \subset C$$

$G^7 = \{G_1^7, G_2^7, \ldots\}$ is a mode of G', where $G_m^7 | m = 1, 2, \ldots$ is the mark class G_m of the combining mode G^7.

The product $R^{BC} \times G_m = \{b_1c_1, b_2c_1, \ldots\} \times G_m$ is considered that the color c_1 is integrated into all marks of the mark class G_m meanwhile scales of G_m are integrated by different brightness $b_1, b_2, \ldots$.

Generally, the integration of generated retinal variables into mark classes can be visually designed with a 2-dimensional matrix, where a dimension indicates mark classes, another indicates generated retinal variables and visual marks. In addition, the integration can also be designed with mathematical expressions. The design with mathematical expression is suitable for graphs visualizing data variable of quantitative characteristics as scales.

3.5 Step 5: Displaying Visual Graph

The graph G visualized from G' by integrating retinal variables is displayed on screen with various modes to enable user to extract information and discover knowledge.

4 Case Studies

4.1 Case Study 1. Visualizing Space-Time Map of Bus

Bus space-time map is considered as a graph representing bus network of a city on space-time cube [14, 15]. The density of marks on the map results in the decrease of visual features and user is difficult to extract information. The efficiency of the map is improved by integrating retinal variables into its marks in accordance with the following process.

Step 1. Grouping Marks of Bus Space-Time Map. The marks of bus space-time map is divided into the mark classes.

- *The class of stations.* Bus stations of all routes are grouped into the mark class of station.

- *The class of space-time points.* Space-time points are marks of points associating bus stations with time points, where each space-time point associates with a station and a time point when a bus calls at the station. All space-time points are grouped into a mark class of space-time points.
- *The class of ground trajectories.* Ground trajectories are polylines connecting bus stations of the same route. Ground trajectories of all routes are grouped into a mark class of ground trajectories.
- *The class of space-time trajectories.* Space-time trajectories are polylines connecting space-time points of the same trip. Space-time trajectories of all routes are grouped into a mark class of space-time trajectories.
- *The class of route.* Each route are constituted by a ground trajectory, stations combining with the ground trajectory, space-time points, and space-time trajectories of the route.

Table 2. The table of the integration of generated retinal variables into mark classes.

Generated retinal variables	Visual Marks	Mark classes of				
		stations	space-time points	ground trajectories	space-time trajectories	routes
Shapes ↓	Point	●	●			
	Line			/	/	
Symbols ↓	Square	▢				
	Dash				⋰	
	Arrow			↗		
Colors ↓	Red	■	●	↗	⋰	Route 1
	Green	■	●	↗	⋰	Route 2
	Blue	■	●	↗	⋰	Route 3

Step 2. Constituting Generated Retinal Variables. The shapes of point and line are used to indicate marks of bus space-time map on displayed plane. The symbols of dash, arrow, triangle, square, and filled circle are designed to integrate into marks of lines or points. The color variable is designed to integrate into marks of bus routes.

Step 3. Processing the Intersections of Mark Classes. In a bus space-time map, some bus stations are shared by different routes. The marks indicating these stations need to be processed to connect simultaneously to different routes. In other words, each common station must be integrated the visual marks of all routes which it belongs to.

Step 4. Integrating Generated Retinal Variables into Mark Classes. The shape of point is assigned to class of stations and class of space-time points. The shape of line is assigned to the class of ground trajectories and the class of space-time trajectories to represent route trajectories and trip trajectories, respectively. The symbol of square is integrated into the mark class of stations to represent bus stations. The symbol of dash is integrated into the mark class of trip trajectories to represent trip trajectories. The symbol of arrow is integrated into the mark class of route trajectories to represent route trajectories and the direction of bus movement on the route. All constituents of a route are integrated by a color to differentiate a route from others. The integration generated retinal variables into mark classes is designed on a table (see Table 2).

Step 5. Displaying Visual Map. After being integrated retinal variables, the bus space-time map is improved its efficiency because of the increase of visual features (see Fig. 3).

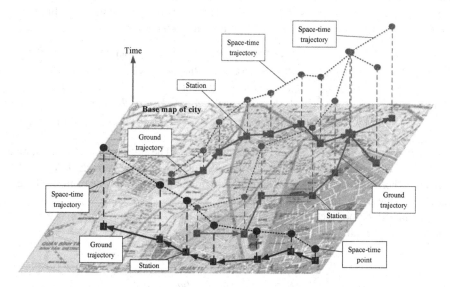

Fig. 3. An illustration of the integration of retinal variables into bus space-time map

4.2   Case Study 2. Representing the Data of Hand-Foot-Mouth Epidemic

The happening of hand-foot-mouth epidemic in Binhduong province during 2012–2014 is represented as a multidimensional graph on a multidimensional cube [16, 17]. The graph represents four data variables, the number of patients, rainfall, humidity, and temperature which share the reference variable of time. The graph can be improved the efficiency by integrating retinal variables into graph to increase visual features.

Step 1. Grouping Marks of Graph. The marks representing the data of happening of hand-foot-mouth epidemic are divided into 4 mark classes corresponding to 4 data variables, the number of patients (P), rainfall (R), humidity (H), temperature (T). It is necessary to consider the relation among data variables because they together refer to time variable. Each of P, R, H, T variables is divided into 3 mark classes as subset of P, R, H, T, respectively, called scales, corresponding to 3 groups of values of data. Maximal scale involves marks representing the values of local maxima and their neighbors, minimal scale involves marks representing the values of local minima and their neighbors, and medial scale involves remainder.

Step 2. Constituting Generated Retinal Variables. The mark classes representing 4 data variables share the visual mark of bar shape to indicate the value of data. Each qualitative mark class as the number of patients, rainfall, humidity, temperature is integrated by a color (a visual mark of color variable). Each quantitative mark class as scales is additionally integrated by a visual mark of brightness variable.

$R^S = \{bar\} = \{barP, barR, barH, barT\}$, where $barP$ is the class of marks shaped bars representing the number of patients; $barR$ is the class of marks shaped bars representing rainfall; $barH$ is the class of marks shaped bars representing humidity; $barT$ is the class of marks shaped bars representing temperature.

$R^C = \{c_1, c_2, c_3, c_4\} = \{red, green, blue, orange\}$ is the generated color variable.
$R^B = \{b_1, b_2, b_3\} = \{dark, medium, light\}$ is the generated brightness variable.
$R^{BC} = \{b_1, b_2, b_3\} \times \{c_1, c_2, c_3, c_4\}$ is the product of two retinal variables.
$R^{BC} = \{\{b_1, b_2, b_3\}c_1, \{b_1, b_2, b_3\}c_2, \{b_1, b_2, b_3\}c_3, \{b_1, b_2, b_3\}c_4\}$
$R^{BC} = \{\{b_1c_1, b_2c_1, b_3c_1\}, \{b_1c_2, b_2c_2, b_3c_2\}, \{b_1c_3, b_2c_3, b_3c_3\}, \{b_1c_4, b_2c_4, b_3c_4\}\}$

Step 3. Processing the Intersections of Mark Classes. The intersection of a qualitative mark class with scales is processed by the product of brightness variable and color variable, where color variable is integrated into qualitative mark classes and brightness variable is integrated into scales.

Integrating the product of generated retinal variables into mark classes to represent simultaneously qualitative mark classes and scales:

$$R^{BCS} = R^{BC} \times R^S$$
$$R^{BCS} = R^{BC} \times \{barP, barR, barH, barT\}$$

Step 4. Integrating Generated Retinal Variables into Mark Classes. Mark classes representing the number of patient composed of qualitative marks and scales are integrated by the generated retinal variable:

$R^{BCP} = \{dark.red.barP, medium.red.barP, light.red.barP\}$ composed of 3 visual marks corresponding to 3 scales of the variable of the number of patients.

Mark classes representing rainfall composed of qualitative marks and scales are integrated by the generated retinal variable:

$R^{BCR} = \{dark.green.barR, medium.green.barR, light.green.barR\}$ composed of 3 visual marks corresponding to 3 scales of the variable of rainfall.

Mark classes representing humidity composed of qualitative marks and scales are integrated by the generated retinal variable:

$R^{BCH} = \{dark.blue.barH, medium.blue.barH, light.blue.barH\}$ composed of 3 visual marks corresponding to 3 scales of the variable of humidity.

Mark classes representing temperature composed of qualitative marks and scales are integrated by the generated retinal variable:

$R^{BCT} = \{dark.orange.barT, medium.orange.barT, light.orange.barT\}$ composed of 3 visual marks corresponding to 3 scales of the variable of temperature.

Step 5. Displaying Visual Graph. The dark colors representing the maximum marks of the number of patients, rainfall, humidity emphasizes the relation among variables. The marks of dark colors of visual graph representing the data of hand-foot-mouth epidemic in Binhduong are perceived the correlation among the variables of the number of patients, rainfall, humidity. The variable of temperature is not perceived any correlation. If this correlation is confirmed by bigger dataset, the result may be used to predict the happening of hand-foot-mouth epidemic when viewing visual graph representing data in real time (Fig. 4).

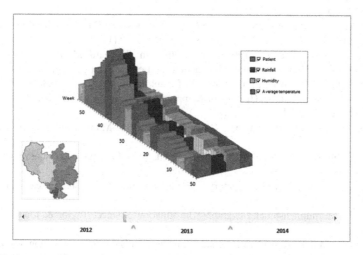

Fig. 4. The visual graph representing the dataset of hand-foot-mouth epidemic in Binhduong province, Vietnam, during 2012–2014, shows the relation among the number of patients, rainfall, and humidity, meanwhile temperature does not affect the number of patients [16, 17].

5   Conclusion

The efficiency of a graph representing visually a dataset depends on human perception. The visual features are utilized to estimate objectively the efficiency of a visual graph according to the level of human perception of the significance of graph. The visual features of a graph are improved when retinal variables are suitably integrated into marks of graph. Graphs of good visual features enable user to extract valuable information and/or discover new knowledge by viewing and thinking.

The paper proposed a process of integrating retinal variables into graph representing multivariate data to increase visual features of the graph. Marks of graph are grouped into mark classes by qualitative and quantitative characteristics, where qualitative mark classes refer to nominal characteristics and quantitative mark classes refer to the values of data variables. Generated retinal variables used to integrate into graphs are formed from basic retinal variables. In that, each generated retinal variable is a subset of a basic retinal variable or a product of basic retinal variables. The process is illustrated with the visualization of bus space-time map and the multidimensional graph representing the data of happening of hand-foot-mouth epidemic in Binhduong province, Vietnam, during 2012–2014.

Acknowledgment. The paper is sponsored by Hochiminh City Open University, Vietnam.

References

1. Few, S.: Tapping the power of visual perception. Perceptual Edge, pp. 1–8, 4 September 2004
2. Dastani, M.: The role of visual perception in data visualization. J. Vis. Lang. Comput. **13**, 601–622 (2002)
3. Green, M.: Toward a Perceptual Science of Multidimensional Data Visualization: Bertin and Beyond. ERGO/GERO Human Factors Science. Citeseer (1998)
4. Few, S.: Data visualization for human perception. In: Soegaard, M., Dam, R.F. (eds.) The Encyclopedia of Human-Computer Interaction, 2nd edn. Aarhus, Denmark (2014)
5. Bertin, J.: General theory, from semiology of graphics. In: Dodge, M., Kitchin, R., Perkins, C. (eds.) The Map Reader. Theories of Mapping Practice and Cartographic Representation, pp. 8–16. Wiley (2011)
6. Bertin, J.: Semiology of Graphics: Diagrams, Networks, Maps. University of Wisconsin (1983)
7. Card, S.: Information visualization. In: Chi, Ed. (ed.) Information Visualization, PARC 2007, pp. 510–543 (2007)
8. Jensen, J.R., Jensen, R.R.: Introductory Geographic Information Systems. Pearson Education (2013)
9. Raper, J.: Multidimensional Geographic Information Science. Taylor & Francis, London (2000)
10. Carpendale, M.S.T.: Considering Visual Variables as a Basis for Information Visualisation. Department of Computer science, University of Calgary, Calgary, AB, Canada (2003)
11. Wagemans, J., et al.: A century of gestalt psychology in visual perception II. Conceptual and theoretical foundations. Psychol. Bull. **138**, 1218–1252 (2012)

12. Nguyen, H.T., Pham, T.M.T., Nguyen, T.A.T., Tran, A.V.T., Tran, P.V., Pham, D.V.: Two-stage approach to classifying multidimensional cubes for visualization of multivariate data. In: Cong Vinh, P., Alagar, V. (eds.) ICCASA/ICTCC-2018. LNICST, vol. 266, pp. 70–80. Springer, Cham (2019). https://doi.org/10.1007/978-3-030-06152-4_7

13. Alexandre, D.S., Tavares, J.M.R.S.: Introduction of human perception in visualization. Int. J. Imaging Robotics™, **4**, 60–70 (2010)

14. Nguyen, H.T., Duong, C.K.T., Bui, T.T., Tran, P.V.: Visualization of spatio-temporal data of bus trips. Presented at the IEEE 2012 International Conference on Control, Automation and Information Science, ICCAIS 2012, Hochiminh City, Vietnam (2012)

15. Nguyen, H.T., Ngo, D.N.T., Bui, T.T., Huynh, C.N.T., Tran, P.V.: Visualizing space-time map for bus. In: 6th International Conference on Context-Aware Systems and Applications, and Nature of Computation and Communication, ICCASA 2017, Tam Ky, Vietnam, pp. 38–47 (2017)

16. Nguyen, H.T., Tran, A.V.T., Nguyen, T.A.T., Vo, L.T., Tran, P.V.: Multivariate cube integrated retinal variable to visually represent multivariable data. In: EAI Endorsed Transactions on Context-aware Systems and Applications, vol. 4, pp. 1–8 (2017)

17. Nguyen, H.T., Tran, A.V.T., Nguyen, T.A.T., Vo, L.T., Tran, P.V.: Multivariate cube for representing multivariable data in visual analytics. In: Cong Vinh, P., Tuan Anh, L., Loan, N.T.T., Vongdoiwang Siricharoen, W. (eds.) ICCASA 2016. LNICST, vol. 193, pp. 91–100. Springer, Cham (2017). https://doi.org/10.1007/978-3-319-56357-2_10

An Approach of Taxonomy of Multidimensional Cubes Representing Visually Multivariable Data

Hong Thi Nguyen[1], Truong Xuan Le[2], Phuoc Vinh Tran[2(✉)], and Dang Van Pham[3,4]

[1] University of Information Technology, Vietnam National University - HCMC, Ho Chi Minh City, Vietnam
hongnguyen1611@gmail.com
[2] Hochiminh City Open University, 35 Ho Hao Hon, Dist. 1, Ho Chi Minh City, Vietnam
{truong.lx, phuoc.tvinh}@ou.edu.vn,
phuoc.gis@gmail.com
[3] Nguyen Tat Thanh University, Ho Chi Minh City, Vietnam
pvdang@ntt.edu.vn
[4] Graduate University of Science and Technology, Hanoi, Vietnam

Abstract. In data visualization, graphs representing multivariable data on multidimensional coordinates shaped cubes enable human to understand better the significance of data. There are various types of cubes for representing different datasets. The paper aims at classifying kinds of cubes to enable human to design cubes representing multivariable datasets. Mathematically, the functional relations among five groups of variables result in the way to structure cubes. The paper classifies cubes as three kinds by the characteristics of datasets, including non-space, 2D-space, and 3D-space multidimensional cubes. The non-space multidimensional cubes are applied for non-space multivariable datasets with variables of objects, attributes, and times. The 2D-space multidimensional cubes are applied for the datasets of movers or objects located on ground at time units. The 3D-space multidimensional cubes are applied for the datasets of flyers or objects positioned in elevated space at time units. The correlation in space and/or time shown on the cubes enables human to discover new valuable information.

Keywords: Multidimensional cube · Multivariable data · Multivariate data · Graph representing data · Data visualization

1 Introduction

A graph representing visually multivariable data is estimated as to be effective if it enables well to extract interesting information and/or discover new knowledge. Technically, the effectiveness of graph depends on the structure of the cube representing it. In other words, the structure of cube affects the effectiveness of graph representing a dataset. Mathematically, the structure of cube representing graph has to be appropriate for the characteristics of dataset [1]. Meanwhile, various types of multidimensional cubes (multivariate cubes, visualization cubes, and so on) have been

© ICST Institute for Computer Sciences, Social Informatics and Telecommunications Engineering 2019
Published by Springer Nature Switzerland AG 2019. All Rights Reserved
P. C. Vinh and A. Rakib (Eds.): ICCASA 2019/ICTCC 2019, LNICST 298, pp. 90–104, 2019.
https://doi.org/10.1007/978-3-030-34365-1_8

proposed to represent visually multivariable datasets as graphs on planar screen. In a cube, each data variable is represented as an axis and each data value or data tuple is represented as a planar mark on screen [1–8].

The issue to be solved is how to structure an effective cube representing a multivariable dataset. The main idea is to classify the cubes representing multivariable data by the characteristics of dataset. Data variables of datasets are grouped into five variable groups including objects, attributes, time, 2D-space, and 3D-space, where each variable or variable group is independent or dependent on others, mathematically. The relations among variable groups are studied to constitute the types of structures of cubes. A taxonomy of multidimensional cubes enables designers to structure coordinates representing a dataset as an effective graph responding analytical questions. The combination of basic cubes composed of non-space cube, 3D-cube, and space-time cube results in three types of multidimensional cubes to represent multivariable datasets, including non-space multidimensional cube, 2D-space multidimensional cube, and 3D-space multidimensional cube.

This paper is structured as follows. The next section depicts the relations among entities by 3W-Triad, OTL-Triad, OATL-Quad, OATL-Pentad and classifies multidimensional cubes according to the groups of the relations. The third section depicts the structure of non-space multidimensional cube and its utilization for data analysis along with an illustration. The fourth section depicts the structure of 2D-space multidimensional cube and its utilization for data analysis along with two case studies. The fifth section depicts the structure of 3D-space multidimensional cube and its utilization for representing flight data. Finally, the sixth section is the conclusion of the paper.

2 Representing the Relations Among Entities

2.1 The 3W-Triad

While representing temporal dynamics in geographic information systems, Peuquet proposed the triad framework representing the relations of questions What, When, and Where [9]. In that, a vertex of the triad is known if the two remainders are given

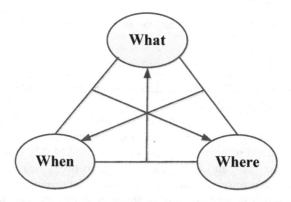

Fig. 1. The 3W-triad representing the relation What-When-Where.

(Fig. 1), i.e. When + Where → What; What + When → Where; What + Where → When. The 3D-triad relations are consistent with forming analytical questions at elementary level of spatio-temporal data analytics.

2.2   The OTL-Triad

While analyzing the movement of objects, Andrienko et al. considered that three sets of data suitable for studying movement are objects, times, and locations, among which the relation can be represented as a triad [10]. The relations in Objects-Times-Locations triad (OTL-Triad) represent the spatial and temporal characteristics of objects (Fig. 2). An object relating with time is considered as a temporal object of which the existent time is determined during observation. An object relating with a location is considered as a spatial object of which the spatial position is indicated during its existence. An object relating to a spatio-temporal position is considered as a spatio-temporal object of which spatio-temporal position is determined during its existence and within observational area. A moving object is a spatio-temporal object of which spatial position changes over time. Attributes of objects are not mentioned in OTL-triad.

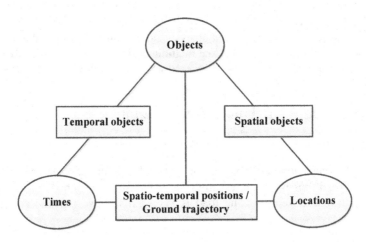

Fig. 2. The OTL-triad representing the relation Objects-Times-Locations.

2.3   The OATL-Quad

In geographic information systems, a dataset is structured by the following sets, objects, attributes, times, and 2D-space. In that, *objects* is the set of bounded and homogenous entities [11], *attributes* are the sets of inherent characteristics of objects, *times* is the set of time units which are instants or time intervals [12], and *2D-space* is the set of objects shaped points, lines, polygons on ground [9, 12]. In the OATL-quad (Fig. 3), the relation between objects and times or between objects and 2D-space defines temporal objects or spatial objects, respectively, the relations between attributes and objects are inherent relations, an attribute is-of objects and an object is-of attributes. As inherent characteristics of objects, attributes together with objects in OATL-quad refer to times or 2D-space. Objects referring simultaneously to times and 2D-space are spatio-temporal objects or moving objects (movers).

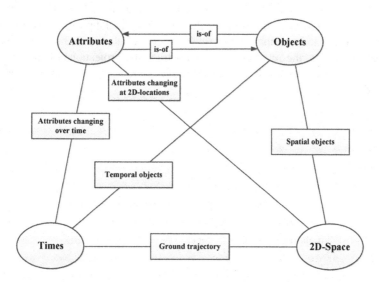

Fig. 3. The OATL-quad representing the relation of Objects-Attributes-Times-2D-Space.

2.4 The OATL-Pentad

OATL-pentad is developed from OATL-quad, where 3D-space is the set of locations positioned in elevated space. The relations among variables in dataset are depicted as OATL-pentad (Fig. 4). In that, *attributes* and *objects* are the variables depending on the reference variables of *times*, *2D-space* or *3D-space*. The dependence of *attributes*, *objects*, and the combination of *objects* and *attributes* on reference variables results in the cases of relations as follows.

- *Referring to time:* The relation of 6 represents the dependence of attributes on time. The relation set of 1, 2, 6 represents the dependence of the combination of objects and their attributes on time.
- *Referring to 2D-space:* The relation of 10 represents the positions of objects on ground. The relation of 5 represents the variation of attributes at ground locations. The relation set of 1, 2, 6, 10 represents different objects at ground and time positions, called spatio-temporal objects, of which the attributes change over time. The relation set of 2, 8, 10 represents the movement of objects on ground, where the ground position of each object changes over time and the relation of 8 traces their ground trajectories. The relation set of 1, 2, 6, 8, 10 represents the ground position and attributes of objects changing over time. The relation set of 5, 6, 8 represents attributes changing at 2D-locations and over time.

– *Referring to 3D-space:* The relation of 7 or the relation set of 7, 4, 10 represents the spatial positions of objects in elevated space, where the relation of 4 indicates the projections of objects on ground. The relation set of 2, 3, 7 or 2, 3, 7, 4, 8 represents the flight of objects in elevated space, where the relation of 3 traces trajectories, the relation of 4 traces the projections of trajectories on ground. The relation set of 2, 3, 7, 1, 6 or 2, 3, 7, 4, 8, 1, 6 represents the change of spatial positions of objects and the variation of their attributes over time, where the relation of 3 traces trajectories in elevated space, the relations of 3 and 4 trace the projections of trajectories on ground, the relations of 4 and 8 trace spatio-temporal trajectories referring to ground.

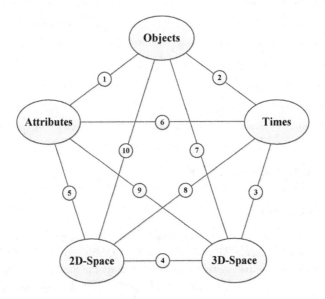

Fig. 4. The OATL-pentad representing the relations of Objects, Attributes, Times, 2D-space, 3D-space in a dataset.

2.5   The Types of Multidimensional Cubes

The functional relations of variables in the studied set of multivariable data shown in OATL-Pentad indicate three reference variables, times, 2D-space, 3D-space and three dependent variables, objects, attributes, and the combination of objects and attributes. The relations are represented in coordinates structured as cubes displayed on planar screen. The cubes are divided into three types according to three reference variables, non-space multidimensional cube, 2D-space multidimensional cube, 3D-space multidimensional cube.

– *Non-space multidimensional cubes:* The non-space multidimensional cubes are designed to represent the dependence of attributes on time by the relation of 6, the dependence of the combination of objects and their attributes on time by the relation set of 1, 2, 6.

– *2D-space multidimensional cubes:* The 2D-space multidimensional cubes without time are designed as traditional maps to indicate the locations of objects on ground by the relation 10, or as topographic maps to represent attributes changing at ground locations by the relation of 5, e.g. the map of landform, the map of temperature. The 2D-space multidimensional cubes with time are designed as multidimensional maps to represent the variation of attributes over time at some different ground positions by the relation set of 1, 2, 6, 10. The 2D-space multidimensional cubes with time are designed as space-time cube to represent objects moving on ground by the relation set of 2, 8, 10. The 2D-space multidimensional cubes with time are designed to represent objects moving on ground and their attributes changing over time by the relation set of 1, 2, 6, 8, 10.

– *3D-space multidimensional cubes:* The 3D-space multidimensional cubes are designed to represent the positions of objects in elevated space by the relation of 7 or the relation set of 7, 4, 10. The 3D-space multidimensional cubes are designed to represent the flight of objects by the relation set of 2, 3, 7, and the flyers together with their attributes changing over time by the relation set of 1, 2, 6, 3, 7, 4, 8.

3   The Non-space Multidimensional Cube

3.1   Structure of Non-space Multidimensional Cube

Non-space multidimensional cube is modified from parallel coordinates by rotating the axis representing the shared-reference variable by 90° to the direction perpendicular to the plane of parallel coordinates (Fig. 5a). For a non-space multidimensional cube, an axis is utilized to represent time which is the shared-reference variable, where time units associating with different attributes are synchronized. The other parallel axes are

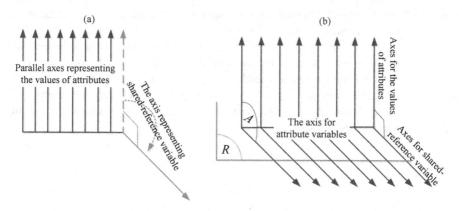

Fig. 5. (a) Non-space multidimensional cube is modified from parallel coordinates by rotating the axis for shared-reference variable; (b) Structure of non-space multidimensional cube with *A* is attribute plane and *R* is relation plane.

utilized to represent attributes or objects referring to time units on time axis. The plane *A* constituted by a time axis and an attribute axis is defined as an attribute plane to represent the values of an attribute or the existence of an object associating with time units (times). The relation plane *R* perpendicular to and moved along time axis shows the correlation between attributes over time (Fig. 5b).

3.2   Non-space Multidimensional Cube for Visual Analytics

For analyzing visually data, human can perceive information and significance of data by viewing graphs on attribute and relation planes of non-space multidimensional cube to answer local, global, and relative questions. Interacting to *A* and *R* planes and viewing the marks on it, human can answer:

- *Local questions:* Local questions are answered by viewing marks on *A* planes. On an *A* plane of a non-space multidimensional cube representing attributes, each mark refers to a value of the attribute of *A* and a time. On an *A* plane of a non-space multidimensional cube representing objects, each mark refers to the title of the object of *A* and a time during the existence of the object.
- *Global questions:* Global questions are answered by viewing marks on *A* planes. Human can perceive the characteristics of an attribute of *A* and answer global questions while viewing the variation of the attribute over time on this *A* plane.
- *Relative questions:* Relative questions are answered by interacting to *R* plane and viewing the marks on it. Moving the *R* plane along the time axis and viewing the marks on it, human can perceive and discover the correlation between attributes.

3.3   Case Study 1: The Non-space Multidimensional Cube Representing Epidemic Data in a Province

The dataset about the hand-foot-mouth epidemic in Binhduong province, Vietnam, during 2012–2014 is constituted by data variables referring time as the number of patients, the average rainfall, the average humidity, and the average temperature (Fig. 6) [2, 3]. Because the dataset does not include spatial data, we represented it on non-space multidimensional cube, where the time units referred by different data variables are synchronized to share the time axis of the cube with all data variables. The non-space multidimensional cube representing dataset of the hand-foot-mouth epidemic enables to answer analytical questions. Especially, moving the relation plane R along the time axis, human may discover the correlation between the number of patients and rainfall and humidity; but there is no correlation between the number of patients and average temperature.

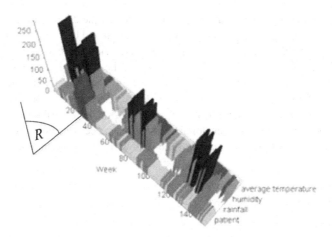

Fig. 6. Non-space multidimensional cube represents the hand-foot-mouth epidemic in Bin-hduong province, Vietnam, where the marks on relation plane R show the possible correlation between the number of patients and rainfall and humidity [2, 3].

4   The 2D-Space Multidimensional Cube

4.1   Structure of 2D-Space Multidimensional Cube

Generally, a 2D-space multidimensional cube is constituted by combining a non-space multidimensional cube with a space-time cube, where the time axis is shared with the cubes. A 2D-space multidimensional cube is used as a 3D-map to represent objects or attributes referring ground locations, as a multidimensional map to represent dataset of attributes referring ground locations and time, as a cube representing objects moving on ground.

For representing the variation of an attribute at locations on ground, the 2D-space multidimensional cube is structured as a 3D-map with 3 orthogonal axes, where two axes indicate locations on ground as a map, another indicates the values of the attribute. According to geographic information science, Thiesen polygon and Delauney triangle enable to represent the variation of attribute at locations on ground [13, 14]. The 2D-space multidimensional cube is suitable for representing terrain, the distribution of temperature or humidity on ground, etc.

For representing the variation of attributes over time at locations on ground, a 2D-space multidimensional cube is structured as a multidimensional map by combining a space-time cube with one or more non-space multidimensional cubes (Fig. 7). The space-time cube is utilized as a map to indicate locations on ground and its time axis is shared with attributes represented at the locations. The attributes at different locations are represented as time-reference variables on different non-space multidimensional cubes. After synchronizing time units on the time axes of non-space multidimensional cubes with time unit on the time axis of space-time cube, the non-space multidimensional cubes are combined with the space-time cube at suitable locations on ground map to form a 2D-space multidimensional cube.

For representing objects moving on ground, a space-time cube is utilized to indicate the ground positions of the objects changing over time [15, 16]. For representing movers along with their attributes, a 2D-space multidimensional cube is utilized to indicate spatio-temporal positions of the objects and the variation of the attributes over time. In studying the movement, attributes changing at locations can transfer to changing over time because locations of objects change over time. The 2D-space multidimensional cube representing movers along with their attributes is formed by combining a non-space multidimensional cube with a space-time cube, where the non-space multidimensional cube shares the time axis with the space-time cube.

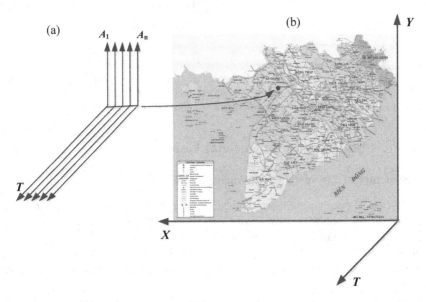

Fig. 7. The 2D-space multidimensional cube, designed as a multidimensional map, is the combination of a space-time cube (Fig. b) with one or more non-space multidimensional cubes (Fig. a) at different spatial positions indicated on the map. (Map source: https://www.google.com.vn/search?source=hp&ei=nuH4XPXpBJyQwgP7yLzQBw&q=b%E1%BA%A3n+%C4%91%E1%BB%93+vi%E1%BB%87t+nam&oq=b%E1%BA%A3n+%C4%91%E1%BB%93+&gs_l=psy-ab.1.0.0l10.1616.6227..9236…4.0..0.79.622.11……0….1..gws-wiz…..0..0i131j0i10.YPYjVWaCMaY)

4.2   The 2D-Space Multidimensional Cubes for Visual Analytics

For analyzing data represented visually on a 2D-space multidimensional cube, human can perceive the information and significance of data by viewing graphs and marks on the cube or on planes parallel or perpendicular to the plane of map.

– *Local questions:* For a cube structured as a 3D-map, the values of an attribute is inferred from the values recorded at indicated spatial positions by approaches of Thiesen or Delauney. For a cube structured as a multidimensional map, the value of an attribute at a spatio-temporal position is indicated on the attribute plane of this attribute of the non-space multidimensional cube at the corresponding spatial position. For a cube representing moving objects, the spatio-temporal position of an object is indicated on the space-time cube and the value of an attribute of an object at a time unit is indicated on the non-space multidimensional cube making up 2D-space multidimensional cube.

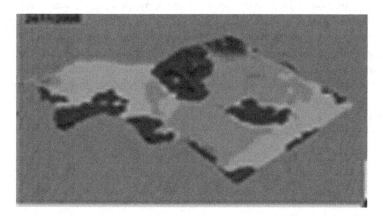

Fig. 8. The 3D-map of flood water level is represented visually by integrating the retinal variable of color [17].

- *Global questions:* For a cube structured as a 3D-map, the variation of an attribute at locations within a given spatial zone is perceived by the visual features of graph integrated by retinal variables (Fig. 8). For a cube structured as a multidimensional map, the variation of an attribute over time at a spatial position is studied on the plane of the attribute at the spatial position. For a cube representing moving objects, the ground and spatio-temporal trajectories are perceived on the space-time cube making up the 2D-space multidimensional cube, the variation of an attribute of the moving object over time is perceived on the non-space multidimensional cube making up the 2D-space multidimensional cube.
- *Relative questions:* The 2D-space multidimensional cube structured as a multidimensional map enables to discover the spatial and temporal correlations, the exchange the temporal for spatial correlation and vice versa. The 2D-space multidimensional cube representing moving objects enables to design spatio-temporal trajectories as well as to estimate the attribute correlation of different objects moving together within the same zone.

4.3 Case Study 2: The 2D-Space Multidimensional Cube Representing Epidemic Data at Several Locations

The dataset of the happening of dengue fever epidemic in Angiang, Soctrang, Tiengiang provinces, Vietnam, during 2009–2012 is constituted by data variables referring to time and spatial positions of the provinces [5]. The dataset is divided into three data subsets, each of which is located at a province. Three non-space multidimensional cubes are designed to represent the variables of the number of patients, rainfall, humidity, and average temperature changing over time, where each cube represents the subset of a province. These three cubes are combined with the space-time cube at the locations of corresponding provinces and share the time axis with the space-time cube (Fig. 9a).

It is easy to answer local and global questions by viewing the marks representing data on attribute planes of data variables at provinces. Technically, the relation plane parallel to the map plane indicates the topology relation of the durations of the epidemic happenings at different provinces. The time topology of happenings in Angiang and Soctrang enables human to infer the possible spatial correlation between Angiang and Soctrang. The discovery need to be considered whether there is an epidemical vector from Angiang to Soctrang because Angiang is upstream from Soctrang on Mekong riverside and the epidemic in Angiang happens at the end of the epidemic in Soctrang (Fig. 9b).

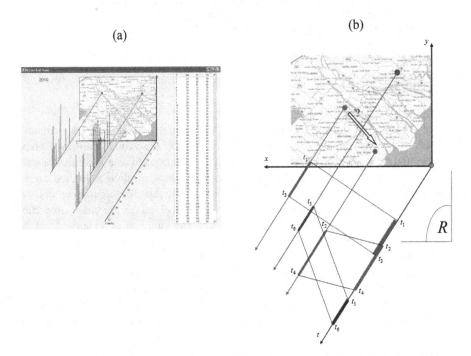

Fig. 9. (a) The 2D-space multidimensional cube represents the dengue fever epidemic in Angiang, Soctrang, Tiengiang provinces, Vietnam, during 2009–2012: (b) The time topology of the epidemic happenings in the provinces shows the possible spatial correlation between the epidemic happenings in Angiang and in Soctrang [5] (Map source: http://www.vietbando.com/maps/?t=0&st=0&l=9&kv=10.0378237,105.853271).

4.4   Case Study 3: The 2D-Space Multidimensional Cube Representing Moving Objects

The dataset of Napoleon's campaign in 1812 to Moscow comprises the data variables of the locations and the times of battles, the number of soldiers going to and coming out each battle, air temperature on retreating. The Napoleon's army is mathematically modeled as a moving object of which the attribute is the number of soldiers. The dataset is composed of the variables of space, time, and the number of soldier dependent on time. In addition, air temperature may be considered as an attribute dependent on time.

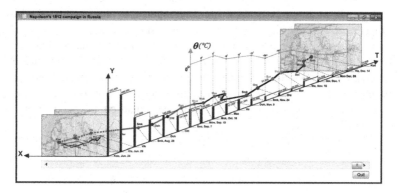

Fig. 10. Napoleon's march to Moscow in 1812 [7]

A 2D-space multidimensional cube may be utilized to represent the dataset (Fig. 10). In that, the space-time cube represents the march of Napoleon's army and the non-space multidimensional cube represents the number of soldiers changing over time. The space-time cube represents the march of the army as a space-time line of which the projection on map represents the line of march on ground. The non-space multidimensional cube represents the number of soldiers of the army coming in and coming out a battle. The space-time cube is combined with the non-space multidimensional cube to form the 2D-space multidimensional cube representing the Napoleon's campaign in 1812. The representation shows the loss of troops at each battle and the possible correlation between air temperature with the loss of soldier on retreating.

5   The 3D-Space Multidimensional Cube

5.1   Structure of 3D-Space Multidimensional Cube

A 3D-space multidimensional cube representing objects in elevated space is constituted by combining a 3D-cube and a non-space multidimensional cube. A 3D-space multidimensional cube for representing flyers is constituted by combining a 3D-cube, a space-time cube, and a non-space multidimensional cube (Fig. 11). In that, the 3D-cube shares ground map with the space-time cube, the non-space multidimensional cube shares the time axis with the space-time cube.

5.2   The 3D-Space Multidimensional Cube for Visual Analytics

- *Local questions:* A 3D-space multidimensional cube representing the data of objects in elevated space enables human to perceive the attributes of the objects at different positions in elevated space. A 3D-space multidimensional cube representing the flight data of flyers enables human to perceive the elevated positions as well as the projections on ground and attributes of the flyers at different time positions. Human views marks on cubes making up 3D-space multidimensional cube to answer local questions.
- *Global questions:* A 3D-space multidimensional cube representing the data of objects in elevated space enables human to perceive the heights of objects as buildings or towers by viewing on the planes parallel to ground map. A 3D-space multidimensional cube representing the flight data of flyers enables human to perceive the state of the flight as well as attributes of an flyer during studied time. Human views on 3D-cube to cognize the trajectories of flyers in elevated space and its projections on ground, views on space-time cube to cognize its spatio-temporal trajectories, and views on non-space multidimensional cube to cognize the variations of attributes over time.

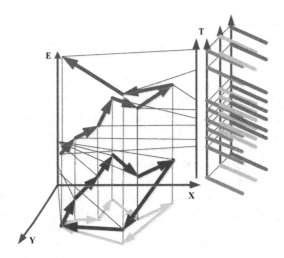

Fig. 11. The 3D-space multidimensional cube for representing flyers

6   Conclusion

The paper analyzed the relations among groups of variables making up a dataset to classify multidimensional cubes as non-space multidimensional cube, 2D-space multidimensional cube, 3D-space multidimensional cube. The non-space multidimensional cube represents dataset of the relations between objects, attributes, and time. The 2D-space multidimensional cube is designed to represent dataset of happening changing over time at some locations, and represent dataset of mover of which ground position and attributes change over time. The 3D-space multidimensional cube is designed to represent objects located in elevated space and flyers having attributes and positions in elevated space changing over time.

The paper summarized the case studies from previous studies to illustrate the effectiveness of types of multidimensional cubes. The non-space multidimensional cube representing the dataset of hand-foot-mouth epidemic in Binhduong province, Vietnam, shows the correlation between the number of patients and rainfall, humidity. The 2D-space multidimensional cube representing the dataset of dengue fever epidemic in Angiang, Soctrang, Tiengiang provinces, Vietnam, shows the spatial correlation between the happenings in Angiang and Soctrang, where the spatial correlation between Angiang and Soctrang provinces is inferred from the temporal correlation between two happenings of epidemic in two provinces.

Acknowledgment. This paper is sponsored by Hochiminh City Open University.

References

1. Thi Nguyen, H., Thi Pham, T.M., Thi Nguyen, T.A., Thi Tran, A.V., Vinh Tran, P., Van Pham, D.: Two-stage approach to classifying multidimensional cubes for visualization of multivariate data. In: Cong Vinh, P., Alagar, V. (eds.) ICCASA/ICTCC -2018. LNICST, vol. 266, pp. 70–80. Springer, Cham (2019). https://doi.org/10.1007/978-3-030-06152-4_7

2. Nguyen, H.T., Tran, A.V.T., Nguyen, T.A.T., Vo, L.T., Tran, P.V.: Multivariate cube integrated retinal variable to visually represent multivariable data. EAI Endorsed Trans. Context-Aware Syst. Appl. **4**, 1–8 (2017)

3. Nguyen, H.T., Van Thi Tran, A., Thi Nguyen, T.A., Vo, L.T., Tran, P.V.: Multivariate cube for representing multivariable data in visual analytics. In: Cong Vinh, P., Tuan Anh, L., Loan, N.T.T., Vongdoiwang Siricharoen, W. (eds.) ICCASA 2016. LNICST, vol. 193, pp. 91–100. Springer, Cham (2017). https://doi.org/10.1007/978-3-319-56357-2_10

4. Nguyen, H.T., Tran, P.V.: Multidimensional cube for representing flight data in visualization-based system for tracking flyer. In: The 5th International Conference on Control, Automation and Information Sciences, Ansan, Korea, pp. 132–137 (2016)

5. Tran, P.V., Nguyen, H.T., Tran, T.V.: Approaching multi-dimensional cube for visualization-based epidemic warning system - dengue fever. Presented at the 8th International Conference on Ubiquitous Information Management and Communication, ACM IMCOM 2014, Siem Reap, Cambodia (2014)

6. Nguyen, H.T., Tran, T.V., Tran, P.V., Dang, H.: Multivariate cube for visualization of weather data. Presented at the IEEE 2013 International Conference on Control, Automation and Information Science, ICCAIS 2013, Nha Trang, Vietnam (2013)

7. Tran, P.V., Nguyen, H.T.: Multivariate-space-time cube to visualize multivariate data. Int. J. Geoinformatics **8**, 67–74 (2012)

8. Tran, P.V., Nguyen, H.T.: Visualization cube for tracking moving object. Presented at the Computer Science and Information Technology, Information and Electronics Engineering (2011)

9. Peuquet, D.J.: It's about time: a conceptual framework for the representation of temporal dynamics in geographic information systems. Ann. Assoc. Am. Geogr. **84**, 441–461 (1994)

10. Andrienko, G., Andrienko, N., Bak, P., Keim, D., Kisilevich, S., Wrobel, S.: A conceptual framework and taxonomy of techniques for analyzing movement. J. Vis. Lang. Comput. **22**, 213–232 (2011)

11. Yuan, M.: Representing complex geographic phenomena in GIS. Cartogr. Geogr. Inf. Sci. **28**, 83–96 (2001)

12. Yuan, M., Nara, A., Bothwell, J.: Space–time representation and analytics. Ann. GIS **20**, 1–9 (2014)

13. Jensen, J.R., Jensen, R.R.: Introductory Geographic Information Systems. Pearson Education, London (2013)

14. Chang, K.-T.: Introduction to Geographic Information Systems. McGraw-Hill, New York (2008)

15. Andrienko, N., Andrienko, G., Pelekis, N., Spaccapietra, S.: Basic concepts of movement data. In: Giannotti, F., Pedreschi, D. (eds.) Mobility, Data Mining and Privacy: Geographic Knowledge Discovery, pp. 15–38. Springer, Heidelberg (2008). https://doi.org/10.1007/978-3-540-75177-9_2

16. Nguyen, H.T., Ngo, H.T., Nguyen, X.V., Nguyen, D.N., Tran, P.V.: An approach to representing movement data. Int. J. Inf. Electron. Eng. **3**, 283–287 (2013)

17. Tran, P.V., et al.: Technical report of Vietnam's national project researching the application of GIS for socio-economic development in Mekong delta during 2001–2005. Vietnam' Ministry of Science and Technology (2005)

A System and Model of Visual Data Analytics Related to Junior High School Students

Dang Van Pham[1,2](✉) [iD] and Phuoc Vinh Tran[3]

[1] Faculty of Information Technology, Nguyen Tat Thanh University,
Hochiminh City, Vietnam
pvdang@ntt.edu.vn, pvdang.tps@gmail.com
[2] Graduate University of Science and Technology,
Vietnam Academy of Science and Technology, Hanoi, Vietnam
[3] Ho Chi Minh City Open University, Hochiminh City, Vietnam
phuoc.tvinh@ou.edu.vn, phuoc.gis@gmail.com

Abstract. The assessment of students' learning ability for career guidance in the future is a huge challenge. The development stage of students' learning ability is considered from the sixth grade to the ninth grade. Student's transcripts from grade 6 to grade 9 are used to assess students' learning abilities. A transcript comparison of grades 6 through 9 is essential for each parent and analyst from there they can guide their children to comprehensive development of knowledge. The objective of this paper is to visually analyze student data using visual analysis approach, proposes a visual analysis system for data discovery with many variables (VAS), a visual data analysis model, visual data analysis criteria, visual data variables, multidimensional cube representing student data, and some visual data analysis questions based on visual graphs related to Junior High School students (JHSSs). Visual analysis of student data helps parents or analysts observe and extract useful information that they interact visual on visual graphs by asking themselves or answering the visual data analysis questions themselves when observing visual graphs by the retina to guide their children to choose the right knowledge chain and future jobs. Visual graphs represent the correlation between subjects and especially the comparison of a subject in the academic years together to help parents and analysts see clearly the trend of the development of students' learning abilities by visual data analysis model.

Keywords: Visual graphs · Students' learning ability · Visual analysis system (VAS) · Visual data analysis model · Visual data analysis criteria · Visual data analysis questions

1 Introduction

The direction of knowledge chain and future careers for each student is a very important job. In order to properly orient knowledge chain and careers for students, studying at all levels such as Education of Primary (EP), Junior High School (JHS), and High School (HS) is always the primary concern of parents, especially the level of JHS, students have qualities that develop in many directions, students' learning ability manifests in many ways and always change over time. In order to assess the inner

© ICST Institute for Computer Sciences, Social Informatics and Telecommunications Engineering 2019
Published by Springer Nature Switzerland AG 2019. All Rights Reserved
P. C. Vinh and A. Rakib (Eds.): ICCASA 2019/ICTCC 2019, LNICST 298, pp. 105–126, 2019.
https://doi.org/10.1007/978-3-030-34365-1_9

learning abilities of each student, people use the academic results table in the classes at the same level to assess. The multi-column transcript shows data on student scores in the learning process for each academic year. Therefore, the transcript is a data table for each academic year that is shown in a desultory way at the same level of study. When parents or analysts look at transcripts, not everyone also understands the future development direction of their child or knows how their development trends are. From there, giving directions to help their children develop some subjects according to their ability and aptitude and have a solid knowledge of their learning and career guidance.

Assessing the students' learning ability of JHS is a necessary job for parents and analysts. Assessing the learning capability of JHSSs, we should evaluate all 4 grade years of JHS. The transcript for a school year only evaluates that student is average, fairly good, good, poor, or weak at a subject. Relying on transcripts for a school year to assess how the student learns does not yet speak of the student's true learning abilities. JHSSs are in the stages of comprehensive development both physically and intellectually, qualities develop in many directions, at this time the learning capability of students newly exposes in many ways and always changes over time. Selecting the results of studying classes at the same level to assess students' learning ability chains is always the right choosing and doing.

The objective of this paper is to visually analyze students' data by using visual analysis approach, proposes a VAS and visual data analysis model related to JHSSs. The visual analysis of the JHSSs' data set will help parents or analysts to know developmental trends of students in the future. The visual analysis of student data helps parents to orient their children to develop comprehensive learning capabilities in the future. This paper focuses on building visual data variables, proposes visual data analysis criteria, multidimensional cube representing student data, provides some visual data analysis questions, and visual graphs that can help answering some visual data analysis questions from parents or analysts that understand the meaning of students' learning outcomes when observation of visual graphs by visual viewing – thinking method.

The remainder of this paper is organized as follows. Section 2 presents an overview of related research works, comments, and suggestions. Section 3 visually presents student data using visual analysis method, proposes a visual analysis system (VAS), visual data analysis model, and visual analysis criteria of student data of JHS. Section 4 performs the results of visual analysis of student data of JHS using some visual data analysis questions based on visual graphs. Section 5 presents the conclusion of the paper and suggests the direction of development.

2   Overview

2.1   The Concepts

2.1.1   Types of Data

Data are values such as numeric, string, image, date, audio, light, etc. They are collected from various places such as schools, businesses, individuals, etc. In this study, we focused on collecting data at a JHS and performing data classification into data types such as nominal data, ordinal data, and ratio data. Nominal data are the type of data based on attributes whose data are not unequal but only differences or equalities about rank [1–3]. In this paper, nominal data are used to indicate the differences in subjects and are applied to the subject variables. Ordinal data the type of data based on the attributes of these attributes whose data are unequal, different, and equal [1–3]. In this paper, ordinal data are used to measure attitudes, opinions, preferences, perceptions, and views, ordinal data are used to represent the preceding order of time and are applied for a temporal variable. Ratio data are the type of data based on the properties that data of these properties can perform arithmetic operations such as addition, subtraction, multiplication, and division, comparison operations differences, and equal data between properties [1–3]. More specifically, ratio data allows comparing the difference in the ratio of data values, order ranking, and distance comparison. In this paper, ratio data are used for calculations such as addition, subtraction, multiplication, and division, comparison scores with each other and are applied to score variables.

2.1.2 Visual Data

Visualization is the conversion of data and information into images. Visualization is an essential tool to help us understand data. The purpose of visualization is to describe and develop previously unknown ideas to help people perceive useful information, information and knowledge that are hidden within the data through transmitted retina perception into the human brain. Vision helps people to receive information from visual models, and the brain processes to help people get useful information when looking at visual graphs.

Visual data use visual techniques to convert data into visual objects such as points, lines, or graphic object bars that are displayed on 2-dimensional (2D) computer screens. Visual data are conveying information and knowledge clearly and semantically by means of graphics. People can perceive information and knowledge by graphics better than text, numbers, scripts, etc. Users observe graphic images to extract information and seek knowledge to serve specific purposes and serve timely decision making.

2.1.3 Visual Features

Data are visualized in the form of graphic images or visual graphs that help users, analysts, etc. to perform information discovery and seek hidden knowledge within the data. A visual graph must ensure visual features. We conduct surveys and have found some visual features as follows [4–6].

- Ordinal: For user-specific purposes, users can observe visual graphs to explore information and knowledge. Therefore, a visual graph is called data visualization when it meets user requirements. A visual graph must be ordered so that users can observe before, after, over, below, left, right, large, and small.
- Selective: For user-specific purposes, users can observe visual graphs to explore information and knowledge. Therefore, a visual graph is called visual data when it satisfies user requirements. In there, a visual graph must have selective so that users can select as a certain element or detect the location of an object on the visual

graphs, can identify differences in the objects on the visual graphs and retrieve some characteristics of the object on the visual graphs.

- Associative: For user-specific purposes, users can observe visual graphs to explore information and knowledge. Therefore, a visual graph is called visual data when it satisfies user requirements. In there, a visual graph must be associated so that users can group objects that are related to each other on visual graphs to extract information and knowledge.
- Quantitative: For user-specific purposes, users can observe visual graphs to explore information and knowledge. Therefore, a visual graph is called visual data when it satisfies user requirements. In there, a visual graph must be quantitative so that users can identify the ratio of two values when they are visualized representation.
- Lengthy: For user-specific purposes, users can observe visual graphs to explore information and knowledge. Therefore, a visual graph is called visual data when it satisfies user requirements. In there, a visual graph must have lengthy so that the user can identify the length relative to the number of elements of a variable represented on a coordinate axis, then the user can perceive each element on the visual graphs.

2.1.4   Visual Analytics

Visual analytics is a fundamental foundation in the field of analytical psychological science. This area has facilitated people to discover information and seek knowledge from data by visual interaction techniques between people and computers through a graphical interface [7]. People use visual techniques and visual analysis tools to discover information and knowledge from data, simultaneously, have an insight into the big data sets that are related to each other that these data sets aren't heterogeneous, vague, rich, diverse and always changing characteristics by the time. The field of visual analysis is an area that goes through professions and assists people to gain a broad sense of large data sets through assessment, strategic planning, and decision making timely. In visual analysis, there are visual interactions and visual representation techniques, these techniques are used to take advantage of the human's retinal to acquire information and knowledge when people observe visual graphs by methods of viewing - thinking intuitiveness. Therefore, the main goal of visual analysis is to support the maximum of the reasoning process and analyze human data conjunction with computers through the creation of argument methods, techniques for visual data analysis and visual representation of data to help maximize the ability to perceive, understand, and reasoning of humans, in which humans play a major role in the process of amplifying knowledge from data.

2.2   Related Works

Making decisions and making decisions in a timely manner as well as carrying out human daily tasks effectively depends on who receives information or knowledge in which context or background and how reliable is it? Therefore, human always desire to find the best methodologies and visual data analysis tools to support users to extract more information as well as perceive more hidden knowledge inside data. Until now, the scientific achievements of knowledge discovery from data have been studied very much by scientists. In it, there are fields such as data visualization, visual analytics, exploratory data analysis, data mining, knowledge discovery in databases, etc. In this paper, we perform systematization some of the research works related to these areas to demonstrate that data scientists are very interested in these areas, especially when human increasingly aim toward awakening the mind (also or effecting the mind or touching the mind) every human being to support policy making, decision doing, and decision making.

Data visualization is a process of creating images that represent diverse data sources, qualitative or quantitative data, where users can extract information and seek hidden knowledge within the data. Data visualization having input parameter is a variety of data sources and having the output parameter is a visual graph, the visual graph must be as simple as possible, good suggestions for users to see the entire range of visual data, do not miss important information, not to misunderstand the meaning does not exist in the data, must take advantage of the retinal viewing ability of human beings and humans can apply the visual viewing - thinking method to view visual graphs. To date, many models of data visualization systems (also or data visualization processes) and data visualization processes have been proposed by many authors groups.

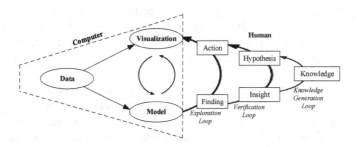

Fig. 1. Model generates knowledge from data [8]

The model arising from knowledge in the field of visual analysis is proposed by Sacha et al. [8] (see Fig. 1). The main purpose of this model is to propose the role of human participating in the process of knowledge development and the rest is a visual analysis system due to the computer performed automatically. The Shacha team divided the model into two main phases, the first stage illustrating a system of visual analysis, the remaining stage illustrating the human join in the process of knowledge development. Human implement the process of generating knowledge that includes sub-processes: the mining process, the testing process, and the process of generating knowledge. The two stages in the model that generate knowledge from data are active interactions between human and computers, in which human play a central role in controlling the whole process.

The process of visual analysis (also known as the visual analysis system model) was proposed by Keim et al. [9], this process combines the model method and visualization method with the main purpose is to help human participate in the process of knowledge mining from data. This process is divided into two main branches, the first branch, human using the visualization method to discover knowledge from data, the second branch, human using the model method to discover knowledge from data. Between these two branches, model methods and visualization methods are mutually supportive in the process of discovering knowledge from data. With the model method, the data is analyzed automatically when the user requires, while the visualization methods, human play a major role in the process of knowledge mining from data. The strength of the visualization method is thanks to the knowledge of existing data analysis expertise of experts in many fields, thanks to the knowledge and experience available in many professional areas that experts have can extract a lot of information and find knowledge in many interdisciplinary branches.

The process of visual analysis proposed by Keim authors [10] is converted from the visualization model proposed by Wijk [11], this process clearly demonstrates the three stages of the knowledge discovery process from data. Stage 1, the process of receiving raw data sources, the original data must be classified and analyzed by data analysis techniques. Stage 2, visualization method will be applied to convert the analyzed data into visual image to help users easily feel. Stage 3, users can apply viewing - thinking methods to perceive or deeply recognize visual images to crystallize into knowledge, from existing knowledge and newly acquired knowledge, human can simultaneously apply to generate new knowledge based on existing assumptions and continue to perform deeper analysis and discovery knowledge from data by the technical charac-teristics applied to the visualization method of stage 2. In the second stage, the application of visual data analysis technical characteristics is very important, normally human interact on visual representation images will be easier to understand the nature of data.

The reference visualization model is still considered as the classic model proposed by Card et al. [12]. The main purpose of the reference visualization model is to model the steps needed to turn data into an interactive visual form. In particular, the model is divided into two main stages, stage 1 is data formed in order from large data sources converted into data table structures, stage 2 is visual form formed in order from visual abstraction to transform into views. In the reference visualization model, the order is converted from stage 1 to stage 2 by visual mappings controlled by the user. In stage 1, the user controls with data transformations, stage 2, the users control with view transformations. So, in this model, the role of human is very clear, human can decide when to perform transformations, data format, choose which visual structure to use, and choose the way which displays.

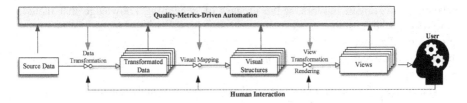

Fig. 2. Visualization process automatically adjusts to quality [13]

The automatic visualization process of quality adjustment [13] (see Fig. 2) is extended by Bertini authors group from the [12] reference visualization model, this group suggests adding at the top of the one-layer reference visualization model automatically adjusting to quality. This layer obtains information from rectangular-shaped boxes of each stage in the reference visualization process [12] and influences the processes of the reference visualization process through the data that the visualization process automatically adjusts according to the calculated quality. Users are always in control of the entire process and the end result is that users get visual structures and different display ways.

The data analysis system developed by Thi Nguyen authors (see Fig. 3) [6] expanded from the model of knowledge generation from data proposed by Sacha et al. [8], and the model of visual analysis system proposed by Keim et al. [9]. The data visualization system is capable of transforming data into information and knowledge by model methods in data analysis to build mathematical models combined with visualization methods along with human's contributions participate in the process of information discovery and knowledge search from data. In particular, the data visualization system highlights the principle with the strategy of knowledge discovery from data, data is converted into information by model method combined with visualization methods, human and computers work together through the use of existing human knowledge and experience to participate in the process of extracting information and discovering knowledge from data by means of visualization or called visual perception method.

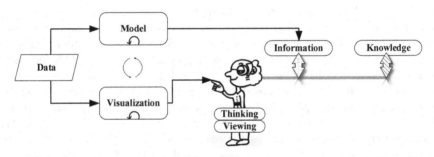

Fig. 3. The system analyzes data by model and visual method with human contribution [6].

Through the systematization of models and processes related to the field of visualization and the field of visual analysis above, we have some comments as follows. The models and processes meet some of the problems of converting data sources into information and knowledge. Models and processes have combined the interaction between computers and humans join in the process of information and knowledge discovery. The models and processes are all focused on using computer technology as the main, while the participation of people in the process of information discovery and knowledge search only speaks of basic interactions like selection, search, and control only. There is no model or process that provides clear criteria or methodology to support users in the process of information discovery and knowledge search from data.

The data analysis system proposed by Thi Nguyen authors [6] refers to the contribution of humans to the process of information and knowledge discovery from data, but human contributions are not grouped how this presents in a specific way.

Through some observations above, we find that the above models or processes are mainly focused on building processes or stages of information and knowledge discovery from data. However, in order for people to make good decisions and make timely and breakthrough decisions, people must know how to apply their existing knowledge and experience to apply to processes is a key to success. The philosophy of von Szent-Gyorgyi *"Discovery consists of seeing what everybody has seen and thinking what nobody has thought."* [14] indicates that each person needs to participate directly in the process of information discovery and knowledge search from data. Based on the above observations and based on the philosophy of Albert von Szent-Gyorgyi, this paper proposes to build a VAS of multiple variables based on visual graphs, building visual graphs, visual data analysis model, and visual data analysis criteria related data for JHSSs. These proposals will be detailed in the next sections of this paper.

3   A System and Model of Visual Data Analytics of JHSSs Data

3.1   Proposing a Visual Analytics System for Data Discovery with Many Variables Based on Visual Graphs

The discovery of information and the search for knowledge from visual graphs by viewing – thinking method are great challenges in the fields of visual analysis. In order to assist people in discovering information and seeking knowledge from data when observing visual graphs effectively, this paper proposes to build a VAS for multivariable data discovery based on visual graphs (see Fig. 4), this system was expanded from a visual analysis model proposed by the group of authors Keim [9], a model of knowledge generation proposed by the group of authors Sacha [8], automatic quality-adjusted visualization process proposed by the group of authors Bertini [13], data analysis system by visualization method combined with a model method that namely mathematical model together with human contributions [6], and the process of knowledge discovery in the databases with data mining techniques [15]. This system is divided into two main layers, the first layer is managed by computers, and the second layer is carried out by humans. The first layer is divided into two main branches, branch 1 applies visualization method in visual data discovery, and branch 2 applies the model method in the process of knowledge discovery in the database. Branch 1, with the visualization method, the reference visualization model [12] coordinates with the model method in data analysis to render into visual graphs. Branch 2, with the model method and the process of knowledge discovery in the databases [15] cooperates with visualization methods in data analysis to crystallize information and knowledge. Branch 2, with the model method and the process of knowledge discovery in the database [15], cooperates with visualization methods in data analysis to crystallize information and knowledge based on visual graphs.

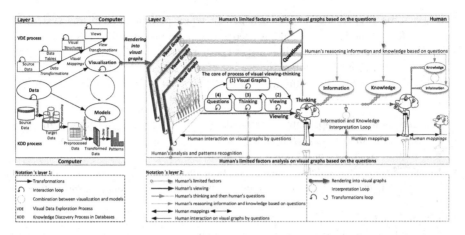

Fig. 4. Visual analytics system (VAS) for data discovery with many variables based on visual graphs

The paper is based on the philosophy of von Szent-Gyorgyi [14] to propose the construction of the second layer to attach to the existing visual data analysis system, this newly built system is called a visual analysis system for data discovery with many variables based on visual graphs, this new system is called VAS for the purpose of serving people to make visual interactions on visual graphs (see Fig. 4), by asking themselves questions and answering their own questions in themselves information discovery process and knowledge search from data. Indeed, humans are always inherently able to see-understand, capable of reasoning or interpretation, being able to remember according to the deductive mechanism or the ability to recall memories, and there are other possibilities. However, people still have limited factors that need to be analyzed need to be studied to show the limited factors of people to overcome on the second layer of this visual analysis system, both methodological and other restricted factors. The philosophy of von Szent-Gyorgyi [14] shows that people need to participate directly in the process of knowledge discovery from data. Therefore, on the second layer of this visual analysis system, the paper analyzes the restricted factors of humans when people interact on visual graphs by relying on asking or answering your own questions. It can be said that data analysis cannot be performed if no questions are asked. Questions are the first step and the basis for promoting the process of visual analysis of data conducted.

Also in the second layer of this VAS (see Fig. 4), we propose to build a core of process of visual viewing - thinking following these steps, step **(1)** with human appearance and visual graphs, step **(2)** human view visual graphs, step **(3)** human think visual graphs and render into information and knowledge, step **(4)** then people interact visually on visual graphs by asking themselves or answering the data analysis questions themselves when observing visual graphs, and continue to repeat step **(1)** if people need to explore information and seek knowledge from visual graphs for the next time. This is an infinite process of a data processing flow in a visual data discovery system with many variables based on visual graphs. In addition, on the second layer of this system, there are some limited factors for each person when participating in this system to perform information discovery and knowledge search on visual graphs based on asking yourself or answering the questions myself when observing the visual graphs. The restricted factors of humans following we are shown that need to be clearly analyzed (see Fig. 4). In particular, the limited factors 1, 2, 3, 4, and 5 were conducted in the next sections of this paper.

- **Limited factor 1:** People interact on visual graphs by posing questions themselves or answering themselves with visual data analysis questions in the process of information discovery and knowledge search.
- **Limited factor 2:** People rely on a visual data analysis model combined with visual data analysis criteria to ask themselves or answer the visual data analysis questions themselves.
- **Limited factor 3:** People use questions and answers in which questions must be classified and stratified into a visual data analysis question system as well as user answers.
- **Limited factor 4:** People use visual viewing – thinking method to ask themselves or answer the visual data analysis questions themselves.
- **Limited factor 5:** People interact on visual graphs with different viewing angles by using visual data analysis criteria to see and better understand the nature of data.
- **Limited factor 6:** People use questions that are reasoned previously or answers to perform analyzes and discoveries that add information and knowledge to existing ones.
- **Limited factor 7:** People use the loop to deduce information and knowledge that was discovered the previous time to perform analysis and discovery to add useful information and knowledge for the next time.
- **Limited factor 8:** People look at visual graphs and then analyze and recognize patterns based on visual graphs for the purpose of discovering information and searching for hidden knowledge on visual graphs.
- **Limited factor 9:** People receive visual graphs by eyes, sense of viewing, human eyes as a means of receiving more data than other means, sense of hearing, gnawing, tasting, and touching. Sensing visual visuals from the eyes performed at different levels of treatment need to be shown.

3.2   Visual Cube Representing Student Data

In this section, we introduce data variables related to students of JHS. Temporal variable (var_T), in turn, is school years of sixth, seventh, eighth and ninth grade. Subject variable (var_Sub), in turn, is Mathematics (M), Physics (P), Biology (B), Literature (L), History (H), Geography (G), Foreign languages (FL), Civic education (CE), and Technology (T). Score variable (var_Sco) is the average of the subjects. From these data variables, we construct visual variables for each variable as a coordinate (0x, 0y, 0z). Then, we built a multidimensional cube representing student data based on the data variables defined above.

3.2.1 Data Variables Related to Students

School and parents monitor the learning process of JHSSs through the academic transcripts that the school records over the school years. A transcript is a data table made up of multiple columns and rows to show students' learning outcomes by school year. The transcript represents the school years of grade 6, grade 7, grade 8 and grade 9; subjects as M, P, B, L, H, G, FL, CE, T, Informatics, Chemistry, Physical education, Music, and Art; Each subject corresponds to an average of that subject.

In order to fully appreciate the academic ability of JHSSs, we need to rely on the subjects that students are fully learning in the four school years of 6th through 9th grade. In the scope of the paper, we focus on surveying and researching a number of subjects as M, P, B, L, H, G, FL, CE, and T (see Table 1). These subjects are assessed by number scores very clearly, there are other subjects that students can only study for two years, those subjects are as chemistry and informatics. If we only assess the students' learning ability trend but only base on two years of study, the learning results do not fully reflect the students' learning ability. In addition, a number of other subjects such as gymnastics, music, and fine arts are not studied in this paper because these subjects are assessed as having achieved or not achieved in the results of the end of the school year but it does not assess students' true learning ability.

Table 1. Data table show the average score of each student in 4 years of JHS [vnedu.vn]

Y (Year)	FN (Full Name)	M (Mathematic)	P (Physics)	B (Biology)	L (Literature)	H (History)	G (Geography)	FL (Foreign Language)	CE (Civic Education)	T (Technology)
C_6	Pham	9.0	7.0	6.5	6.0	6.0	6.5	10	8.0	7.0
C_7	Thao	8.5	8.0	5.0	9.0	9.0	8.0	10	9.0	9.5
C_8	Nguyen	9.8	9.2	8.5	7.0	7.0	5.0	9.0	7.0	7.6
C_9		10	9.5	7.0	9.5	9.5	8.1	10	9.0	9.5
C_6	Pham	5.4	5.0	6.1	5.7	5.8	6.3	3.9	6.7	6.0
C_7	Dang	6.5	7.8	4.5	5.5	5.5	6.9	4.0	5.5	5.5
C_8	Khoi	8.5	6.2	8.8	5.7	6.8	6.2	7.7	5.9	5.8
C_9		9.8	7.2	9.4	7.7	7.8	6.6	9.7	6.9	5.8

Table 1 is shown as follows, the school year column contains data elements {C_6, C_7, C_8, C_9} are the school years {Class 6, 7, 8, and 9} respectively; the full name used to contain the student's first and last name; M, P, B, L, H, G, FL, CE, and T columns used to contain student's scores from 0.0 to 10 marks; on each line of Table 1 (except for the first line), each unit of time {C_6, C_7, C_8, C_9} will combine with full name {Pham Thao Nguyen, Pham Dang Khoi, etc.}, and the average score of each subject {M, P, B, L, H, G, FL, CE, T} indicates the students' learning ability in each grade 6, 7, 8, and 9.

Through the data analysis in Table 1, we found that the school year column (Y) is a unit of time considered as an independent variable; the columns of M, P, B, L, H, G, FL, CE, and T are dependent variables that change over time; the var_Sco, in turn, include the scores of the subjects. The variable is a data set whose components are the elements of the set. Therefore, in Table 1, elements of the set include subjects such as M, P, B, L, H, G, FL, CE, and T; school years like C_6, C_7, C_8, C_9; average grades of subjects such as M, P, B, L, H, G, FL, CE, and T. Therefore, the data variable is a variable data value, the data value can be a decimal form (e.g. a score), a string form (e.g. subject, time). The paper presenting the data variable used includes the following variables as temporal variable (var_T), subject variable (var_Sub), and score variable (var_Sco).

The var_T shows the school years, with the unit is class and the school years from [2014–2015] to [2017–2018] respectively is the 6th, 7th, 8th and 9th grade. The JHS program is stipulated every student that will learn in 4 years, every year a student is allowed to take a class, the class is arranged in order from grade 6, grade 7, grade 8, then finally grade 9, students are not allowed to learn beyond class. Due to the order of such classes, the var_T is an ordered data type, the var_T consists of elements C_6, C_7, C_8, C_9. Let var_T is the temporal variable and call t_1, t_2, t_3, t_4 are the set of elements of var_T. The var_Sub includes combinations of subject elements such as M, P, B, L, H, G, FL, CE, and T. The var_Sub only shows the difference between subjects or equally in the hierarchy. Let var_Sub is the subject variable and call m_1, m_2, $m_3, ..., m_9$ are the set of elements of var_Sub. The var_Sco shows average scores with numerical values from 0.0 to 10.0 scores of subjects. For score variables, we can perform basic calculations such as adding, subtracting, multiplying, dividing, and performing comparisons between numerical scores. Therefore, the var_Sco is the ratio of data type. The var_Sco consists of a set of values of $\{0.0, 3.6, 3.7, ...10\}$. Let var_Sco be a score variable and call $s_1, s_2, s_3, ...s_n$ is a set of elements of var_Sco.

- The var_T = $\{C_6, C_7, C_8, C_9\}$, with C_6, C_7, C_8, C_9 turn in order is grade 6, grade 7, grade 8, and grade 9, in it: $(t_1, t_2, t_3, t_4) \in$ var_T, $t_1 = \{C_6\}, t_2 = \{C_7\}, t_3 = \{C_8\}, t_4 = \{C_9\}$.
- The var_Sub = {M, P, B, L, H, G, FL, CE, T}, in it: $(sub_1, sub_2, sub_3, ... sub_9)$ var_Sub, $sub_1 = \{M\}$, $sub_2 = \{P\}$, $sub_3 = \{B\}$, $sub_4 = \{L\}$, $sub_5 = \{H\}$, $sub_6 = \{G\}$, $sub_7 = \{FL\}$, $sub_8 = \{CE\}$, $sub_9 = \{T\}$.
- The var_Sco = $\{0.0, 3.6, 3.7, ...10\}$, with $0.0, 3.6, 3.7, ...10$ is the numerical value indicating the average score, in it: $(s_1, s_2, s_3, ...s_n) \in$ var_Sco, $s_1 = [0.0–2.0]$, $s_2 = [2.0–4.0]$, $s_3 = [4.0–6.0]$, $s_4 = [6.0–8.0]$, $s_5 = [8.0–10]$.

Users can perform the assessment of JHSSs' results through observing visual graphs. The visual graph is a graph showing students' learning data into images that make it easy for observers. In order for the observation to gain more information and knowledge, the user must combine with the regulations in assessing students' learning outcomes, which are clearly stated in the circular 58 of Ministry of Education and Training (MET) [16]. In order for the observation to gain more information and knowledge, the user must combine with the regulations in assessing students' learning outcomes, which are clearly stated in the circular 58 of the MET. The provisions in circular 58 combined with visual graphs observation will help the observer understand better the learning process of JHSSs. These provisions are expressed in the following terms.

- Students' learning ranking is divided into 5 categories as good, fair, average, weak, and poor is defined in item 2, article 5, chapter 3 in circular 58 of the MET.
- Evaluating in a way that scores for some subjects such as M, P, B, L, H, G, FL, CE, and T through tests are given the scores on a scale of 0 to 10 scores specified in point d, clause 1, article 6, chapter 3 in circular 58 of the MET.

- The calculation of the subject results for each semester and the whole school year for the subjects assessed by giving the scores specified in point a-b-c, clause 1, article 10, chapter 3 in circular 58 of the MET.
- The calculation of the score average of the semester or the whole school year gives in the integer or decimal number being taken to the first decimal after rounding the number specified in clause 3, article 11 in the circular 58 the MET.
- Ranking semester and a whole year of students are defined in article 13, chapter 3 in circular 58 of the MET. To classify students, it must be based on the following classification criteria.
  - Good: If the average score is 8.0 or higher and there are no subjects that the average score is below 6.5 points and the other rules are attached.
  - Fair: If the average score is 6.5 or higher and there are no subjects, the average score is below 5.0 and the other rules are attached.
  - Average: If the average score is 5.0 or higher and there are no subjects, the average score is below 3.5 and the other rules are attached.
  - Weak: If the average score is 3.5 or higher and there are no subjects, the average score is below 2.0 and the other rules are attached.
  - Poor: The other cases.

3.2.2 Proposing a Visual Data Analysis Model of JHSSs Data

Visual variables are divided into two types, plane variables and retinal variables [4]. In which, plane variables are dimensions, in a plane variable coordinate system is the coordinate system; retinal variables include variables such as magnitude, brightness, fineness, color, direction, and shape; retinal variables enhance capacity the visualization of data for people to observe, perceive the most information from data, extract useful information from data.

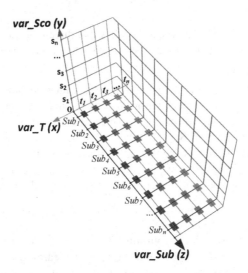

Fig. 5. Visual data analysis model of 3 student data variables based on 3D coordinate system

From the data variables described above, we propose to build a visual data analysis model of JHSSs' data through three variables including temporal variables (var_T), subject variables (var_Sub), and score variables (var_Sco). The construction of visual data analysis model of JHSSs' data by visual images will help people to observe easily and increase the ability to extract a lot of potential information inside the data. Each data variable will be represented as a plane variable and the corresponding visual variable. The visual data analysis model of JHSSs' data (see Fig. 5) helps users to visualize student data intuitively, from which users can answer some analytical questions themselves and evaluate development orient of students' learning ability of JHS. Each data variable is represented as a visual variable and a visual variable is represented on a column of the visual data analysis model.

With the visual analysis of student data based on three data variables (see Fig. 5), it will allow users to observe and extract a lot of potential information within student data. With y coordinate axis denotes var_Sco are score average of the whole school year of the subjects. With x coordinate axis denotes var_T changes of the school year. With z coordinate axis denotes var_Sub. Each of the three values of the var_Sub, var_Sco, and var_T will be represented as a column in the 3-dimensional (3D) space Oxyz (see Fig. 5). In which, the position in the Oxz plane represents the value pair of the var_Sub and var_T; y coordinate axis represents the height of the var_Sco, the value of the var_Sco will always change over time; the relationship of altitude of the same var_Sub that changes over time will help the observer see the change of the var_Sub of that student over the school years. Based on the visual data analysis model of three data variables (var_T, var_Sub, var_Sco) of students (see Fig. 5), we propose and develop some visual data analysis criteria used to observe students' learning outcomes that help users discover information and seek knowledge from student data.

Criteria 1: Users can combine a set of any three values in $\{(sub_1, \ldots sub_n), (t_1, \ldots t_n), (s_1, \ldots s_n)\} \in 3$ variables (var_T, var_Sub, var_Sco) together to discover students' learning information. For example, a combination of three values (sub_3, t_1, s_3) in $\{(sub_1, \ldots sub_n), (t_1, \ldots t_n), (s_1, \ldots s_n)\} \in 3$ variables (var_T, var_Sub, var_Sco) located in the Oxz plane, this combination of a value three (sub_3, t_1, s_3) constitutes the learning result of a subject (sub_3) of a class (t_1) with an average score (s_3) of a student, see Fig. 5.

Criteria 2: Users can combine a set of any three values of three variables (var_T, var_Sub, var_Sco), we can choose a set of three values in the Oxz plane to observe the learning results of a student. For example, we choose the set of three values of three variables (var_T, var_Sub, var_Sco) as follows $\{(sub_1, t_4, s_5), (sub_2, t_4, s_4), (sub_3, t_4, s_5), (sub_4, t_4, s_4), (sub_5, t_4, d_4), (sub_6, t_4, s_3), (sub_7, t_4, s_5), (sub_8, t_4, s_3), (sub_9, t_4, s_3)\}$ in the Oxz plane. Combining these triple set at the same time (t_4) will help observers discover the learning outcomes of the subjects on the same school year (t_4), see Fig. 5.

Criteria 3: Users can combine sets of three values $\{(sub_1, \ldots sub_n), (t_1, \ldots t_n), (s_1, \ldots s_n)\} \in$ (var_T, var_Sub, var_Sco), and then can perform comparison operations $(=, <, \leq, >, \geq, \neq)$ based on proportional values (var_Sco of $s_1, s_2, s_3 \ldots s_n$) to discover information and seek knowledge from results learning of students. Compare pairs of value in turn $\{(\mathbf{sub_1, t_1, s_3})$ and $(\mathbf{sub_1, t_4, s_5})$ based on var_Sco s_3 and s_5; $(\mathbf{sub_2,}$

t_1, s_3) and (**sub$_2$**, **t$_4$**, **s$_4$**) based on var_Sco s_3 and s_4; (**sub$_3$**, **t$_1$**, **s$_3$**) and (**sub$_3$**, **t$_4$**, **s$_5$**) based on var_Sco s_3 and s_5; (**sub$_4$**, **t$_1$**, **s$_3$**) and (**sub$_4$**, **t$_4$**, **s$_4$**) based on var_Sco s_3 and s_4; (**sub$_5$**, **t$_1$**, **s$_3$**) and (**sub$_5$**, **t$_4$**, **s$_4$**) based on var_Sco s_3 and s_4; (**sub$_6$**, **t$_1$**, **s$_3$**) and (**sub$_6$**, **t$_4$**, **s$_3$**) based on var_Sco s_3 and s_3; (**sub$_7$**, **t$_1$**, **s$_2$**) and (**sub$_7$**, **t$_4$**, **s$_5$**) based on var_Sco s_2 and s_5; (**sub$_8$**, **t$_1$**, **s$_3$**) and (**sub$_8$**, **t$_4$**, **s$_3$**) based on var_Sco s_3 and s_3; (**sub$_9$**, **t$_1$**, **s$_3$**) and (**sub$_9$**, **t$_4$**, **s$_3$**) based on var_Sco s_3 and s_3}, see Fig. 5.

Criteria 4: Users can select sets of any three values $\{(sub_1, \ldots sub_n), (t_1, \ldots t_n), (s_1, \ldots s_n)\}$ ∈ three variables (var_T, var_Sub, var_Sco) according to any subject $(sub_1, \ldots sub_n)$ in each school year $(t_1, \ldots t_n)$. For example, the user selects the set of three value sets $\{(sub_3, t_1, s_3), (sub_3, t_2, s_2), (sub_3, t_3, s_5), (sub_3, t_4, s_5)\}$ ∈ 3 variables (var_T, var_Sub, var_Sco) by subject (sub_3) to explore information and seek knowledge from students' learning result, see Fig. 5.

Criteria 5: Users can select sets of any three values $\{(sub_1, \ldots sub_n), (t_1, \ldots t_n), (s_1, \ldots s_n)\}$ ∈ three variables (var_T, var_Sub, var_Sco) in two any subjects $(sub_1, \ldots sub_n)$ in each school year $(t_1, \ldots t_n)$, then it is possible to perform arithmetic comparisons $(=, <, \leq, >, \geq, \neq)$ on the proportional value var_Sco to discover information and search for knowledge from the students' learning ability, see Fig. 5.

3.3   Multidimensional Cube Representing Student Data

As observed in Table 1 above, we noticed the structure of this data table is like a 2D matrix consisting of columns and lines. Each column represents an attribute that includes a set of values of the variable and each row is a data set representing a relationship between variables. Visual data is studied as a transformation of an element of the table's data variable into a visual variable as an axis or in other words each axis represents an element of the variable. Each axis displays the data of a column as an element of the data variable. The intersecting axes of var_T, var_Sub, and var_Sco create a multidimensional cube that visually represents student data.

Currently, graphs have many forms, including column graphs, line graphs, pie graphs, bar graphs, etc. In particular, one of the most common graphs used to compare numerical values is the column graph. In a column graph, the data is arranged in columns and rows on the worksheet. Column graphs often display genres across the horizontal axis and numerical values along the vertical axis. Because the column graph has advantages in data analysis, this type of graph is used to denote the values of the subject variables such as the average score of the school year of M, P, B, L, H, G, FL, CE, and T in JHS year. The columns indicate differences in height, color, and similarity in the width of the columns.

In order for a visual analysis of JHS data for good results, we performed a visual representation of JHSSs' data on 2D column graphs or 3D column graphs. For a 2D column graph (see Fig. 6), on each column of the graph shows the subject value, the different colors represent the class by each subject, in this graph the data variables are continuous representation on one axis, this should make it difficult for the user to observe and compare the relationship of the data when the data table has many data.

In order to assess the inner learning abilities of each student, it is necessary to rely on the students' learning outcomes of the JHS years, the data variables must be represented on the same visual graph by visual data analysis model. The 2D column graph has the above limitations, to solve the limitations of 2D column graphs, a 3D coordinate axis system is attached to data variables, it is called visual data analysis model of three student data variables based on 3D coordinate system (see Fig. 5). In it, the x coordinate axis represents the var_T (unit is the class), the z axis coordinate represents the var_Sub in turn, and the coordinate axis expresses the average score of the students' subjects. For 3D column graphs (see Fig. 5), on each column represents the average score of each subject by grade 6, grade 7, grade 8, and grade 9, the subjects are shown visually of each individual school year makes it easy for users to observe and compare the subject of the school year compared to the same subject in other school years, or to compare the subjects together in same school year, see Figs. 7 and 8 representing Pham Thao Nguyen's and Pham Dang Khoi's student learning outcomes in turn.

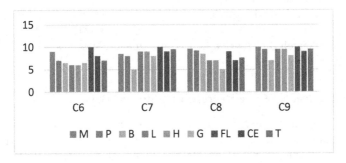

Fig. 6. 2D visual graph showing Pham Thao Nguyen's student learning results (Color figure online)

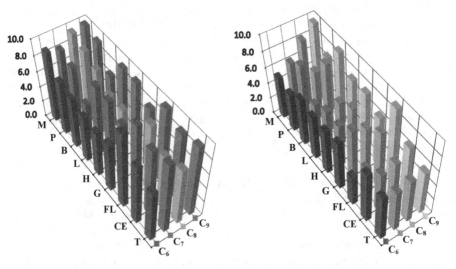

Fig. 7. 3D visual graph showing Pham Thao Nguyen's student learning results

Fig. 8. 3D visual graph showing Pham Dang Khoi's student learning results

4 Analyzing Student Data

4.1 Analyzing Data by Questions

Every object that existing in this real world has a certain use meaning, people perceive it through visual recognition to view - think visually from the existing image of objects in the real world. From there, people will ask visual data analysis questions because of the need to explore objects. The visual data analysis question consists of two main parts as hypothesis and conclusion. In it, people play a major role in the process of analyzing information discovery and finding knowledge from data by applying data analysis process including the following steps [17].

- Step 1: Build questions. In this step, the researcher builds visual data analysis questions to find information or knowledge from the data based on visual graphs.
- Step 2: Choose analytical methods. The analytical method consists of two main methods, which is the method of using model method and visualization method. The modeling method is to use mathematical models to explore information and knowledge from data. Visualization method is a method of combining computer and human knowledge to extract information and knowledge from data by viewing – thinking way.
- Step 3: Prepare data to apply the method. In this step, data is collected through a specific origin. Data is collected, then discarded unnecessary data types and left only the data types for thematic analysis.
- Step 4: Apply methods for data sets which were collected. After the data is available, we apply the method selected in step 2 to the analytic process of existing data.
- Step 5: Explain and evaluate the results. Researchers observe and extract information and knowledge by looking at visual graphs. Information and knowledge are extracted when observing visual graphs, and then perform the evaluation of achieved results.

In the above process, building a question is an initial step, a basis for promoting the data analysis process. It can be said that data analysis cannot be performed if no questions are asked. Through a survey of research works, we found many author groups propose ways to classify data analysis questions. Based on the relevance of the question with data variables and data variable values, Bertin divided analytical questions into three levels, elementary level, intermediate level, and the overall level [4]. In which, the question at the elementary level relates to a value of a variable, the question at the intermediate level relates to a value group of a certain variable, the question is at an overall level related to can variables. Andrienko classifies analytical questions into two levels, elementary questions, and synoptic questions [17]. In addition, approach the use of data variables and data of data variables to answer questions for information extraction or knowledge search objectives, the authors Thi Nguyen et al. classified the analysis question into three levels [6], elementary questions related a value of a data variable, variation questions related to a group or whole value of a certain variable to understand the properties or rules of variable variation, correlation questions related many data variables to find the correlation between data variables to detect new rules of relationship between attributes.

4.2   Visual Data Analysis Questions

To visually analyze the data of JHSSs, the paper proposes to build a visual data analysis model of JHSSs through data variables analyzed by visual analysis approach (see Fig. 5). To assess the true learning abilities of a student, we perform visual analysis of student data on visual graphs, thereby posing some questions to verify the visual graph is reasonable and effective. Users can ask questions to analyze student data and can answer this question based on visual graphs, from which users extract useful information by viewing - thinking visual graphs to serve specific purposes. To better understand the visual graph, let's look at a visual graph that visually demonstrates a student's learning score data and poses some questions to analyze data of JHSSs and see the student's development trend.

Users ask questions and answer questions themselves when observing the visual graphs in Figs. 7 and 8 for the purpose of exploring information and seeking knowledge from visual graphs of visual analysis JHSSs. Types of questions that users can ask include primary questions, variable questions, and correlated questions, along with five visual data analysis criteria proposed by the paper in Sect. 3.2.2. These types of questions have been detailed below and now we perform a visual analysis of student data below.

Visual data analysis questions are questions asked by users, analysts, or etc. when observing things, phenomena, etc. Visual data analysis questions used to explore information and knowledge in existing large data sets. Because of the essence of the data that users or analysts can be ask for appropriate analytical questions as they observe, the visual data analysis questions are divided into different categories and each segment question and the data area consists of two parts as the hypothetical part and the conclusion part. To highlight the students' learning ability development trend of JHSSs, the paper incorporates the criteria for visual data analysis of student data in Sect. 3.2.2 and the types of questions of the author group Thi Nguyen [6] to study data analysis of JHSSs as follows.

4.2.1   Coordinating the Type of Primary Questions and Criteria 1

Question 1: How many marks does Pham Dang Khoi get when he learns Foreign Language (**FL**) in grade 9? See Figs. 8 and 9.

- Supposition: Pham Dang Khoi, **FL**, grade 9
- Conclusion: Marks
- Looking at Fig. 8, parents or analysts extract Pham Dang Khoi's student learning results is shown in Fig. 9 based on coordinating between primary questions type and criteria 1 for parents results in Fig. 9.

Question 2: Pham Thao Nguyen has the results of learning in grade 7 which is the average subject and which subject is good? See Figs. 7 and 10.

- Supposition: Pham Thao Nguyen, grade 7.
- Conclusion: Which is the average subject and which subject is good?
- Looking at Fig. 7, parents or analysts extract Pham Thao Nguyen's student learning results is shown in Fig. 10 based on coordinating between type of primary questions and criteria 1 for parents results in Fig. 10.

4.2.2   Coordinating the Type of Variation Questions and Criteria 4, Criteria 5

Question 3: In the 6th, 7th, 8th, and 9th grade, how does Pham Dang Khoi tend to develop Mathematic (M)? See Figs. 8 and 11.

- Supposition: The 6th, 7th, 8th, and 9th grade, Pham Dang Khoi, **M**.
- Conclusion: Tend to develop **M**.
- Looking at Fig. 8, parents can see that the direction of Pham Dang Khoi's development of **M** is shown in detail in Fig. 11 depend on combining between type of variation questions and criteria 4 and 5 for supporting parents and analysts results in Fig. 11.

4.2.3   Coordinating the Type of Correlation Questions and Criteria 2, Criteria 3

Question 4: Which subjects are Pham Dang Khoi good at in grade 9? What relationships do they have with each other? See Figs. 8 and 12.

- Supposition: Pham Dang Khoi, good subjects, grade 9
- Conclusion: Subject, the relationship between subjects
- Looking at Fig. 8, parents can know that which subjects Pham Dang Khoi good at in grade 9 are and what relationships they have with each other are detailed in Fig. 12 rely on coordinating between type of correlation questions and criteria 2 and 3 for serving parents and analysts results in Fig. 12.

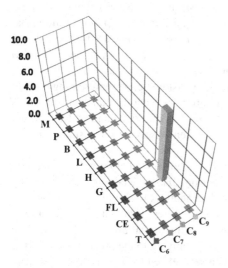

Fig. 9. Results of visual analysis Pham Dang Khoi's data

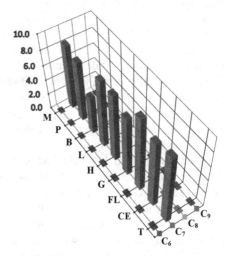

Fig. 10. Results of visual analysis Pham Thao Nguyen's data

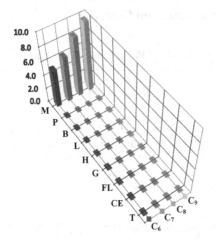

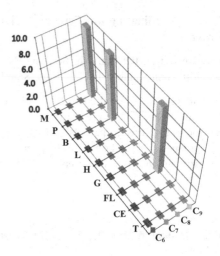

Fig. 11. Results of visual analysis Pham Dang Khoi's data

Fig. 12. Results of visual analysis Pham Dang Khoi's data

5 Conclusion

This paper has systematized the research works related to the areas of data visualization, visual analysis and processes of data visualization or visual analysis. This paper proposes to build a VAS, visual data analysis model and visual data analysis criteria for JHSSs' data whereby the paper applies to information discovery and knowledge search from JHSSs' data. Parents or data science analysts use VAS, visual data analysis model, visual data analysis criteria and visual graphs in combination with visual analysis of student data for information discovery, and seeking knowledge towards the knowledge chain as well as the future career for each student. This paper has also focused on building student-related data variables to become visual variables, then proposing visual data analysis criteria and multidimensional cube representing student data. Based on the visual graphs, we build a number of visual data analysis questions that help parents or analysts answer visual data analysis questions and understand the meaning of students' learning outcomes of JHS when observing the visual graph by visual viewing - thinking method.

With a VAS of multivariate data based on visual graphs to help parents or analysts discover information and search for knowledge from JHSSs data when observing the visual graph an effective way. With the visual data analysis model of multivariate data coordinated with the visual graph, it helped us build some visual data analysis criteria of JHSSs data, these criteria combine the provisions in circular 58 of the MET to help parents or data science analysts use it as a basis for applying to the process of exploring information and searching knowledge from data sets related to JHSSs. The visual data analysis model of JHSSs' multivariate data is shown in separate academic years to help parents or analysts perform arithmetic comparisons between subjects of this school year compared to subjects of another school year or making comparisons of subjects together in the same school year is easy.

In addition, the VAS and visual data analysis model of JHSSs' multivariate data can also be developed and expanded to compare the learning outcomes of many students in the same subject and class, or at the same level and specially developed for the High School student data set or develop and apply to the management data set in the University aimed at the knowledge chain as well as career orientation for future pupils and students.

References

1. Stuart, C.K., Jock, M., Ben, S.: Readings in Information Visualization: Using Vision to Think. Academic Press, Norwell (1999)
2. Card, S.T., Mackinlay, J.D., Scheiderman, B.: Readings in Information Visualization, Using Vision to Thinks. Graphic Press, Cheshire (1990)
3. Stevens, S.S.: On the theory of scales of measurement. Science **103**, 677–680 (1946)
4. Bertin, J.: General theory, from semiology of graphics. In: Dodge, M., Kitchin, R., Perkins, C. (eds.) The Map Reader. Theories of Mapping Practice and Cartographic Representation. Wiley, pp. 8–16 (2011)
5. Nguyen, H.T., Tran, A.V.T., Nguyen, T.A.T., Vo, L.T., Tran, P.V.: Multivariate cube integrated retinal variable to visually represent multivariable data. EAI Endorsed Trans. Context.-Aware Syst. Appl. **4**, 1–8 (2017). https://doi.org/10.4108/eai.6-7-2017.152757
6. Thi Nguyen, H., Thi Pham, T.M., Thi Nguyen, T.A., Thi Tran, A.V., Vinh Tran, P., Van Pham, D.: Two-stage approach to classifying multidimensional cubes for visualization of multivariate data. In: Cong Vinh, P., Alagar, V. (eds.) ICCASA/ICTCC -2018. LNICST, vol. 266, pp. 70–80. Springer, Cham (2019). https://doi.org/10.1007/978-3-030-06152-4_7
7. Thomas, J.J., Cook, K.A.: Illuminating the path the research and development agenda for visual analytics. National Visualization and Analytics Center – NVAC (2005)
8. Sacha, D., Stoffel, A., Stoffel, F., Kwon, B.C., Ellis, G., Keim, D.A.: Knowledge generation model for visual analytics. IEEE Trans. Vis. Comput. Graph. **20**(12), 1604–1613 (2014). https://doi.org/10.1109/tvcg.2014.2346481
9. Keim, D., Kohlhammer, J., Ellis, G., Mansmann, F.: Mastering the Information Age: Solving Problems with Visual Analytics. Eurographics Association, Goslar (2010). ISBN 978-3-905673-77-7
10. Keim, D., Andrienko, G., Fekete, J.-D., Görg, C., Kohlhammer, J., Melançon, G.: Visual analytics: definition, process, and challenges. In: Kerren, A., Stasko, John T., Fekete, J.-D., North, C. (eds.) Information Visualization. LNCS, vol. 4950, pp. 154–175. Springer, Heidelberg (2008). https://doi.org/10.1007/978-3-540-70956-5_7
11. Wijk, J.J.: The value of visualization. In: IEEE Visualization, p. 11 (2005)
12. Card, S.T., Mackinlay, J.D., Scheiderman, B.: Readings in Information Visualization, Using Vision to Think. Academic Press, Norwell (1999)
13. Bertini, E., Tatu, A., Keim, D.: Quality metrics in high-dimensional data visualization: an overview and systematization. IEEE Trans. Vis. Comput. Graph. **17**(12), 2203–2212 (2011). https://doi.org/10.1109/TVCG.2011.229
14. von Szent-Gyorgyi, A.: American (Hungarian-born) Biochemist (Nobel Laureate, 1937) who said: "Discovery consists of seeing what everybody has seen and thinking what nobody has thought" ed. by Irving Good, The Scientist Speculates (1962)

15. Fayyad, U., Piatetsky-Shapiro, G., Smyth, P.: From data mining to knowledge discovery in databases. AI Mag. **17**(3), 37 (1996)
16. Ministry of Education and Training (MET), Abstract: "Released circular regulations in assessing and ranking of Secondary School Students and High School Students" in menu of legal documents at page 20, Effect: in force. https://en.moet.gov.vn/document/legal-docu ments/Pages/detail.aspx?ItemID=744. Published date: 12/15/2011, Date to: 01/26/2012, Official number: 58/2011/TT-BGDĐT. Accessed Apr 2019
17. Andrienko, N., Andrienko, G.: Exploratory Analysis of Spatial and Temporal Data – A Systematic Approach, p. 2006. Springer, Heidelberg (2006)

CDNN Model for Insect Classification Based on Deep Neural Network Approach

Hiep Xuan Huynh[1] , Duy Bao Lam[2], Tu Van Ho[1(✉)] ,
Diem Thi Le[1] , and Ly Minh Le[1]

[1] Can Tho University, Can Tho, Vietnam
{hxhiep,hvtu,ltdiem,leminhly}@ctu.edu.vn
[2] Mekong University, Long Hồ, Vietnam
lambaoduy84@gmail.com

Abstract. The Mekong Delta has made great progress in rice production over the past ten years. Intensive cultivation with multi-cropping brings many benefits to farmers as well as the food export industry. However, this is also an opportunity for raising epidemic outbreak, Brown Plant-hoppers can directly damage by sucking the rice's vitality, and they can cause the wilting and complete drying of rice plants, a noncontagious disease known as "Hopper-burn". In this article, we propose the CDNN model for insect classification based on Neural Network and Deep Learning approach. First, insect images are collected and extracted features based on Dense Scale-Invariant Feature Transform. Then, Bag of Features is used for image representation as feature vectors. Lastly, these feature vectors are trained and classified using CDNN model based on Deep Neural Network. The approach is demonstrated with experiments, and measured by a large amount of Brown Plant-hoppers and Ladybugs samples.

Keywords: Bag of Features · Brown Plant-hoppers · Classification · Deep neural network · Dense SIFT · Insect · Ladybugs

1 Introduction

Rice cultivation plays a very important role for farmers in Vietnam. There are many insect pests attack rice tree [23], they would destroy the rice crop. Especially, Brown Plant-hopper (BPH), a small insect pest causes extensive crop damages. It has high reproductive capacities. Besides Hopper-burn, BPH also causes serious diseases in rice crop, such as "Rice yellow dwarf disease". In the other hand, predators (beneficial insect such as ladybug, ladybird, and spider) kill and feed on several to many individual insect pest during their lifetimes, they are bio-control groups in agriculture. Without these predators, insect pests would grow and destroy crops quickly [8].

Classification of living insects is on the agenda for several reasons. First, due to climate change, it is important to understand how insects distribute or response. Second, the significant development of insects leads to unbalancing some surrounding conditions. Nevertheless, it is necessary to have agricultural specialists to identify insects. In case of lacking domain experts, a requests for insect recognition and classification to be carried out more efficiently have become pressing. In response, image-

P. C. Vinh and A. Rakib (Eds.): ICCASA 2019/ICTCC 2019, LNICST 298, pp. 127–142, 2019.
https://doi.org/10.1007/978-3-030-34365-1_10

based technology is used to improve the wide range of applications especially in agriculture, ecology and environmental science [5]. It generally can be utilized in prevention of plant disease and insect pests, plant quarantine and as an essential part of eco-informatics research. Insect classification has to be taken into a serious measure because insect presents an especially severe threat and it can cause many negative effects on agriculture in a short period of time.

This paper proposes a novel approach by developing a CDNN model of classifying insects in images based on Neural Network [11, 20] and Deep Learning [3, 16, 35]. Image features are extracted by Dense Scale-Invariant Feature Transform (Dense SIFT) [6] and represented as feature vectors by Bag of Features (BoF) [19, 26, 28, 29]. The research contributes to building a sampling BPH light trap surveillance network in the Mekong Delta, Vietnam [2], helping reduce crop damage caused by insect pests.

The rest of this article is presented as follows. Section 2 depicts some previous work relating to insect image classification. Insect images representation based on the BoF model is presented in the next section. System of insect classification is proposed in Sect. 4. Section 5 illustrates some results of the classification method. The last section is our conclusion and future plans.

2 Related Work

There have been many research of insect detection or classification in image data. Zhu and Zhang [21] introduced a method to classify insects by using color histogram and Gray Level Co-occurrence Matrix (GLCM) of wing images. First, the image of lepi-dopteran insect is preprocessed to get the ROI (Region of Interest); then the color image is converted from RGB (Red-Green-Blue) to HSV (Hue-Saturation-Value) space, and the 1D color histograms of ROI are generated from hue and saturation distributions. Afterward, the color image is converted to grayscale one, rotated and transformed to a standard position, and their GLCM features are extracted. Matching is first undergone by computing the correlation of the histograms vectors between testing and template images. Then, their GLCM features are further matched when the cor-relation is higher than certain threshold.

According to Hassan et al. [27], several methods used in machine vision learning in detecting and classifying insects based on their features, colors, and shape. Each method has the advantages and disadvantages in detecting insects. Among the method used, color histogram seems to be the best approach in classifying and recognizing species of insects. In the method, each acquired image is divided into several same size squares and each of the square of images has its own histogram. Even though the detected insects is not in the same position in the trained image, the system still can identified which type of insect based on the color histogram.

To improve the classification accuracy, Xie et al. [12] develop an insect recognition system using advanced multiple task sparse representation and multiple-kernel learning (MKL) techniques. As different features of insect images contribute differently to the classification of insect species, the multiple-task sparse representation technique can combine multiple features of insect species to enhance the recognition performance.

In [5], Lu *et al.* proposed a hybrid approach called discriminative local soft coding (DLSoft) which combines local and discriminative coding strategies together. This method used neighbor codewords for getting a local soft coding and class-specific codebooks (sets of codewords) for a discriminative representation. On obtaining the vector representation of image via spatial pyramid pooling of patches, a linear SVM classifier is used for classifying images into species.

Shapes and sizes can be used to detect BPHs in images by using morphology operations [7, 17]. The experimental results show that the proposed approach is suitable for detecting and counting BPHs in images.

3   Insect Images Representation

3.1   Characteristics of Insect Images

Two interested insect species (see Fig. 1) are BPH [23] and Ladybugs [8], they have an average size of about 4-10 mm, and their characteristics can be identified by morphological. For example, BPH has a yellowish brown body and their head overhangs towards the front, their wings are transparent and the front wings have a black spot on the back side.

(a)   **(b)**

Fig. 1. RGB insect image: adult BPH [23] (a) and Ladybug [8] (b)

Insect images were taken by 1280 × 720 pixels resolution. Before extracting feature, insect images were converted to grayscale and stored in grayscale image matrix, each cell of matrix has value between 0 and 255 (see Fig. 2).

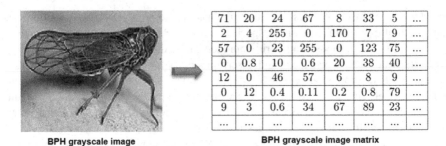

BPH grayscale image   **BPH grayscale image matrix**

Fig. 2. BPH grayscale image stored in a matrix

3.2 Bag of Features Model

Insect image representation is the key step in classification, its performance directly affects the insect classification results. Bag of Features (BoF) [19, 26, 28, 29] approach can be motivated by an analogy to learning methods using the Bag-of-Words (BoW) [36] representation for text categorization. BoF methods have been applied to image classification, object detection, image retrieval, and even visual localization for robots. BoF approaches are characterized by the use of an orderless collection of image features. Due to its simplicity and performance, the BoF approach has become well-established in the field.

BoF model is designed for representation insect image features as feature vectors. The main idea is to reduce storage space and minimize computation. This model includes 3 main functions as described in Fig. 3: (1) extracting insect image features based on Dense SIFT algorithm, (2) vector quantization using the variant of the K-means algorithm, and (3) constructing bag of features by applying the Spatial Pyramid Matching framework.

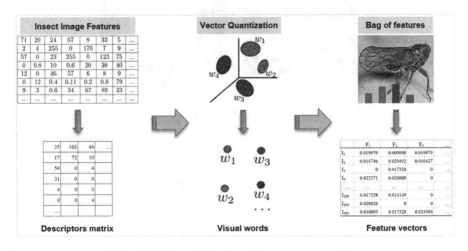

Fig. 3. BoF model for insect images representation

Extracting Insect Image Features

Scale-Invariant Feature Transform (SIFT) [13] provides a set of features of objects in an image. These features are invariant with the change of scale, rotation, view, noise or light intensity in an acceptable level. This method archives high efficiency in image recognition [14]. Four major stages of computation used to generate the set of image features are involved in the following order:

- Scale-space extrema detection: the first stage of computation searches over all scales and image locations. It is implemented efficiently by using a difference-of-Gaussian function to identify potential interest points that are invariant to scale and orientation.
- Keypoint localization: at each candidate location, a detailed model is fit to determine location and scale. Keypoints are selected based on measures of their stability.
- Orientation assignment: one or more orientations are assigned to each keypoint location based on local image gradient directions. All future operations are performed on image data that has been transformed relative to the assigned orientation, scale, and location for each feature, thereby providing invariance to these transformations.
- Keypoint descriptor: the local image gradients are measured at the selected scale in the region around each keypoint. These are transformed into a representation that allows for significant levels of local shape distortion and change in illumination.

Dense SIFT [1, 6, 31, 33] is derived from the SIFT [13, 14], the most significant difference between them is that Dense SIFT assumes all the significant points are evenly distributed. Therefore, the selection of keywords in all areas of the image is dense and standardized.

Dense SIFT operation starts with segmenting a grayscale image into small segments, each of these segment is further divided into smaller segments. For each of these segments, which represent the neighborhoods around the feature point (center of the segment), the image gradients were calculated. A smoothed weighted histogram of eight orientation bins (corresponding to eight directions) is created based on the sum of gradient value. Consequently, a descriptor of a local region (keypoint) is formed by calculating the gradient magnitude and orientation around the keypoint.

These descriptors are set in a Gaussian window. They are accumulated into orientation histograms in 4×4 sub regions of which the length of each arrow depicts the number of orientation bins inside a region. A best results are achieved with a 4×4 array of histograms with 8 orientation bins in each, the local descriptor results in a 128-dimensionl vector. After extracting, each insect image feature is represented by a descriptors matrix.

Vector Quantization

Vector quantization [4] is a classical quantization technique from signal processing that allows the modeling of probability density functions by the distribution of prototype vectors. It works by dividing a large set of points (vectors) into groups having approximately the same number of points closest to them. Each group is represented by its centroid point, as in K-means and some other clustering algorithms.

A variant of the K-means algorithm [9] is used for grouping descriptor vectors in descriptors matrix to the set of clusters. K-means algorithm is a popular and unsupervised learning algorithm. The goal of the K-means clustering algorithm is to minimize the sum of squared Euclidean distances [11] between each point and the nearest cluster center. In this paper, Dense SIFT feature of each insect image has average feature descriptors number about few ten thousand descriptors. Therefore, in this section we initialize number of clusters with value 1000. Then, clustering process is done by a variant of the K-means algorithm [9], this algorithm applies a technique based acceleration the triangular inequality. Besides, we use k-dimensional tree algorithm [18] for enhancing performance of vector quantization. The results of this phase is the number of descriptor vectors in each cluster, and each cluster is a word in visual words.

Constructing Bag of Features
Visual words is used for constructing feature vectors which represent insect images. The number of descriptor vectors in each cluster are calculated and built a spatial histogram of visual words. Visual words are associated into a spatial histogram by applying the Spatial Pyramid Matching framework [28]. This method combines the technique of generating visual words into the Pyramid matching plan. For each level of space, the pyramid apply a method for matching a series of grids. At each level, the number of histogram matches is counted in each grid and a weighted sum is collected for all resolutions. The result is a histogram for each image taking into account the relative location of image features. It should be pointed out that level of a spatial pyramid L = 0 is equivalent to a standard BoF implementation. After this process, a feature vector which represents an insect image Dense SIFT feature, is obtained.

4   Insect Classification

The system handles insect classification including 3 main phases with functions described in Fig. 4:

- Data phase: real insects are caught and taken their pictures. Some preprocessing tasks are done in order to remove unnecessary points in image.
- BoF representation phase: BoF model is used for image feature extraction and representation as feature vectors.
- Classification phase: these feature vectors are trained by CDNN model and applied for insect images classification.

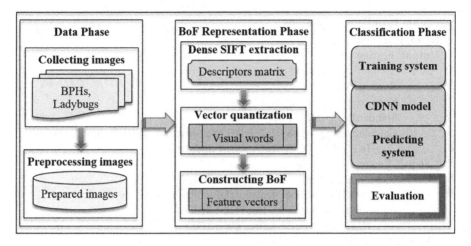

Fig. 4. System of insect classification

4.1 Data Phase

Insect image samples (see Fig. 5) are collected from adult BPH images and ladybug images by using a camera with [1280 × 720] resolution in different views. After preprocessing, information relating to these insects is kept, others are removed.

Fig. 5. BPH image samples

4.2 BoF Representation Phase

Bag of features (BoF) model is designed for representation phase. The number of keypoints is used to form feature vectors. Therefore, feature vector $F = \{F_1, F_2,..., F_{4000}\}$ represents for each insect image. The steps for BoF representation are as follows:

Algorithm 1: BoF Representation
Input: Insect image
Output: Feature vector
1:    Step 1: Extracting insect image features
2:            Reading insect image
3:            Converting insect image to grayscale
4:            Standardizing image size
5:            Calculating keypoints (KEYPTS) and (descriptors) DESCRS
6:                [KEYPTS, DESCRS] = DSift.calculate(img)
7:    Step 2: Vector quantization
8:            Clustering descriptor vectors (WORDS)
9:                WORDS = Elkan_Kmeans(DESCRS, numWords)
10:           Building a k-dimensional tree (KDTREE)
11:               KDTREE = build_kdtree (WORDS)
12:   Step 3: Constructing bag of features
13:           Computing a spatial histogram of visual words
14:               HIST = compute_Histogram(KEYPTS, WORDS)
15:           Reducing a spatial histogram to single
16:               HIST = single(HIST / sum(HIST))

4.3 Classification Phase

Classification phase as described in Fig. 4 includes 4 main functions: (1) CDNN model, (2) training system, (3) predicting system (testing system), and (4) evaluation. In this section, CDNN model and training system are described. Predicting system and evaluation will be presented in the next part.

CDNN Model

Deep neural networks [10, 16] are distinguished from the more commonplace single-hidden-layer neural networks by their depth. The traditional neural network has at most 3 layers: input, hidden, output while a deep neural networks has more than 1 hidden layers. The principle of deep neural networks is that nodes in a layer is trained by specific features based on outputs of the previous layer. The more layers the network has, the more complex features can recognize because it is able to combine features in previous layers.

CDNN model which is designed for insect images classification consists of many layers of interconnected neurons, it is a straight forward neural network as described in Fig. 6. In this model, each layer has a specific role and responsibility.

- Input layer: plays an input role to match inputs relevant to feature vectors of insect images. The number of nodes in the input layer is fixed with number of insect image feature vectors. For example, feature vectors $F = \{F_1, F_2,..., F_{4000}\}$ represents for insect images, the number of nodes in the input layer is n = 4000 nodes.
- Hidden layers: is the middle layers, the number of hidden layer and the number of nodes in each hidden layer is designed for the purpose of increasing the accuracy of

the model. CDNN model must has at least 2 hidden layers. In this paper, the experiment is designed in two scenarios: using 2 hidden layers and 3 hidden layers.

- Output layer: is a linear classification which is relevant to the output space. The number of nodes in the output layer is class numbers which needs for classification, this model has two classes (PBHs and Ladybugs).

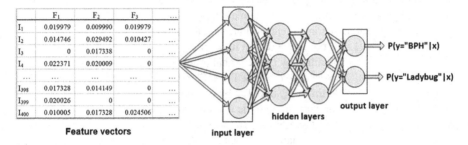

Fig. 6. CDNN model with 2 hidden layers

Training System

The training protocol of CDNN model applies parallel distributed and multi-threaded in H2O Deep Learning [3]. Loss function based on Mean squared error loss [3]:

$$L(W, B \mid j) = \frac{\sum_{i=1}^{n} (t_j - o_j)}{n}$$

Where:

- W is the collection $\{w_i\}_{1:N-1}$, where W_i denotes the weight matrix connecting layers i and i + 1 for a network of N layers.
- B is the collection $\{b_i\}_{1:N-1}$, where b_i denotes the column vector of biases for layer i + 1.
- j is training sample.
- n is number of training samples.
- t_j is value the predicted output (target output).
- o_j is output value of the network (actual output).

The process of minimizing the loss function $L(W, B \mid j)$ is a parallelized version of stochastic gradient descent (SGD). The gradient $\nabla L(W, B \mid j)$ updated with back-propagation algorithm [34]. The SGD method is fast and optimal memory but not easily parallelizable without becoming slow, Hogwild update method [15] is used for resolving this problem.

Bias units are included in each non-output layer of the network. The weights linking neurons and biases with other neurons fully determine the output of the entire network. Learning occurs when these weights are adapted to minimize the error on the labeled training data.

Let the constant α is the learning rate to control the step sizes during gradient descent. Avg_n represents the final averaging of these local parameters across all nodes to obtain the global model parameters and complete training. The following steps outline the training protocol of CDNN model:

Algorithm 2: The training protocol of CDNN model
1:    Step 1: Initialing global parameters: Weights (W) and Biases (B)
2:    Step 2: Distributing training data T to all nodes
3:    Step 3: Repeat until convergence criterion reached:
4:            3.1. For nodes $n \in T_n$, do in parallel:
5:                    Obtain copy of the global model parameters W_n, B_n
6:                    Select active subset $T_{na} \subset T_n$
7:                    Partition T_{na} into T_{nac} by cores n_c
8:                    For cores n_c on node n, do in parallel
9:                        Get training sample $i \in T_{nac}$
10:                       Update all weights $w_{jk} \in T_n$, biases $b_{jk} \in B_n$
11:                       $w_{jk} = w_{jk} - \alpha \dfrac{\partial L(W,B|j)}{\partial w_{jk}}$
12:                       $b_{jk} = b_{jk} - \alpha \dfrac{\partial L(W,B|j)}{\partial b_{jk}}$
13:                   3.2. Updating global parameters
14:                       $W, B = Avg_n W_n, Avg_n B_n$
15:                   3.3. Optionally score the model on train/validation scoring sets

In all of the CDNN model nodes, input data is distributed and training on all nodes, weight and bias are calculated in parallel on each node until weights and biases (W, B) obtained by averaging.

5   Experimental Results and Discussion

In all experiments, the learning rate is $\alpha = 0.005$ to control the step sizes during gradient descent. Weights and biases are randomly initialized. Accuracy and error rate are calculated by confusion matrix [30].

5.1   Data Used

Experiments were performed on BPH images and Ladybug images. All experimental data are describe in Table 1.

Table 1. Experimental data.

Insect name	Training sets	Testing sets	Total
BPH	200	100	300
Ladybug	200	100	300

All insect images in the training dataset and testing dataset were extracted Dense SIFT features and applied BoF model for feature vectors. Training feature vectors and testing feature vectors are described in Tables 2 and 3. The test labels are not assigned.

Table 2. Training feature vectors.

	F_1	F_2	F_3	...	F_{3999}	F_{4000}	Label
I_1	0.019979	0.009990	0.019979	...	0.098386	0.101874	BPH
I_2	0.014746	0.029492	0.010427	...	0.261088	0	BPH
I_3	0	0.017338	0	...	0.478497	0.484118	BPH
I_4	0.022371	0.020009	0		0.255067	0.086062	BPH
...	...	...	...	...	...	...	...
I_{398}	0.017328	0.014149	0	...	0	0	LDBUG
I_{399}	0.020026	0	0	...	0.440688	0.106440	LDBUG
I_{400}	0.010005	0.017328	0.024506	...	0	0.159446	LDBUG

Table 3. Testing feature vectors

	F_1	F_2	F_3	...	F_{3999}	F_{4000}	Label
I_1	0.086084	0.026476	0.026476	...	0	0	
I_2	0	0.088023	0.191645	...	0	0	
I_3	0.011362	0.039360	0.093003	...	0.017302	0.028255	
I_4	0.415988	0.009997	0.009997		0	0.295634	
...	...	...	...	...	...	...	
I_{198}	0.185016	0	0	...	0.102334	0.053099	
I_{199}	0.407395	0	0	...	0.145924	0.387371	
I_{200}	0.010005	0	0.015688	...	0.048343	0.016114	

5.2 Tool Used

The experimental tool is installed in Matlab [22] and VLFeat 0.9.20 [33]. BOF model is used to represent insect image as feature vectors. These feature vectors are imported into R tools [25, 32] with H2O Deep Learning package [3] for classification. Experiments are operated on the computer with the configurations: Intel Core i7-4710HQ, CPU 2.50 GHz, Memory 16 GB RAM, Ubuntu 16.04 LTS operating system.

5.3 Scenario 1: Insect Classification in CDNN Model with 2 Hidden Layers

In this scenario, we evaluate CDNN model with 2 hidden layers. A number of neurons are customized in specific cases.

Case 1. Each hidden layer has 10 neurons (10, 10). Figure 7 illustrates number of BPH and ladybugs after classifying with the accuracy 91.5%.

```
> summary(predictions, exact_quantiles=TRUE)
 predict      BPH                    LDBUG
 BPH   :117  Min.    :5.392e-08   Min.    :1.625e-07
 LDBUG:  83  1st Qu. :1.313e-06   1st Qu. :2.133e-06
             Median  :9.999e-01   Median  :1.370e-04
             Mean    :5.432e-01   Mean    :4.568e-01
             3rd Qu. :1.000e+00   3rd Qu. :1.000e+00
             Max.    :1.000e+00   Max.    :1.000e+00
```

Fig. 7. Summary of classification in case 1:2 hidden layers (10, 10).

Case 2. A number of neurons in each hidden layer are adjusted, each hidden layer has 20 neurons (20, 20). Figure 8 illustrates number of BPHs and ladybugs after classifying with the accuracy 93%.

```
> summary(predictions, exact_quantiles=TRUE)
 predict      BPH                    LDBUG
 BPH   :114  Min.    :1.381e-08   Min.    :3.845e-08
 LDBUG:  86  1st Qu. :5.690e-07   1st Qu. :7.520e-07
             Median  :9.991e-01   Median  :8.938e-04
             Mean    :5.205e-01   Mean    :4.795e-01
             3rd Qu. :1.000e+00   3rd Qu. :1.000e+00
             Max.    :1.000e+00   Max.    :1.000e+00
```

Fig. 8. Summary of classification in case 2:2 hidden layers (20, 20).

Continuing experiments by adjusting the number nodes in 2 hidden layers of CDNN model. Table 4 shows the results of execution time and Mean squared errors (MSE) in different neural networks, predictable result in 2 classes (BPHs and Ladybugs) based on insect feature vectors, as well as the percentage of classification accuracy and the error rate.

Table 4. Summary of classification in Scenario 1: CDNN model with 2 hidden layers

Id	Number of nodes	Execution time (sec)	Mean squared errors (MSE)	Result PBHs; Ladybugs	Accuracy (%)	Error (%)
1	10, 10	3.437	1.304558e−09	117; 83	91.5	8.5
2	20, 20	3.568	1.111752e−10	114; 86	93.0	7.0
3	40, 40	4.631	2.224379e−11	114; 86	93.0	7.0
4	80, 80	6.224	7.733223e−12	111; 89	94.5	5.5
5	100, 100	10.276	2.35158e−12	109; 91	95.5	4.5

The result in Table 4 concludes that, in the Deep neural network with 2 hidden layers, the more the number of nodes in a layer is, the more the accuracy increases (but the error decreases).

5.4   Scenario 2: Insect Classification in CDNN Model with 3 Hidden Layers

In this scenario, we evaluate CDNN model with 3 hidden layers. A number of nodes in hidden layers are also adjusted in specific cases. Table 5 shows the summary of classification in Deep neural network with 3 hidden layers.

Table 5. Summary of classification in Scenario 2: CDNN Model with 3 Hidden Layers

Id	Number of nodes	Execution time (sec)	Mean squared errors (MSE)	Result PBHs; Ladybugs	Accuracy (%)	Error (%)
1	50, 50, 50	17.554	0.04597361	114; 86	93.0	7.0
2	100, 50, 50	22.214	0.03883661	106; 94	97.0	3.0
3	100, 100, 50	28.162	0.02325019	106; 94	97.0	3.0
4	100 ,100, 100	28.312	0.02747581	107; 93	96.5	3.5
5	200, 100, 100	58.002	0.03568920	109; 91	95.5	4.5

The result in Table 5 shows that when adjustment the number of nodes in the Deep neural network with 3 hidden layers, the rate of accuracy classification increases. The best result (accuracy rate 97% with smallest MSE) achieves with the number of nodes (100, 100, 50). However, when the number of nodes in 3 hidden layers adjusts to (200, 100, 100), the accuracy classification rate decreases (95.5%). This problem is called overfitting [24], a large number of nodes in hidden layers affects classification results.

5.5   Discussion

In comparing the accuracy, Fig. 9 illustrates the accuracy prediction (percentage) of the classification in different networks. In Deep neural network with 2 hidden layers, the accuracy increases corresponding to the increment of number of nodes. Similarly, in 3 hidden layers network, there is a rise of accuracy when the number of nodes increases. However, when increasing the number of classes to (200,100,100), the accuracy prediction rate tends to decrease. There is a distinction between the accuracy of 2 hidden layers and 3 hidden layers network. Obviously, accuracies of 3 hidden layers network are better than those of 2 hidden layers ones since they require one more layer to train and classify feature vectors. In short, the accuracy of a network is ratio with the number of hidden layers as well as the number of nodes in a hidden layer (with the appropriate number of nodes).

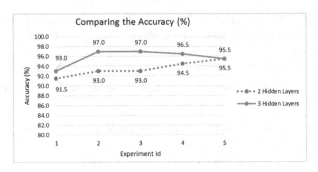

Fig. 9. Comparing the accuracy (%)

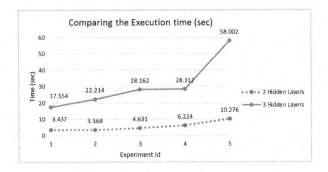

Fig. 10. Comparing the execution time (sec)

In comparing the execution time, Fig. 10 demonstrates convincingly that when the number of nodes in the hidden layer increases, the execution time increases as well. Further more, in all cases of experiment, execution times in 3 hidden layers network are longer than those in 2 hidden layers network.

6   Conclusion

We have advocated proposed the CDNN model to classify insect images using Bag of features and Deep Neural Networks approach. Insect image features are extracted and saved to descriptors matrix based on Dense SIFT. Vector quantization is done with a variant of the K-means algorithm, each cluster is a vocabulary of visual words. A spatial histogram is built with spatial pyramid matching, feature vector is the result at the end of this process. These feature vectors become the input of CDNN model which is applied for classifying insect image. The accuracy of the classification process can be increased by adjusting the number of nodes in a layer as well as the number of hidden layers in a network. Experiments show that the model is suitable for classification in static insect images. The best result (accuracy rate 97% with smallest MSE) achieves in case of using CDNN model 3 hidden layers with the number of nodes (100, 100, 50).

We believe that there would be tremendous benefit to an insect identification application and hope that this work will provide a starting point for further work on such a technology. It is intended that the proposed method will serve as a corner stone for research into real-time monitoring and tracking insects or other living organisms with the participation of experts in the field of information technology and agriculture.

References

1. Chavez, A.J.: Image classification with dense sift sampling an exploration of optimal parameters. Kansas State University, Manhattan (2012)
2. Tran, A.C., Tran, N.C., Huynh, H.X.: An approach to detecting brown plant hopper based on morphological operations. In: Vinh, P.C., Barolli, L. (eds.) ICTCC 2016. LNICST, vol. 168, pp. 52–61. Springer, Cham (2016). https://doi.org/10.1007/978-3-319-46909-6_6
3. Candel, A., LeDell, E., Parmar, V., Arora, A.: Deep Learning with H_2O, 5th edn. H2O.ai (2016)
4. Gersho, A., Gray, R.M.: Vector Quantization and Signal Compression. The Springer International Series in Engineering and Computer Science. Springer, Berlin (1992). https://doi.org/10.1007/978-1-4615-3626-0
5. Lu, A., Hou, X., Liu, C.-L., Chen, X.: Insect species recognition using discriminative local soft coding. In: Proceedings of the 21st International Conference on Pattern Recognition (ICPR2012), pp. 1221–1224. IEEE, Tsukuba (2012)
6. Vedaldi, A., Fulkerson, B.: VLFeat: an open and portable library of computer vision algorithms. In: Proceedings of the 18th ACM International Conference on Multimedia, pp. 1469–1472. ACM, New York and Firenze (2010)
7. Lam, B.H., Van Tran, H., Huynh, H.X., Pottier, B.: Synchoronous networks for insects surveillance. In: Proceedings of the Sixth International Symposium on Information and Communication Technology, pp. 163–170, Hue City (2015)
8. Shepard, B.M., Barrion, A.T., Litsinger, J.A.: Friends of the rice farmer: helpful insects, spiders, and pathogens. International Rice Research Institute (1987)
9. Elkan, C.: Using the triangle inequality to accelerate k-means. In: Proceedings of the Twentieth International Conference on Machine Learning (ICML-2003), pp. 147–153. AAAI Press, Washington, DC (2003)
10. Szegedy, C., Toshev, A., Erhan, D.: Deep neural networks for object detection. In: Neural Information Processing Systems Conference (2013)
11. Christopher, M.: Bishop: Pattern Recognition and Machine Learning. Springer, New York (2006)
12. Xie, C., et al.: Automatic classification for field crop insects via multiple-task sparse representation and multiple-kernel learning. Comput. Electron. Agric. **119**, 123–132 (2015)
13. David, G.: Lowe: distinctive image features from scale-invariant keypoints. Int. J. Comput. Vis. **60**, 91–110 (2004)
14. Lowe, D.G.: object recognition from local scale-invariant features. In: Proceedings of the 7th IEEE International Conference on Computer Vision, pp. 1150–1157. IEEE (1999)
15. Niu, F., Recht, B., Re, C., Wright, S.J.: Hogwild: a lock-free approach to parallelizing stochastic gradient descent. In: Advances in Neural Information Processing Systems, pp. 693–701 (2011)
16. Larochelle, H., Bengio, Y., Louradour, J., Lamblin, P.: Exploring strategies for training deep neural networks. J. Mach. Learn. Res. **10**, 1–40 (2009)

17. Lim, J., Cho, J., Nam, T., Kim, S.: Development of a classification algorithm for butterflies and ladybugs. In: TENCON 2006 - 2006 IEEE Region 10 Conference, pp. 51–63. IEEE, Hong Kong (2006)
18. Bentley, J.L.: Multidimensional binary search trees used for associative searching. Commun. ACM **18**, 509–517 (1975)
19. Sivic, J., Zisserman, A.: Video google: a textretrieval approach to object matching in videos. In: Proceedings Ninth IEEE International Conference on Computer Vision, pp. 1470–1477. IEEE, Nice (2003)
20. Du, K.-L., Swamy, M.N.S.: Neural Networks and Statistical Learning. Springer, London (2014). https://doi.org/10.1007/978-1-4471-5571-3
21. Zhu, L.Q., Zhang, Z.: Auto-classification of insect images based on color histogram and GLCM. In: Seventh International Conference on Fuzzy Systems and Knowledge Discovery, Yantai, Shandong, China, pp. 2589–2593 (2010)
22. MathWorks Homepage. http://www.mathworks.com. Accessed 25 June 2018
23. Pathak, M.D., Khan, Z.R.: Insects pests of rice. International Rice Research Institute (1994)
24. Srivastava, N., Hinton, G., Krizhevsky, A., Sutskever, I., Salakhutdinov, R.: Dropout: a simple way to prevent neural networks from overfitting. J. Mach. Learn. Res. **15**, 1929–1958 (2014)
25. RStudio Homepage. https://www.rstudio.com. Accessed 25 June 2018
26. López-Sastre, R.J., Renes-Olalla, J., Gil-Jiménez, P., Maldonado-Bascón, S.: Visual word aggregation. In: Vitrià, J., Sanches, J.M., Hernández, M. (eds.) IbPRIA 2011. LNCS, vol. 6669, pp. 676–683. Springer, Heidelberg (2011). https://doi.org/10.1007/978-3-642-21257-4_84
27. Hassan, S.N.A., Rahman, N.S.A., Htike, Z., Win, S.L.: Advanced in automatic insect classification. Electr. Electron. Eng.: Int. J. **3**(2), 51–63 (2014)
28. Lazebnik, S., Schmid, C., Pomce, J.: Beyond bag of features: spatial pyramid matching for recognizing natural scene categories. In: 2006 IEEE Computer Society Conference on Computer Vision and Pattern Recognition, pp. 2169–2178. IEEE, New York (2006)
29. O'Hara, S., Draper, B.A.: Introduction to the bag of features paradigm for image classification and retrieval. arXiv:1101.3354v1 (2011)
30. Visa, S., Ramsay, B., Ralescu, A., Knaap, E.V.D.: Confusion matrix-based feature selection. In: Proceedings of The 22nd Midwest Artificial Intelligence and Cognitive Science Conference 2011, Cincinnati, Ohio, USA, pp. 120–127 (2011)
31. Vo, T., Tran, D., Ma, W.: Tensor decomposition of dense SIFT descriptors in object recognition. In: European Symposium on Artificial Neural Networks, Bruges, Belgium, vol. 1, pp. 319–324 (2014)
32. The R Project for Statistical Computing Homepage. https://www.r-project.org. Accessed 25 June 2018
33. VLFeat Homepage. http://www.vlfeat.org. Accessed 25 June 2018
34. LeCun, Y.: A theoretical framework for back-propagation. In: Proceeding of the 1988 Connectionist Model Summer School, pp. 21–28. Morgan Kaufmann, Pittsburg (1988)
35. Bengio, Y.: Deep learning of representations: looking forward. In: Dediu, A.-H., Martín-Vide, C., Mitkov, R., Truthe, B. (eds.) SLSP 2013. LNCS (LNAI), vol. 7978, pp. 1–37. Springer, Heidelberg (2013). https://doi.org/10.1007/978-3-642-39593-2_1
36. Harris, Z.S.: Distributional structure. Word **10**, 146–162 (1954)

Predicting of Flooding in the Mekong Delta Using Satellite Images

Hiep Xuan Huynh[1], Tran Tu Thi Loi[2], Toan Phung Huynh[1(✉)],
Son Van Tran[3], Thu Ngoc Thi Nguyen[3], and Simona Niculescu[4]

[1] Cantho University, Cantho 94000, Vietnam
{hxhiep, hptoan}@ctu.edu.vn
[2] Fsoft Cantho, Can Tho, Vietnam
tutran5985@gmail.com
[3] Kiengiang Medical College, Rạch Giá 91000, Kiengiang, Vietnam
tvsonkl3@gmail.com, ntngocthu@gmail.com
[4] Université de Bretagne Occidentale - UBO, Brest, France
simona.niculescu@univ-brest.fr

Abstract. Flooding is a natural risk, large floods have occurred almost every year. These are major issues that researchers are interested and to identify flooded areas or assess the risk of flooding, the researchers using image LiDAR or image RADAR to flood mapping, flood risk management, observation and change detection in floodable area. However, flood modeling or flood assessment don't solve the problem of flood risks. Therefore, in this paper we propose a new approach of processing methodology based on time series analysis that enables predicting of the floodable areas in the Mekong Delta using new satellite images such as Lansat 7 ETM+, Landsat 8 OLI and sentinel-2 MSI.

Keywords: Assess the risk of flooding · Satellite image · Modeling of image classification · Time series analysis · Random forest · Decision trees · Determining and predicting the flooding area

1 Introduction

Flood inundation is the natural disaster, damage to human life and agriculture [13]. In the near years, the flood inundation changes due to the effect of climate change. Therefore, we need the best solutions for monitoring and management to forecast flooding capacity and also to limit obstacles to people and productions.

Nowaday, most of the researchers have mapped the floods [25] by using normalized difference water index are used to separate water and soil [8]. Supervised learning methods and classification algorithms such as decision trees [10], support vector machine [5], random forest [11] applied to the remote sensing images have successfully implemented image classification showing that the uniform pixels are grouped in layers.

Remote sensing technology such as radar remote sensing sensor (SAR) [20] seems to be one of the fastest and most effective ways to observe and provide information on flooding levels but it is expensive and not available for public use. Meanwhile Landsat

P. C. Vinh and A. Rakib (Eds.): ICCASA 2019/ICTCC 2019, LNICST 298, pp. 143–156, 2019.
https://doi.org/10.1007/978-3-030-34365-1_11

images (Landsat 7 ETM+, Landsat 8 OLI) and optical images (Sentinel-2 MSI) are provided free of charge by NASA, is one of the scientific achievements that is widely used for all fields because it has high time resolution and rich spectral information. Landsats images known in flood mapping [15], followed and monitored major flood by repeating of period cycle. It is capable of quickly assessing the change of objects [15] in monitoring the situation of floods events [21], and previously flooded areas could be identified based on spectral attribute changes between before floods and after floods [24]. Beside, Sentinel-2 optical is a new approach for improving the area to be analyzed such as the mapping of restored areas relevant for the classification of wetland vegetation [22].

The aim of this paper use new satellite images such as Landsat 7 ETM+, Landsat 8 OLI and sentinel-2 MSI [3] to analyze the objects of the images based on normalized difference water index (NDWI) [19], and establish region of interest (ROI) [18]. Combination with supervised classification algorithm, random forest [11] classify and generalise for all images. The classification results accurate with overall accuracy from 90% to 100% in before floods, during floods and after floods periods in the Mekong Delta with new satellite images.

This paper is organized as follows. The first section is introduction. The second presents about regions of interest for flooding. The third and fourth section introduces the discovering floods area and determine flooding disposition over time. The fifth section present results experiment. And the end is conclusion and future work.

2   Regions of Interest for Flooding

2.1   Image Characteristics

Digital image is a two-dimensional matrix that is displayed in the form of small squares of equal size, each square has a value (numeric type) representing a color. There are two types of images that we observe are grayscale images (each pixel counts from 0 to 255, which means that there are 8 bits or 1 byte to represent each of these pixels) and color image, a combination of three colors such as green, blue, red. Each color is between 0 and 255, meaning that each pixel needs 24 bits or 3 bytes to be represented as illustrated in Fig. 1.

The spectral characteristics of objects such as soil, clear water, turbid water and vegetation are described as follows:

- Clear river water absorbs a lot and is less reflective, so its color is very dark on the image.
- Turbid water is more reflective than the clear water because its reflexivity depends on the ability of the objects in the water to reflect (such as silt or algae)
- Soil is very reflective and the ability to reflect depends on the length of the wavelength
- Vegetation are reflected at 0.54 mm wavelength and infrared. The spectral reflectance of vegetation in the infrared is many times larger than the visible light.

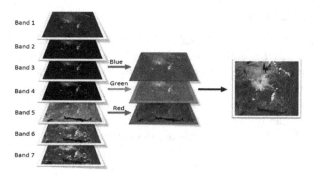

Fig. 1. Color image with combination of band red, green, blue (Color figure online)

Pixel images are square and display a certain area on an image as illustrated in Fig. 2. It is important to distinguish between pixel size and spatial resolution, they can not be interchangeable. If a sensor has a spatial resolution of 20 m and an image from that sensor is displayed at full resolution, each pixel represents an area of 20 m × 20 m on the ground. In this case the pixel size and resolution are the same. However, it is possible to display images of pixel size other than resolution. Landsat image have 30 m × 30 m resolution.

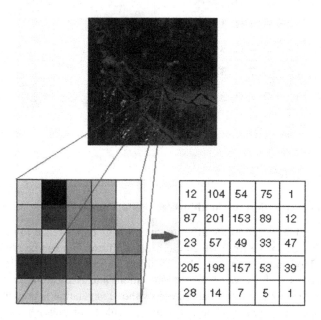

Fig. 2. Number of regions (Source: CCRS/CCT)

2.2   Creating Regions of Interest

Region of interest (ROI) [18] is a subset of an image or a set of data is determined for a particular purpose. ROI is used to determine the boundary of an object to be considered. In Fig. 3, the center pixel is used as seed (figure a) for the development area of spectral (figure b) with spectral distance parameter = 0, 1; Similar pixels are selected to create the training area (figure c và figure d). For example, sea water (blue) different soil (grey), river water (turbid water) different sea water (clearer water). Floods often involve rivers, lakes, flooded rice fields or urban areas.

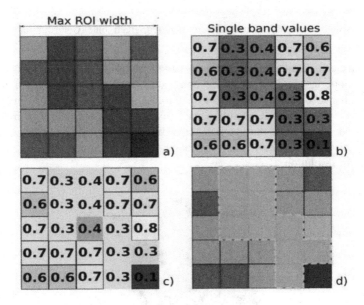

Fig. 3. Region of interest (Source: semi automatic classification manual) (Color figure online)

3   Identity Flood Areas

3.1   Features Extraction in Combined Satellite Images

The mathematical approach to identifying which image bands relate to merge spectral bands into one final image from which the needed information can be obtained and to determine of flood inundation area [16]. With image in Fig. 1 show different multi-band combinations such as water, urban, vegetation, unclassification.

With Blue-Green-Red, this is natural colors show, vegetation is brown and yellow, shorelines and clouds appear white and very difficult to distinguish. Water is white gray, not as easily detected to sparsely vegetated areas and urban.

With Blue-NIR-SWIR1, the vegetation is light green, not clear. The city is bright purple. Clouds are white with a red border, the shadow is black. Red water is easy to mistake with clouds.

With Green-NIR-SWIR2, the vegetation and grasslands is green, the soil is dark brown and urban areas appear in varying shades of purple. Clouds are white with yellow borders, the shadow is black. The water is red brown, shallow water or flooded on rice fields will appear as green yellow.

The multi-band combination [16] will show the object such as water, urban, vegetation, cloud, shadow. Therefore, the merge images is necessary for each request as illustrated in Fig. 4.

Fig. 4. Various features of the area with different band combinations

3.2   Object Extraction with Normalized Difference Water Index

The Normalized difference water index (NDWI) [1] that is shown in Fig. 5 is calculated from Near-Infrared (NIR) and Short Wave Infrared (SWIR) channels. The NDWI allows the separation of two soil and water objects [4], [23] in satellite images. In addition, the NDWI [19] of McFeeters asserted that values of NDWI smaller or equal than to zero are assumed to non-water surfaces, while values greater than zero are assumed to be water surfaces.

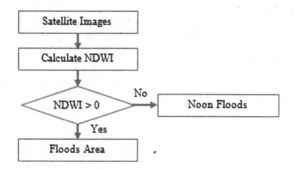

Fig. 5. Flowchart calculate NDWI

The NDWI is calculated using Eq. (1):

$$NDWI = (Green - NIR)/(Green + NIR) \tag{1}$$

Below image (Fig. 6) is the satellite image calculated NDWI with the threshold [1, 1] [2].

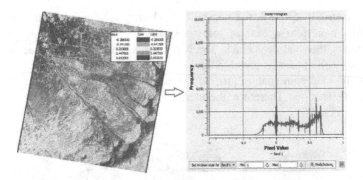

Fig. 6. NDWI for Landsat (ETM+, OLI) with threshold [−1,1]

4   Determine Flooding Disposition over Time

In this study, we used a random forest algorithm in the Orfeo toolbox combining QGIS as well as three different sensors. This algorithm can be used to assign the pixels in the image to the various map classes as illustrated in Fig. 7. This algorithm creates decision trees for each pixel. Each of these decision trees votes on what the pixel should be classified.

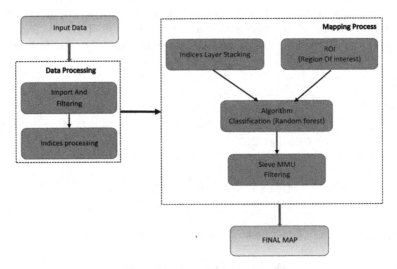

Fig. 7. Supervised classification for floods area

The method of determining the period before floods, during floods and after floods, is observation of remote-sensing images from 2014–2016 to determine the distribution of floods over time. The next, images classification based on NDWI [26] (extract the flooding) and supervised classification (random forest) will separate water, urban, vegetation and unclassification each class. It can also be seen that, over time, the reflectance of the water area changes slightly (Fig. 8).

Therefore, the determine flooding disposition over time is divided into three period:

- Before floods (Jan to Aug): water in areas such as rivers, lakes or seas has not change spectral information.
- During floods (Sep to Oct): flooding in medium or high level as in 2000 and 2010, the highest flood peak was October or early November. The spectral information will be change.
- After floods (Nov to Dec): the level of floods decreases and spectral information will be change.

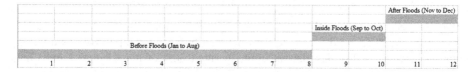

Fig. 8. Time of floods from 2014 to 2016

5 Experiments

5.1 Datasets

The study of flooding using remote sensing images in Landsat 7 ETM+ [12], Landsat 8 OLI [12] and sentinel-2 MSI [3] use the main bands (Table 1) in all the bands of the data set. The projection area is UTM-48, WGS84 coordinates.

Table 1. Band comparison between Landsat 7 ETM+, Landsat 8 OLI and Sentinel-2 MSI

	Landsat 7 ETM+	Landsat 8 OLI	Sentinel-2 MSI bands
Wavelength (micrometer)			
Blue	0.45–0.52	0.45–0.51	0.458–0.523
Green	0.52–0.60	0.53–0.59	0.543–0.578
Red	0.63–0.69	0.64–0.67	0.65–0.68
NIR	0.77–0.90	0.85–0.88	0.785–0.9
SWIR-1	1.55–1.75	1.57–1.65	1.565–1.655
SWIR-2	2.09–2.35	2.11–2.29	2.1–2.28

Landsat 7 [12] images consist of band 1 to band 7 is 30 m and band 8 is 15 m. There are 16 images, but use 6 images in 2000-08-02; 2000-11-06; 2000-12-24; 2001-02-26; 2001-09-06; 2001-12-11.

Landsat 8 OLI will be collected in 2014 and 2017 for floods analysis (there are 68 images, but use 8 images in 2014-02-22; 2014-09-18; 2014-11-05; 2015-05-16; 2015-09-05; 2015-12-26; 2016-07-21; 2017-03-17).

Sentinel 2 MSI [3] is multi-spectral image will be collected in 2015 and 2017 for floods analysis (there are 91 images, but use 7 images in 2015-09-19; 2015-12-28; 2016-02-26; 2016-09-26; 2016-11-12; 2017-03-02; 2017-07-10).

Table 2. Class information

Color	Value	Legend
Blue	1	Water
Green	2	Vegetation
Pink	3	Urban
Black	4	Unclassification

In datasets, we have 4 class are water, vegetation, urban (built-up) and unclassification (cloud, shadow, other,..). A class have 20 polygons, the polygons is divided into two datasets, is learning dataset (training about 30% of the polygons) and validation (testing about 70% of the polygons). The Table 2 is the class information.

5.2   Tool Used

We use combination of Orfeo Toolbox (OTB version 2.14) [7, 14] and Quantum GIS (QGIS version 2.14) [17] with the Grass Plugin. Inside, OTB is a cross-platform software that can process high-resolution optical, multi-spectral, radar images and have some supervised classification algorithms as SVM, random forest is used to classify images based on homogeneous groups of pixels in the remote sensing images. These applications is open source software displays the precision, recall, F-score and kappa indices and can output results as an *.CSV file.

5.3   Study Area

Mekong delta has 12 provinces and Can Tho City. This is the largest rice growing area of Vietnam, the region also has great potential for tourism. However, the region is also affected by floods that occur every year especially Tan Chau and Hong Ngu districts in An Giang and Dong Thap provinces. The Mekong river floods [9] was formed in May and divided into 3 period [15]. July to August is flood water flowing into the channels of Tan Chau, Hong Ngu district. Flood peak happened in September and October (in 2000, 2011 years). In November and December, the water level will be lowered.

5.4   Scenario 1: Determining the Flooding Area

5.4.1   Floods Area in 2000–2001 with Landsat 7 ETM+

The statistics water levels at Tan Chau, Hong Ngu in 2000–2001 [6] rather higher than normal water levels with the maximum water level of 5.06 m and 4.86 m as illustrated in Fig. 9.

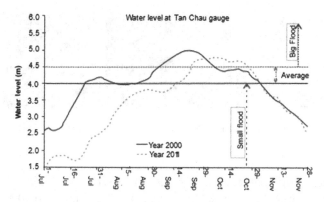

Fig. 9. Flood hydrograph at Tan Chau in 2000 and 2001 [6]

In Fig. 10, water color is clear and widely distributed in flooded areas such as Tan Chau and Hong Ngu district and summarized in Table 3.

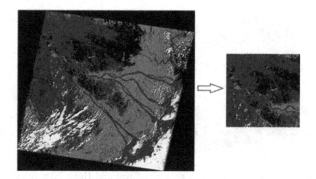

Fig. 10. Result classification of floods area (Tan Chau and Hong Ngu district)

Table 3. Result of area and PixelSum at Tan Chau, Hong Ngu district in 2000

Over time	PixelSum	Area [m²]
Before floods	380981	342747979
During floods	10708276	9637448400
After floods	1628777	1465386081

With below image (Fig. 11), we will see the change of water surface (blue) through the three images, the middle image has the most water because this is the period of floods in October-2000 in Vietnam (Tan Chau, Hong Ngu district).

Fig. 11. Change of floods zone in Feb-2000, Oct-2000, Dec-2000 at Tan Chau and Hong Ngu district

5.4.2   Floods Area in 2014–2016 with Landsat 8 OLI

We predict the time of the floods in 2014–2016, and 2017 similar to 2000 above. The right image in Fig. 12 is combined of bands 4, 5, 6. This images are features related to clear water, turbidity water, and vegetation (tree, rice field và vegetable). The classification image in the left of a period before the floods (Feb-2014), results blue pixels less than green and pink. And it summarized in Table 4.

Fig. 12. Result classification of floods area Tan Chau and Hong Ngu (image in the left)

Table 4. Result average of pixel classification and area water

Over time	PixelSum	Area [m^2]
Before floods	1807200	1626480000
During floods	7547690	6792921000
After floods	6429232	5786308800

5.4.3   Floods Area in 2015–2016 with Sentinel-2 MSI

With Sentinel-2 MSI similar to Landsat-8 OLI, floods season analysis during 2000 was theoretical to analyze the Sentinel-2 image in three stages.

In 2015, the period before the floods, no images have a condition for smaller clouds 10%, during floods (image in Sep-2015) and after floods (image in Dec-2015). In 2016, the period after the floods, no images have a condition for smaller clouds 10%, image in Feb-2016 (before floods) and image in Sept-2016 (during floods) is illustrated in Table 5.

Table 5. Result of area floods

Over Time	Area [m^2]	
	2015	2016
Before floods	–	676784079.39
During floods	1085437975.34	1951083316.47
After floods	1023188829.29	1004844619.61

5.5   Scenario 2: Predicting the Flooding Area

5.5.1   Floods Area in 2017 with Landsat 8 OLI

In this section, we use the Landsat 8 flood classification model (2014–2016) to predict the Landsat 8 image at Mar-2017 as Fig. 13. The results of the classification and prediction accounted for 98.02% of the overall and the lowest water area was 246291280.216 m^2 with 273861 pixels.

Fig. 13. Image classification in March-2017

With the information classified below shows high accuracy 97.59% for water (class 1), 98.59% for urban and 100% for vegetation (class 2 and class 3) and then 96.15% for unclassification (class 4) as Table 6.

Table 6. Result of classification

Class	Area	User accuracy	User accuracy uncertainty
1	246291280.216	97.59	3.3
2	56859209.2352	98.59	2.74
3	2338038201.06	100.0	0.0
4	2349089162.13	96.15	4.27

5.5.2   Floods Area in 2017 with Sentinel-2 MSI

In this section, we use a model to classify floodplains through the phases of Sentinel-2 (2015–2016) to predict the sentinel-2 image by March-2017. The classification and prediction results in 97.67% and overall area is 885939671.67 m^2 with a pixel number of 8861339.

Classification image (Fig. 14) of Sentinel-2 MSI display clearly colors than Landsat-8 OLI, water objects in fixed areas (the river, lake) are classified correctly (blue). Beside, other objects are also categorized into training class (green: vegetation, pink: urban, black: unclassification).

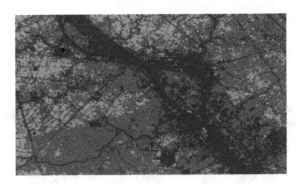

Fig. 14. Image classification in March-2017 (Sentinel-2 MSI) at Can Tho city

With the information classified below shows high accuracy 98.71% for water (class 1), 100% for vegetation and 96.44% for urban (class 2 and class 3) and then 99.58% for unclassification (class 4) as Table 7.

Table 7. The result of classification

Class	Area	User accuracy	User accuracy uncertainty
1	885939671.671	98.71	1.45
2	559115422.744	100	0.0
3	1839076111.51	96.44	2.28
4	26326128.4107	99.58	0.82

6   Conclusion

In this study, we evaluated the performances of the three sensor (Landsat 7 ETM+, Landsat 8 OLI và sentinel-2 MSI) highly effective with random forest classification has been correctly classified in the before floods (Jan to Aug), during floods (Sep to Oct) and after floods (Nov to Dec) in two main areas are Tan Chau and Hong Ngu district.

We chose the greatest flooding times of 2000 to observe and evaluate the flood classification in combination with the flood season in recent years (2014 to 2016). As a result, the area of flooding in Tan Chau and Hong Ngu district, before the floods were lowest, during floods were highest and after floods decreased compared to during the floods.

In addition, we predict that flooding in 2017 in the Can Tho area will result in accurate classification with a probability of 97.67% (Sentinel-2), 98.02% (Landsat 8) and area of floods (March-2017) is 246291280.216 m^2 (Landsat 8), 885939671.67 m^2 (Sentinel-2). We have evaluated Landsat 7 is not as high as Landsat 8 OLI and sentinel-2 MSI when classifying using random forest algorithms. However, the Landsat 7 ETM + image data has more.

References

1. Gao, B.: Ndwi—a normalized difference water index for remote sensing of vegetation liquid water from space. Remote Sens. Environ. **58**(3), 257–266 (1996)
2. Brivio, P.A., Colombo, R., Maggi, M., Tomasoni, R.: Integration of remote sensing data and GIS for accurate mapping of flooded areas. Int. J. Remote Sens. **12**, 429–441 (2002)
3. Dechoz, C., et al.: Sentinel 2 global reference image (2015)
4. Cassé, C., Viet, P.B., Nhung, P.T.N., Phung, H.P., Nguyen, L.D.: Remote sensing application for coastline detection in CA MAU, Mekong delta. In: International Symposium on Geoinformatics for Spatial Infrastructure Development in Earth and Allied Sciences (2012)
5. Cortes, C., Vapnik, V.: Support-vector networks. Mach. Learn. **20**, 273–297 (1995)
6. Duong, V., Van Trinh, C., Nestmann, F., Oberle, P.: Land use based flood hazards analysis for the mekong delta. In: Proceedings of the 19th IAHR-APD Congress 2014, Hanoi, Vietnam (2014)
7. Christophe, E., Inglada, J., Giros, A.: Orfeo toolbox: a complete solution for mapping from high resolution satellite images. In: International Archives of the Photogrammetry, Remote Sensing and Spatial Information Sciences, vol. XXXVII, Part B4, pp. 1263–1268, Beijing (2008)
8. Bonn, F., Dixon, R.: Monitoring flood extent and forecasting excess run off risk with radarsat-1 data. J. Int. Soc. Prev. Mitig. Nat. Hazards **35**(3), 377–393 (2005)
9. Nguyen, H.Q., et al.: Water quality dynamics of urban water bodies during flooding in Can Tho city, Vietnam. Water **9**(4), 260 (2017)
10. Quinlan, J.R.: Induction of decision trees. Mach. Learn. **1**, 81–106 (1986)
11. Breiman, L.: Random forests. Mach. Learn. **45**(1), 5–32 (2001)
12. NASA: What are the band designations for the Landsat satellites? URL https://landsat.usgs.gov/what-are-band-designations-landsat-satellites
13. Natural Disaster Risk Assessment and Area Business Continuity Plan Formulation for Industrial Agglomerated Areas in the ASEAN Region. Japan International Cooperation Agency OYO International Corporation Mitsubishi Research Institute, Inc. CTI Engineering International Co., Ltd. March (2015)
14. OTB Development Team. Orfeo toolbox 5.4. July 2016
15. Dao, P.D., Liou, Y.-A.: Object-based flood mapping and affected rice field estimation with landsat 8 oli and modis data. Remote Sens. **7**(5), 5077–5097 (2015)
16. Potcoava, M.C., Stancalie, G., Raducanu, D.: The using of satellite image data from optic and microwaves data for development of a methodology for identification and extraction of flooded area. Int. Arch. Photogrammetry Remote Sens. **6**, 1185–1190 (2000)

17. QGIS Development Team: QGIS Geographic Information System. Open Source Geospatial Foundation (2009). http://qgis.osgeo.org

18. Brinkmann, R.: The Art and Science of Digital Compositing. The Morgan Kaufmann Series in Computer Graphics, 2 edn., pp. 149–188 (2008)

19. McFEETERS, S.K.: The use of the normalized difference water index (NDWI) in the delineation of open water features. Int. J. Remote Sens. **17**(7), 1425–1432 (1996)

20. Niculescu, S., Lardeux, C., Hanganu, J., David, L., Mercier, G.: Change detection in floodable areas of the Danube delta using radar images. Nat. Hazards J. Int. Soc. Prev. Mitig. Nat. Hazards **78**(3), 1899–1916 (2015)

21. Niculescu, S., Lardeux, C., Hanganu, J.: Synergy between SENTINEL-1 radar time series and Sentinel-2 optical for the mapping of restored areas in Danube delta. In: Proceedings of the International Cartographic Association, vol. 1 (2017)

22. Niculescu, S., Lardeux, C., Guttler, F., Rudant, J.-P.: Multisensor systems and flood risk management application to the danube delta using radar and hyperspectral imagery. Teledetection **9**(3–4), 271–288 (2010)

23. McFeeters, S.K.: Using the normalized difference water index (NDWI) within a geographic information system to detect swimming pools for mosquito abatement: a practical approach. Remote Sens. **5**(7), 3544–3561 (2013)

24. Sakamoto, T., Van Nguyen, N., Kotera, A., Ohno, H., Ishitsuka, N., Yokozawa, M.: Detecting temporal changes in the extent of annual flooding within the cambodia and the vietnamese mekong delta from modis time-series imagery. Remote Sens. Environ. **109**(3), 295–313 (2007)

25. Bertin, X.: A modeling-based analysis of the flooding associated with xynthia, central bay of biscay. Coast. Eng. **94**, 80–89 (2014)

26. Zhou, Y., et al.: Open surface water mapping algorithms: a comparison of water-related spectral indices and sensors. Water **9**, 256–272 (2017)

Development English Pronunciation Practicing System Based on Speech Recognition

Ngoc Hoang Phan[1(✉)], Thi Thu Trang Bui[1], and V. G. Spitsyn[2]

[1] Ba Ria-Vung Tau University, 80, Truong Cong Dinh, Vung Tau,
Ba Ria-Vung Tau, Vietnam
hoangpn285@gmail.com, trangbt.084@gmail.com
[2] National Research Tomsk Polytechnic University,
30, Lenin Avenue, Tomsk, Russia
spvg@tpu.ru

Abstract. The relevance of the research is caused by the need of application of speech recognition technology for language teaching. The speech recognition is one of the most important tasks of the signal processing and pattern recognition fields. The speech recognition technology allows computers to understand human speech and it plays very important role in people's lives. This technology can be used to help people in a variety way such as controlling smart homes and devices; using robots to perform job interviews; converting audio into text, etc. But there are not many applications of speech recognition technology in education, especially in English teaching. The main aim of the research is to propose an algorithm in which speech recognition technology is used English language teaching. Objects of researches are speech recognition technologies and frameworks, English spoken sounds system. Research results: The authors have proposed an algorithm based on speech recognition framework for English pronunciation learning. This proposed algorithm can be applied to another speech recognition framework and different languages. Besides the authors also demonstrated how to use the proposed algorithm for development English pronunciation practicing system based on iOS mobile app platform. The system also allows language learners can practice English pronunciation anywhere and anytime without any purchase.

Keywords: Speech recognition · English pronunciation ·
Hidden markov models · Neural networks · Mobile application

1 Introduction

1.1 Speech Recognition Technology

Speech recognition technology has been researched and developed over the past several decades. In the 1960's this technology was developed based on filter-bank analyses, simple time normalization methods and the beginning of sophisticated dynamic programming methodologies. In this time technology could recognize small vocabularies (10–100 words) of isolated words using simple acoustic phonetic properties of speech sounds [1].

P. C. Vinh and A. Rakib (Eds.): ICCASA 2019/ICTCC 2019, LNICST 298, pp. 157–166, 2019.
https://doi.org/10.1007/978-3-030-34365-1_12

In the 1970's the key technologies of speech recognition were the pattern recognition models, spectral representation using LPC methods, speaker-independent recognizers using pattern clustering methods and dynamic programming methods for connected word recognition. During this time, we able to recognize medium vocabularies (100–1000 words) using simple template-based and pattern recognition methods [1].

In the 1980's the speech recognition technology started to solve the problems of large vocabulary (1000 – unlimited number of words) using statistical methods and neural networks for handling language structures. The important technologies used in this time were the Hidden Markov Model (HMM) and stochastic language model [1]. Using HMMs allowed to combine different knowledge sources such as acoustics, language, and syntax, in a unified probabilistic model.

In the 1990's the key technologies of speech recognition were stochastic language understanding methods, statistical learning of acoustic and language models, finite state transducer framework and FSM library. In this time speech recognition technology allow us to build large vocabulary systems using unconstrained language models and constrained task syntax models for continuous speech recognition and understanding [1].

In the last few years, the speech recognition technology can handle with very large vocabulary systems based on full semantic models, integrated with text-to-speech (TTS) synthesis systems, and multi-modal inputs. In this time, the key technologies were highly natural concatenative speech synthesis systems, machine learning to improve both speeches understanding and speech dialogs [1].

1.2   Key Speech Recognition Methods

Dynamic Time Warping (DTW)

Dynamic time warping (DTW) is an approach that was historically used for speech recognition. This method is used to recognize about 200-word vocabulary [2]. DTW divide speech into short frames (e.g. 10 ms segments) and then it processes each frame as a single unit. During the time of DTW, achieving speaker independence remained unsolved. DTW was applied for automatic speech recognition to cope with different speaking speeds. It allows to find an optimal match between two given sequences (e.g., time series) with certain restrictions.

Hidden Markov Models (HMM)

DTW has been displaced by the more successful Hidden Markov Models-based approach. HMMs are statistical models that output a sequence of symbols or quantities. In HMMs a speech signal can be a piecewise stationary signal or a short-time stationary signal. And speech can be approximated as a stationary process in a short time-scale (e.g., 10 ms).

By the mid-1980s a voice activated typewriter called Tangora was created. It could handle a 20,000-word vocabulary [3]. It processes and understands speech based on using statistical modeling techniques like HMMs. However, HMMs are too simplistic to account for many common features of human languages [4]. But it proved to be a highly efficiency model for speech recognition algorithm in the 1980s [1].

Neural Networks

Neural networks have been used in speech recognition to solve many problems such as phoneme classification, isolated word recognition, audiovisual speech recognition, audiovisual speaker recognition and speaker adaptation [5, 6].

By comparing with HMMs, neural networks make fewer explicit assumptions about feature statistical properties. Neural networks allow discriminative training in a natural and efficient manner, so they are effectiveness in classifying short-time units such as individual phonemes and isolated words [7]. However, because of their limited ability to model temporal dependencies, neural networks are not successfully used for continuous speech recognition.

To solve this problem, neural networks are used to pre-process speech signal (e.g. feature transformation or dimensionality reduction) and then use HMM to recognize speech based on the features received from neural networks [8]. In recently, related Recurrent Neural Networks (RNNs) have showed an improved performance in speech recognition [9–11].

Like shallow neural networks, Deep Neural Networks (DNNs) can used to model complex non-linear relationships. The architectures of these DNNs generate compositional models, so DNNs have a huge learning capacity and they are potential for modeling complex patterns of speech data [12]. In 2010, the DNN with the large output layers based on context dependent HMM states constructed by decision trees have been successfully applied in large vocabulary speech recognition [13–15].

End-to-end Automatic Speech Recognition

Traditional HMM-based approaches required separate components and training for the pronunciation, acoustic and language model. And a typical n-gram language model, required for all HMM-based systems, often takes several gigabytes memory to deploy them on mobile devices [16]. However, since 2014 end-to-end ASR models jointly learn all the components of the speech. It allows to simplify the training and deployment process. Because of that, the modern commercial ASR systems from Google and Apple are deployed on the cloud.

Connectionist Temporal Classification (CTC) based systems was the first end-to-end ASR and introduced by Alex Graves of Google DeepMind and Navdeep Jaitly of the University of Toronto in 2014 [17]. In 2016, University of Oxford presented LipNet using spatiotemporal convolutions coupled with an RNN-CTC architecture. It was the first end-to-end sentence-level lip reading model. And it was better than human-level performance in a restricted grammar dataset [18]. In 2018 Google DeepMind presented a large-scale CNN-RNN-CTC architecture. In the results this system achieved 6 times better performance than human experts [19].

1.3 Speech Recognition Applications

With speech recognition technology computers now can hear and understand what people speak to them and can do what people want they do. The speech recognition technology can be used in a variety way and plays very important role in people's lives. For example, this technology can be used in-car systems or smart home systems to help people do simple thing by voice commands such as: play music or select radio station, initiate phone calls, turn on/off lights, televisions and other electrical devices.

For education, speech recognition technology can be used to help students who are blind or have very low vision. They can use computer by using voice commands instead of having a look at the screen and keyboard [20]. Besides, students who are physically disabled or suffer from injuries having difficulty in writing, typing or working can benefit from using this technology. They can use speech-to-text programs to do their homework or school assignments [21]. Speech recognition technology can allow students to become better writers. They can improve the fluidity of their writing by using speech-to-text programs. When they say to computer, they don't worry about spelling, punctuation, and other mechanics of writing [21]. In addition, speech recognition technology can be useful for language learning. They can teach people proper pronunciation and help them to develop their speaking skills [22].

Recently, all people have their own mobile devices and they can use them anywhere, anytime. Most of mobile apps and devices runs on two main operating systems: iOS and Android OS. These operating systems are equipped with the best speech recognition technology developed by Google or Apple. There are many mobile apps that use these speech recognition technologies for playing games, controlling devices, making phone calls, sending text messages etc.

There are also many software applications to practice English pronunciation on mobile devices. By using these support tools, learners can record all what they say and compare with sample pronunciation of native speakers to correct errors. The applications often display the pronunciation of words, allowing learners to listen to sample pronunciation, then the learners will record their pronunciation and compare themselves with the sample pronunciation. The application has not integrated the voice recognition feature into the software to test the learner's pronunciation.

Because of that, building a mobile app using speech recognition technologies for language pronunciation learning is urgent and perspective. In this paper we present an algorithm that use speech recognition technology to help people determine if they properly pronounce an English sound. The proposed algorithm is used for building mobile app based on speech recognition technology. This algorithm is tested.

2 Proposed Algorithm

In this paper, we propose an algorithm based on speech recognition framework for English pronunciation learning. The framework used to test proposed algorithm in this paper is Apple speech recognition technology [23]. Besides, in this paper we demonstrate how to use the proposed algorithm for development English pronunciation practicing system based on iOS mobile app platform. This proposed algorithm can be applied to another speech recognition framework (e.g. Google speech recognition) and different languages.

The main aim of developing of proposed algorithm to help learners can use speech recognition technologies to test their own English pronunciation and make appropriate adjustments. The application will provide learners with the inherent functions of an English pronunciation training tool and support learners to completely free practice English pronunciation anytime, anywhere.

2.1 Apple Speech Recognition Technology

The Apple speech recognition framework allow to recognize spoken words in recorded or live audio. It can be used to translate audio content to text, handle recognize verbal commands etc. The framework is fast and works in near real time. Besides the framework is accurate and can interpret over 50 languages and dialects [23]. The process of speech recognition task using Apple technology can be presented in Fig. 1.

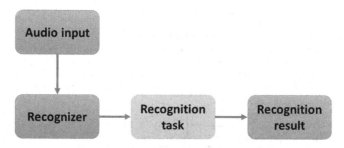

Fig. 1. Process of speech recognition task on speech recognition framework.

Audio Input is an audio source from which transcription should occur. Audio source can be read from recorded audio file or can be captured audio content, such as audio from the device's microphone. The audio input is then sent to Recognizer that is used to check for the availability of the speech recognition service, and to initiate the speech.recognition process. At the end, the process gives the partial or final results of speech recognition [23].

2.2 One-Word Pronunciation Assessment

Based on this speech recognition framework, we propose an algorithm to assess the language learner's pronunciation. The process of pronunciation assessment for one word is presented in Fig. 2.

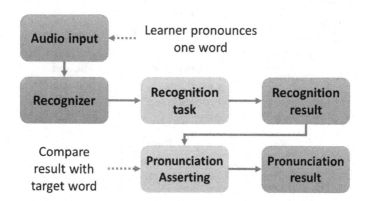

Fig. 2. Process of pronunciation assessment for one word.

At first the language learner pronounces a word which is used to practice pronunciation. Then the learner's pronunciation is handled by speech recognition framework which gives the recognition result. After that, the recognition result is compared with target word to determine if the learner correctly pronounce the target word (Fig. 3).

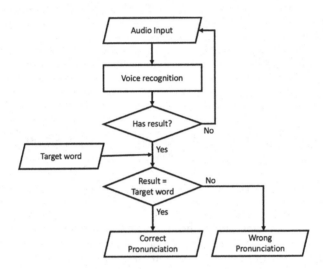

Fig. 3. Learner's pronunciation assessment for one word

2.3   One Sound Pronunciation Assessment

In order to assess one sound pronunciation, we need to assess the pronunciations of list of words which contain the target sound. The process of pronunciation assessment for one sound can be then presented in Fig. 4.

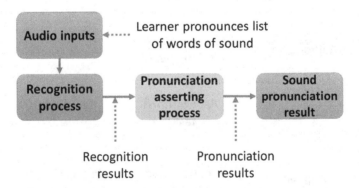

Fig. 4. Process of pronunciation assessment for one sound.

At first the language learner pronounces one word of the list which contains the sound used to practice pronunciation. Then the learner's pronunciation is handled by recognition process. After that the recognition result are processed by pronunciation asserting. The language learner repeats these steps for other words of the list until all words of the list have been pronounced. Based on the pronunciation results of words in the list, we can calculate the sound pronunciation fluency of the language learner by following formula:

Sound pronunciation fluency = Total number of correctly pronounced words /Total number of words in the list.

2.4 English Pronunciation Practicing System

The English language contains 44 sounds divided into three main groups: vowels (12 sounds), diphthongs (8 sounds) and consonants (24 sounds). The vowel sounds consist of two sub-groups: long sounds and short sounds. The consonant sounds consist of three sub-groups: voiced consonants, voiceless consonants and other consonants. The phonemic chart of 44 English spoken sounds is presented in Table 1.

Based on the phonemic chart of spoken English sounds, proposed algorithm for word and sound pronunciation asserting, we developed an iOS app for English pronunciation practicing system. The main aim of this system is to allow language learners can know if they correctly pronounce English sounds. Based on the results, provided by this system, language learners will have proper adjustment to improve their English pronunciation. Besides the app allows language learners can freely practice pronunciation anywhere and anytime.

Table 1. Phonemic chart English sounds

English sounds	Vowels	Short sounds	ɪ	e	æ	ʌ	ʊ	ə	ɒ	
		Long sounds	iː	ɜː	uː	ɔː	ɑː			
	Diphthongs		eɪ	ɔɪ	aɪ	eə	ɪə	ʊə	əʊ	aʊ
	Consonants	Voiceless consonants	p	f	θ	t	s	ʃ	ʧ	k
		Voiced consonants	b	v	ð	d	z	ʒ	dʒ	g
		Other	m	n	ŋ	h	w	l	r	j

The English pronunciation practicing system consists of 44 lessons according to 44 spoken English sounds (Fig. 5a). Each lesson has its own practicing exercises and depending on the sound these exercises normally divided into the following types: the sound is at the beginning of words; the sound is in middle of words; the sound is at the end of words; the sound is followed by a vowel/consonant; the sound is after a vowel/consonant (Fig. 5b).

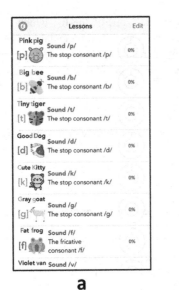
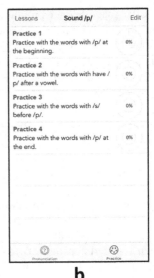

Fig. 5. English pronunciation practicing system: (a) list of lessons, (b) examples of exercise types of sound p.

The language learners must practice with all words in the list of exercise, and then the system will automatic give recognition and pronunciation results according each word (Fig. 6). After that the system calculates the pronunciation fluency for each sound and shows the results to the language learners (Fig. 7).

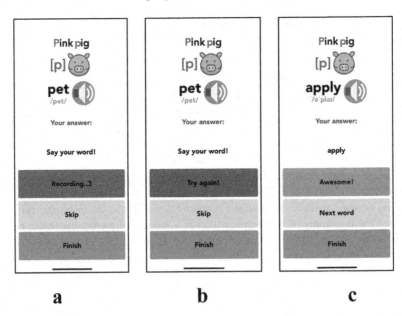

Fig. 6. Example of one practice: (a) practice overview and mode, (b) practice answer mode, (c) pronunciation result of one word.

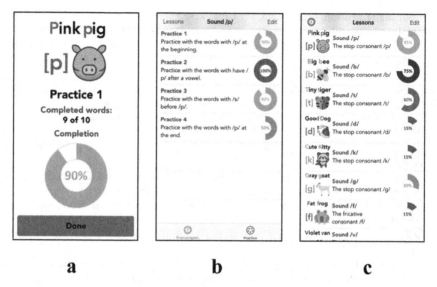

a   b   c

Fig. 7. Example of pronunciation assessment: (a) pronunciation result for one practice, (b) pronunciation result for practices, (c) pronunciation result for sound.

3   Conclusion

In this paper, we propose an algorithm based on speech recognition framework for English pronunciation learning. This proposed algorithm can be applied to another speech recognition framework (e.g. Google speech recognition) and different languages. Besides we also demonstrate how to use the proposed algorithm for development English pronunciation practicing system based on iOS mobile app platform.

This system allows language learners can determine if they correctly pronounce English sounds. Based on these results, the language learners will have proper adjustment to improve their English pronunciation. The system also allows language learners can practice English pronunciation anywhere and anytime without any purchase, which they can not do in the classroom.

References

1. Juang, B.H., Rabiner, L.R.: Automatic speech recognition–a brief history of the technology development (2015). https://web.ece.ucsb.edu/Faculty/Rabiner/ece259/Reprints/354_LALI-ASRHistory-final-10-8.pdf
2. Benesty, J., Sondhi, M.M., Huang, Y.: Springer Handbook of Speech Processing. Springer, Heidelberg (2008). https://doi.org/10.1007/978-3-540-49127-9
3. Jelinek, F.: Pioneering Speech Recognition (2015). https://www.ibm.com/ibm/history/ibm100/us/en/icons/speechreco/
4. Huang, X., Baker, J., Reddy, R.: A Historical perspective of speech recognition. Commun. ACM **57**(1), 94–103 (2014)

5. Hanazawa, T., Hinton, G., Shikano, K., Lang, K.J.: Phoneme recognition using time-delay neural networks. IEEE Trans. Acoust. Speech Sig. Process. **37**(3), 328–339 (1989)
6. Wu, J., Chan, C.: Isolated word recognition by neural network models with cross-correlation coefficients for speech dynamics. IEEE Trans. Pattern Anal. Mach. Intell. **15**(11), 1174–1185 (1993)
7. Zahorian, S.A., Zimmer, A.M., Meng, F.: Vowel Classification for Computer based Visual Feedback for Speech Training for the Hearing Impaired, ICSLP, 2002
8. Hu, H., Zahorian, S.A.: Dimensionality reduction methods for HMM phonetic recognition. In: ICASSP (2010)
9. Sak, H., Senior, A., Rao, K., Beaufays, F., Schalkwyk, J.: Google voice search: faster and more accurate. Wayback Machine (2016)
10. Fernandez, S., Graves, A., Hinton, G.: Sequence labelling in structured domains with hierarchical recurrent neural networks. In: Proceedings of IJCAI (2007)
11. Graves, A., Mohamed, A., Schmidhuber, J.: Speech recognition with deep recurrent neural networks. In: ICASSP (2013)
12. Deng, L., Yu, D.: Deep Learning: Methods and Applications. Found. Trends Sig. Process. **7**(3), 197–387 (2014)
13. Yu, D., Deng, L., Dahl, G.: Roles of pre-training and fine-tuning in context-dependent DBN-HMMs for real-world speech recognition. In: NIPS Workshop on Deep Learning and Unsupervised Feature Learning (2010)
14. Dahl, G.E., Yu, D., Deng, L., Acero, A.: Context-dependent pre-trained deep neural networks for large-vocabulary speech recognition. IEEE Trans. Audio Speech Sig. Process. **20**(1), 30–42 (2012)
15. Deng, L., Li, J., Huang, J., Yao, K., Yu, D., Seide, F.: Recent advances in deep learning for speech research at microsoft. In: ICASSP (2013)
16. Jurafsky, D., James, H.M.: Speech and Language Processing: An Introduction to Natural Language Processing, Computational Linguistics, and Speech Recognition. Stanford University (2018)
17. Graves, A.: Towards end-to-end speech recognition with recurrent neural networks. In: ICML (2014)
18. Yannis, M.A., Brendan, S., Shimon, W.N., de Freitas, N.: LipNet: End-to-End Sentence-level Lipreading. Cornell University (2016)
19. Brendan, S., et al.: Large-Scale Visual Speech Recognition. Cornell University (2018)
20. National Center for Technology Innovation Speech Recognition for Learning (2010). http://www.ldonline.org/article/38655/
21. Follensbee, B., McCloskey-Dale, S.: Speech recognition in schools: an update from the field. In: Technology and Persons with Disabilities Conference (2018)
22. Forgrave, K.E.: Assistive technology: empowering students with disabilities. The Clearing House **7**(3), 122–126 (2002)
23. Apple Inc: Speech framework (2010). https://developer.apple.com/documentation/speech

Document Classification by Using Hybrid Deep Learning Approach

Bui Thanh Hung[(✉)]

Data Analytics and Artificial Intelligence Laboratory
Engineering - Technology Faculty, Thu Dau Mot University,
6 Tran Van On Street, Phu Hoa District, Thu Dau Mot City,
Binh Duong Province, Vietnam
hungbt.cntt@tdmu.edu.vn

Abstract. Text classification is an essential component in a variety of applications of natural language processing. While the deep learning-based approach is becoming more popular, using vectors of word as an input for the models has proved to be a good way for the machine to learn the relation between words in a document. This paper proposes a solution for the text classification using hybrid deep learning approaches. Every existing deep learning approach has its own advantages and the hybrid deep learning model we are introducing is the combination of the superior features of CNN and LSTM models. The proposed models CNN-LSTM, LSTM-CNN show enhanced accuracy over another approach.

Keywords: Document classification · CNN · LSTM · Hybrid deep learning

1 Introduction

Text classification is a traditional topic for natural language processing, in which one needs to assign predefined categories to free-text documents. This task is essential in several applications of natural language processing such as web searching, information filtering, sentiment analysis, etc.... Therefore, it has attracted a remarkable attention from many researchers. Feature representation is a key problem in text classification. The common features based on the bag-of-words model, where unigrams, bigrams, n-grams or some exquisitely designed patterns are typically extracted as features. The range of text classification research goes from designing the best features to choosing the best possible machine learning classifiers. Nowadays, almost all techniques of text classification are based on words, in which simple statistics of some ordered word combinations usually perform the best.

The application of deep learning approaches to text classification or natural language processing in large scale has been explored in literature. Without any knowledge on the syntactic or semantic structures of a language, based on discrete embedding of words, these approaches have been proven to be competitive to traditional models.

In this paper, we focus on hybrid deep learning approached based on Long Short Term Memory (LSTM) and Convolution Neural Network (CNN). We propose two hybrid deep learning models: CNN-LSTM and LSTM-CNN; both of which are

P. C. Vinh and A. Rakib (Eds.): ICCASA 2019/ICTCC 2019, LNICST 298, pp. 167–177, 2019.
https://doi.org/10.1007/978-3-030-34365-1_13

combination of the superior features of CNN and LSTM models. We use pre-trained word embeddings to extract and weight useful affective information in accordance with their contribution to the document classification. This paper will proceed to compare both of those approaches, as well as using either CNN or LSTM separately.

The rest of this paper is organized as follows: Sect. 2 introduces related work on the document classification. Section 3 describes in details, the different approaches and how we applied hybrid deep learning models to the document classification problem. Section 4 shows the experiments, as well as discussion related to the results. Finally, Sect. 5 summarizes our work and future directions.

2 Related Works

There have been a number of studies in the world that have shown positive results in text classification [5, 8, 12, 14]. Three topics: feature engineering, feature selection and using different types of machine learning algorithms are mainly focused on traditional text classification works. The most widely used feature for feature engineering topic is the bag-of-words feature. In addition, part-of-speech tags, noun phrases features have been designed as complex features for machine learning models. Deleting noisy features and improving the classification performance are the advantages of feature selection. However, traditional approaches still have its own weakness which is data scarcity; and this has big impact on the classification accuracy.

Recently, deep neural networks, representation learning and neural models for learning word representations have inspired new ideas for solving text classification problem. Kim [13] used convolution neural networks (CNN) for text classification. Zhang et al. [12] applied a character-level CNN model. Johnson et al. [8] proposed a high-dimensional one hot vector. Socher et al. [9] used recursive neural networks for text classification. Tai et al. [7] applied the structure of a sentence and used a tree structured LSTMs for classification. There are a few works that combine LSTM and CNN structure to for sentence classification. Zhou et al. [3] used a CNN to get a sentence vector and then a recurrent neural network to compose the sentence vectors to get a document vectors. Bui [2] used hybrid deep learning mode CNN-LSTM for Vietnamese keyword extraction.

Our research follows a different approach. We use combination of the superior features of CNN and LSTM in two hybrid deep learning models: CNN-LSTM and LSTM-CNN. Hybrid deep learning LSTM-CNN, CNN-LSTM models are used for text classification. We have done the experiment and also made the comparison with other models which have been published before in the same dataset.

3 The Proposed Model

The proposed model for this work is shown in Fig. 1. The model includes three main steps: Word Embedding, Hybrid Deep Learning Models and Classification. Details of the functionality and responsibility of each layer in our model are as follows:

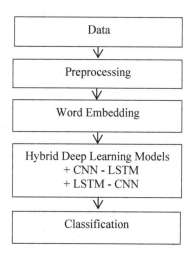

Fig. 1. The proposed model

3.1 Word Embedding

The idea of Word embedding is to capture with them as much as possible structure of the word such as the semantical/morphological/ context/hierarchical/ etc. information and convert it to vectors. Using vector representation for words has been widely known in recent days and Tomas Mikolov's Word2vec algorithm [11] is the most famous one.

We used Skip-gram [11] in this research. Objective of the Skip-gram model is to predict the contexts of a given target-word. Using a window of an arbitrary size n—by capturing n words to the left of the target and n words to its right retrieves the contexts which are immediate neighbours of the target. Skip-gram model is shown in Fig. 2.

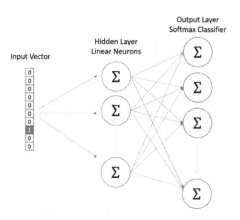

Fig. 2. Skip-gram model

3.2   Hybrid Deep Learning Models

Machine learning methods could be classified into three categories including supervised, semi-supervised and unsupervised. In the wider family of machine learning methods, Deep learning is a member. Recurrent Neural Networks (RNNs) [1, 9] and Convolutional Neural Networks (CNN) [4, 8]. [13] are two most well-known types of deep neural networks. We will describe about Long Short Term Memory (LSTM) [10], Convolutional neural networks (CNN) and Convolutional Neural Networks combined with Long Short Term Memory in hybrid deep learning models: CNN-LSTM, LSTM-CNN as follows:

LSTM

A recurrent neural network (RNN) is a type of advanced artificial neural network. RNNs can use their internal state (memory) to process sequences of inputs [1, 9]. RNNs have shown great successes in many natural language processing tasks. RNNs connect previous information to present task, since the gap between the relevant information and the place that it needs is small, RNNs can learn to use the past information. However, RNNs seem to fail to connect the information since there is still a gap between the relevant information and the words we expect it in terms of Long-Term dependencies, so RNNs has not yet proved to be workable.

A modification of the Recurrent neural networks is Long short term memory (LSTM) [10]. Comparing with the regular feed forward neural network, LSTM ables to retain the knowledge about previous outputs because of the feedback loop present in its architecture. A diagram of a simple LSTM cell is shown in Fig. 3. A large network is made by combining individual cells together. The memory is represented by the cell unit. Five main elements: an input gate i, an output gate o, a forget gate f, a recurring cell state c and hidden state output h compose in the cell. Given a sequence of vectors $(x_1, x_2, ..., x_n)$, σ is the logistic sigmoid function, the hidden state h_t of LSTM at time t is calculated as follows [10]:

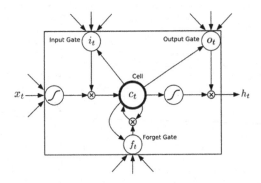

Fig. 3. The long short term memory cell

$$h_t = o_t * tanh(c_t) \tag{1}$$

$$o_t = tanh(Wx_0x_t + Wh_0h_{t-1} + Wc_0c_t + b_o) \tag{2}$$

$$c_t = f_t * c_{t-1} + i_t * tanh(Wx_cx_t + Wh_ch_{t-1} + b_c) \tag{3}$$

$$f_t = \sigma\left(Wx_fx_t + Wh_fh_{t-1} + Wc_fc_{t-1} + b_f\right) \tag{4}$$

$$i_t = \sigma(Wx_ix_t + Wh_ih_{t-1} + Wc_ic_{t-1} + b_i) \tag{5}$$

CNN

CNN includes several major architectural components which are paired with each other in multi-story structure that is: Convolution, Pooling, Activation function (ReLu, Sigmoid, Tanh), and Fully connected [4, 8, 13]. This model is shown in Fig. 4.

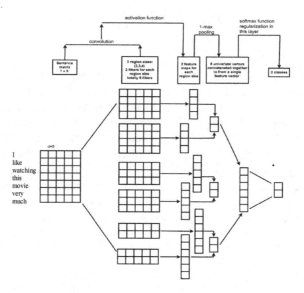

Fig. 4. Convolutional Neural Network (CNN) model

CNN-LSTM

The CNN model focused on extracting spatial information as features, whereas the LSTM model focused on extracting temporal information (from the past to the future). CNN-LSTM model [2, 3, 6], therefore, can combine and use both types of information together. The basic idea is to use the CNN model first to extract the spatial information. Then, instead of flatten them, we feed them directly to the LSTM model for classification. Figure 5 shows CNN-LSTM model.

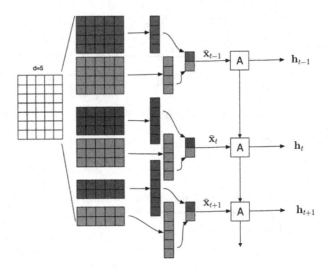

Fig. 5. CNN-LSTM model

LSTM-CNN

LSTM-CNN model combines both types of information: temporal information and spatial information together. The inputs are fed into two LSTM layers at first to capture the temporal information. Next the CNN model focused on extracting spatial information. After the max pooling layer, data is reshaped to a vector again and passed into a fully connection layer with dropout operation before feeding into the output layer. Using the dropout operation to prevent over-fitting and achieve better generalization. To calculate the probabilities of different classes, in the output layer, softmax function is chosen as the active function. The class with the highest probability will be final prediction for inputs. Figure 6 shows LSTM-CNN model.

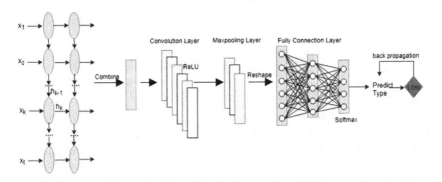

Fig. 6. LSTM-CNN model

3.3   The Classification

Following by [6], with the text vector learned from the CNN-LSTM, LSTM-CNN model, the output layer defined as:

$$y = (W_d x_t + b_d) \tag{6}$$

where

x_t: the text vector learned from the CNN-LSTM, LSTM-CNN models
y: the degree of document class of the target text
W_d, b_d: the weight and bias associated with the CNN-LSTM, LSTM-CNN models.
By minimizing the mean squared error between the predicted document class and actual document class, the CNN-LSTM, LSTM- CNN model are trained. The loss function is defined as follows:

$$L(X, y) = \frac{1}{2n} \sum_{k=1}^{n} \binom{n}{k} \left\| h(x^i) - y^i \right\|^2 \tag{7}$$

$X = \{x^1, x^1, x^2, \ldots, x^m\}$: a training set of document matrix
$y = \{y^1, y^2, \ldots, y^m\}$: a document class ratings set of training sets.

4   Experiments

4.1   Dataset

We conducted a model experiment and its comparison with other models has been published before. We used 7 datasets, gathered by Zhang [12]. These data sets focus on two main aspects: emotional analysis and document classification; let us describe more detail about these datasets.

- DBPedia 2014 (DBP) includes structured information extracted from Wikipedia, this dataset has 14 labels headlines and abstracts of articles on Wikipedia.
- Yahoo! Answers (Yahoo A) includes questions and answers from Yahoo! Web-scope, this dataset has 10 labels.
- AG's news (AG) includes titles and descriptions of the articles newspapers from more than 2000 different sources. This dataset has 4 labels according to the category of each article.
- Amazon reviews (Amazon) includes user product reviews on the "Amazon" web-site. Similar to Yelp, this dataset is divided into 2 episodes: the first episode (Amazon Polarity) consists of 2 labels "positive" and "negative" and the second episode (Amazon Full) has the number of labels corresponding to the star number of the review.

- Yelp reviews 2015 (Yelp) includes location reviews on the "Yelp" website, this data source is divided into 2 Episodes: the first volume (Yelp Polarity) consists of 2 labels, "positive" and "negative" and the second episode (Yelp Full) has the number of labels corresponding to the star number of the review.

Detailed information about the seven datasets is shown in Table 1. Datasets have data for training and testing separately.

Table 1. Overview of the dataset

Dataset	DBP	Yahoo A	AG	Amazon F	Amazon P	Yelp P	Yelp F
Train	560K	1.4M	120K	3M	3.6M	560K	650K
Test	70K	60K	7.6	560K	400K	38K	50K
Classes	14	10	4	5	2	2	5

We preprocessed and cleaned datasets by the following steps:

- Eliminate non-alphabetical characters, numeric characters except spaces
- Separating words, creating dictionaries for numbering words, dictionaries with a maximum size of 50000 words (tokenize)
- Convert words to 300 vector size (based on pre-train word2vec- FastText) [5] and set equal length sentences using padding technique. The maximum length of the sentence is 2.5 times the average length of all sentences in the filtered data set, but will be the lowest limit of 64 and the highest is 150.
- Words not included in the word vector set will be randomly generated with the mean (center) and standard deviation equal to the mean and standard deviation of the vector matrix of the dictionary (50000 words)

4.2   Experiment Setting

The models are set as follows:

- Adam Optimizer is used as the optimization algorithm, the cost function is softmax, learning rate initialized to 0.0005, size Mini-Batch 128.
- Loss calculation algorithm: Categorical cross-entropy.
- The maximum number of training sessions (epoch) is 20. During training, learning rate will be reduced 10 times if accuracy is not improved (minimum 5e-6) and stop training after 5 times with no improvement in accuracy (2 for too large dataset).
- We used word2vec- FastText published in [5] as pre-trained word embeddings.

The parameters of each model and details about how to apply each model in the document classification are described as follows:

LSTM: The input will be fed with 500 time steps. At each time step, one 300-dimensions word embedding will be fed, the result of the current time step will be affected by the result of previous time steps. This way, the temporal information will be extracted by the LSTM, and the final result will be judged based on this information as well.

CNN: to apply this model, we first need to treat the input as a 2-d image, whose each row contains a word, which is also a 300-dimension vector. The CNN model will have a window with size $(x; 300)$ that moves along the rows (moves along each words). 300 is a constant, which is the same as the word-embedding size. x is the kernel size, which is either 2, 3 or 4 in our case. This means we are grouping together 2, 3 or 4 words to get our relevant spatial information. The result will be the spatial information that was extracted. We can then flatten them and feed them to another fully-connected layer. Finally, the output of that layer can be turned into document classification.

CNN-LSTM: For applying this model, the first part (CNN) is done similar to the CNN approach. The output of the CNN part will have the spatial information of groups of words. For a kernel size of 4, which means 4 words per group, CNN will gives an output of 125 features, from the original input of 500 words (each word is a 300-dimensions vector). We then feed these features into the LSTM, one feature per time steps. This brings the number of time steps to 125 as well. The final result should have the temporal information of the spatial information of the original input. We can then turn it into document classification.

LSTM-CNN: In this model, the first part (LSTM) is done similar to the LSTM approach. The output of the LSTM part will have the temporal information of groups of words. We use same parameters of CNN model. After the max pooling layer, data is reshaped to a vector again and passed into a fully connection layer with dropout operation before feeding into the output layer. Softmax function is chosen as the active function. We can then turn probability of temporal information of the spatial information of the original input into document classification.

4.3   Evaluation

We used accuracy score to evaluate the models. This score is calculated by Eq. in (8):

$$Accuracy = \frac{\#number\ of\ true\ predict\ labels}{\#number\ of\ predict\ lables} \tag{8}$$

We compared our models with character-level Convolutional Neural Networks (CNN) [12] (*) and LSTM-bigram (h = 10) [5] (**) since they are attractive models for text classification and did experiment in the same datasets. We used the results of these models published by the authors. In character-level Convolutional Neural Networks (CNN) we used five models named as: Lg. Full Conv. Th., Lg. w2v Conv. Th., LSTM, Sm. Lk. Conv, BoW TFIDF and ngrams TFIDF. Table 2 shows the results and performance of our Hybrid Deep Learning approach in seven datasets compared with the others. The bold number indicates which dataset approaches gives the best result for a particular model (for a column). From the results we saw that our proposed model CNN-LSTM produced the best results in four datasets: AG, Amazon F, Amazon P and Yelp F and LSTM-CNN got the best results in DBP and Yahoo A datasets. To compare the results in seven datasets between our models with the others, we calculated the sum of accuracy of each model in the seven datasets. The result is shown in Fig. 7. From the Fig. 7, we saw that CNN-LSTM model be the first rank, following is LSTM-bigram and LSTM-CNN. To explore more about our hybrid deep learning models CNN-LSTM and LSTM-CNN, we compared in training time per epoch of each model in DBP dataset. By our experiments, CNN-LSTM is three times faster than the LSTM-CNN.

Table 2. Accuracy of our models compared with other, numbers are in percentage.

Model	DBP	Yahoo A	AG	Amazon F	Amazon P	Yelp F	Yelp P
CNN-LSTM	98.68	72.40	**92.60**	**61.32**	**95.48**	**64.34**	95.50
LSTM-CNN	**98.87**	**73.61**	92.32	59.98	95.02	62.25	95.53
LSTM, bigram (**)	98.60	72.30	92.50	60.20	94.60	63.90	**95.70**
Lg. Full Conv. Th. (*)	98.45	70.42	90.49	59.46	94.49	61.96	95.12
Lg. w2v Conv. Th. (*)	98.63	68.77	90.09	56.25	94.20	60.42	95.37
LSTM (*)	98.55	70.84	86.06	59.43	93.90	58.17	94.74
Sm. Lk. Conv (*)	98.15	69.98	89.13	56.34	94.15	58.59	94.46
BoW TFIDF (*)	97.37	71.04	89.64	55.26	91.00	59.86	93.66
ngrams TFIDF (*)	98.69	68.51	92.36	52.44	91.54	54.80	95.44

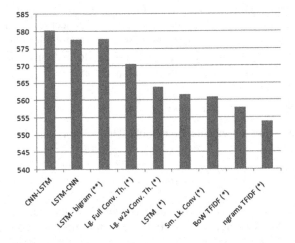

Fig. 7. Sum of accuracy of each model in the seven datasets

5   Conclusion

This paper has presented a solution for document classification using hybrid deep learning approaches. In our experiments, testing with public dataset is positive; the hybrid deep learning approach shows the better result comparing with other approaches. The result shows that CNN-LSTM model is better LSTM-CNN and also performs much faster than LSTM-CNN. In future work, we would like to apply in other deep learning models and explore more features to improve the results.

References

1. Graves, A.: Supervised Sequence Labelling with Recurrent Neural Networks, vol. 385. Springer, Heidelberg (2012). https://doi.org/10.1007/978-3-642-24797-2
2. Hung, B.T.: Vietnamese keyword extraction using hybrid deep learning methods. In proceedings of the 5th NAFOSTED Conference on Information and Computer Science - NICS (2018)
3. Zhou, C., Sun, C., Liu, Z., Lau, F.: A C-LSTM neural network for text classification. arXiv preprint arXiv:1511.08630 (2015)
4. Conneau, A., Schwenk, H., Barrault, L., LeCun, Y.: Very deep convolutional networks for natural language processing. CoRR, vol. abs/1606.01781 (2016)
5. Grave, E., Mikolov, T., Joulin, A., Bojanowski, P.: Bag of tricks for efficient text classification. In Proceedings of the 15th Conference of the European Chapter of the Association for Computational Linguistics, EACL, Valencia, Spain, pp. 427–431 (2017)
6. Wang, J., Yu, L.-C., Lai, K.R., Zhang, X.: Dimensional sentiment analysis using a regional CNN-LSTM model. In: The 54th Annual Meeting of the Association for Computational Linguistics, vol. 225 (2016)
7. Tai, K.S., Socher, R., Manning, C.D.: Improved semantic representations from tree-structured long short term memory networks. In: Proceedings of ACL (2015)
8. Johnson, R., Zhang, T.: Convolutional neural networks for text categorization: shallow word-level vs. deep character-level. arXiv:1609.00718 (2016)
9. Socher, R., et al.: Recursive deep models for semantic compositionality over a sentiment treebank. In: Proceedings of EMNLP (2013)
10. Hochreiter, S., Schmidhuber, J.: Long short term memory. Neural Comput. 9(8), 1735–1780 (1997)
11. Mikolov, T., Chen, K., Corrado, G., Dean, J.: Efficient estimation of word representations in vector space. In: Proceedings of International Conference on Learning Representations (ICLR 2013), Workshop Track (2013)
12. Zhang, X., Zhao, J.J., LeCun, Y.: Character-level convolutional networks for text classification. In: Advances in Neural Information Processing Systems 28: Annual Conference on Neural Information Processing Systems, Montreal, Quebec, Canada, pp. 649–657 (2015)
13. Kim, Y.: Convolutional neural networks for sentence classification. In: Proceedings of the Conference on Empirical Methods in Natural Language Processing, EMNLP 2014, 25–29 October Doha, Qatar, A meeting of SIGDAT, a Special Interest Group of the ACL, pp. 1746–1751 (2014)
14. Yang, Z., Yang, D., Dyer, C., He, X., Smola, A.J., Hovy, E.H.: Hierarchical attention networks for document classification. In: NAACL HLT, The 2016 Conference of the North American Chapter of the Association for Computational Linguistics: Human Language Technologies, San Diego California, USA, pp. 1480–1489 (2016)

A FCA-Based Concept Clustering Recommender System

G. Chemmalar Selvi[1(✉)], G. G. Lakshmi Priya[1],
and Rose Bindu Joseph[2]

[1] Vellore Institute of Technology, Vellore 632014, TN, India
chemmalar06@gmail.com
[2] Christ Academy Institute for Advanced Studies, Bengaluru 560083, India

Abstract. Recommender systems are information filtering software which is capable of resolving the recent issue of internet's information overload. The recommender system generate the recommendation more suitably based on the data gathered either implicitly like user profile, click information, web log history or explicitly like ratings (scale 1–5), likes, dislikes, feedbacks. The most important challenge to the recommender system is the growing number of online users making it a high dimensional data which leads to the data sparsity problem where the accuracy of recommendation depends on the availability of the data. In this paper, a new approach called formal concept analysis is employed to handle the high dimensional data and a FCA-based recommender algorithm, User-based concept clustering recommendation algorithm (UBCCRA) is proposed. The UBCCRA out performs by accurately generating the recommendation for the group-based users called cluster users. The experimental result is shown to prove the cluster recommendation with good result.

Keywords: Recommender system · Collaborative filtering · Clustering · Formal concept analysis · Sparsity

1 Introduction

The torrent increase in the enormous volume of digital information and the count of internet or online users have set a drastic confrontation with the information overload [1] which restricts the need of an hour to access to interest of certain items on the internet. There are few information retrieval systems like Google and YouTube who have targeted this problem and tried to provide likely solutions by finding, filtering, prioritizing and personalizing according to the online users. They simply associate the item contents with the user's profile and interest. This has increased the urge for recommender systems than even ever before.

Recommender Systems are known to be highly predictive and personalized software which is capable of interacting with the overwhelming data flowing in the internet. The Recommender Systems provide more suitable suggestions of items to the online users who are more of skeptical attitude when the choices are plenty around them [2]. They have the ability to predict whether a particular user would like an item or not based on the information acquired explicitly like ratings or implicitly like user

© ICST Institute for Computer Sciences, Social Informatics and Telecommunications Engineering 2019
Published by Springer Nature Switzerland AG 2019. All Rights Reserved
P. C. Vinh and A. Rakib (Eds.): ICCASA 2019/ICTCC 2019, LNICST 298, pp. 178–187, 2019.
https://doi.org/10.1007/978-3-030-34365-1_14

history, weblog or click depth [3]. Thus, they are essential to both service providers as well as to the users [4]. It has well decreased the transaction costs when identifying and preferring the items to buy and has also improved the strong decision making process and quality [5].

The application of faultless recommendation algorithms is very much essential for any recommender system to offer suitable and exact recommendation to its individual users. The recommendation algorithms are broadly classified into content-based [6], collaborative filtering-based [7] and hybrid-based algorithms [8]. In this paper, the application of collaborative filtering-based algorithm is presented by combining a new approach based on Formal Concept Analysis (FCA). In general, the people who buy similar items are formed as clusters which pave the way for performing most prominent and suitable recommendations of new items to be bought. Formal Concept Analysis (FCA) is a mathematical tool which is used for analyzing the large datasets and representation of complex information [9].

In recent years, the application of FCA over recommender system has started evolving. In the paper [10], the author has studied the friends' recommendations by presenting the CCG (concept context graph) which will represent the knowledge context preferably from the social interactions in order to recommend more friends. The concept similarity is computed and ranked among the matching concepts in the concept context graph of the target users for recommendation. The authors [11] discussed the exploration of FCA in the collaborative filtering-based algorithm by representing the relation between the users and items and have constructed two new algorithms for finding neighbours in a collaborative recommender. The algorithm has shown better result in finding out the neighbours without much loss in the result accuracy.

The rest of the paper is organized to explain more in detail about the application of new FCA-based approach over the collaborative filtering-based recommender algorithm. The first section of the paper provides the foundations and terminologies in FCA approach. In the second section, a new FCA-based collaborative filtering–based algorithm is proposed. In the third section, an algorithm to deal with recommender system using collaborative filtering-based is presented by illustrating with the example dataset. Finally, the conclusion of this paper provides the summary of the proposed work and its success in recommender systems.

2   An Overview of Formal Concept Analysis

Formal Concept Analysis (FCA) is a mathematical approach which defines the complex data representation and was first introduced by Wille and Ganter [12]. The one such property of FCA is to tackle uncertainty of data and it has been applied widely in the areas of fuzzy concept, interval–valued fuzzy concept, and rough set, approximate and triadic concept analysis [13–17]. The fundamental aspect of FCA are the formal context and concept hierarchy. The formal context consists of set of objects, set of attributes and binary relation among with objects and attributes. The followings describes the important terminologies in FCA.

Definition 1 Formal Context. A formal context is a triplet (P, Q, R), where P and Q are two nonempty and finite sets, and R is a binary relation on P and Q (Refer Fig. 1).

R	q_1	q_2	q_3	q_4	q_5
p_1	X	X		X	X
p_2	X	X	X		
p_3				X	
p_4	X	X	X		

Fig. 1. Formal context M

Here, P and Q are the set of objects and set of attributes, respectively where $(p, q) \in R$ indicate that the object p has the attribute q and $(p, q) \notin R$ indicate that the object p does not have the attribute q.

Definition 2 Concept-Forming Operators. For every formal context (P, Q, R), the concept-forming operators $\uparrow: 2^P \rightarrow 2^Q$ and $\downarrow: 2^Q \rightarrow 2^P$ for every $A \subseteq P$ and $B \subseteq Q$ as:

$$A^\uparrow = \{q \in Q \mid \text{for each } p \in A : (p, q) \in R\}$$
$$B^\downarrow = \{p \in P \mid \text{for each } q \in B : (p, q) \in R\}$$

The operator $\uparrow$ assigns the subsets of Q to subsets of P. $A^\uparrow$ is the set of all attributes shared by all the objects in A. Analogously, the operator $\downarrow$ assigns the subsets of p to subsets of Q. $B^\downarrow$ is the set of all objects shared by all the attributes in B.

Definition 3 Formal Concept. Formal concept is a pair (A, B) for any formal context (P, Q, R) such that $A \subseteq P$ and $B \subseteq Q$ where $A^\uparrow = B$ and $B^\downarrow = A$.

Here (A, B) is the formal concept if and only if set A consist of only those objects that are shared by all the attributes shared from the set B which is called extent of the concept. Also, set B consist of only those attributes that are shared from the set A which is called intent of the concept.

The corresponding formal context M represented in Fig. 1, contain the following formal concepts:

$C_0 = (\{\}, \{q_1, q_2, q_3, q_4\})$, $C_1 = (\{p_1\}, \{q_1, q_2, q_4, q_5\})$, $C_2 = (\{p_2, p_4\}, \{q_1, q_2, q_3\})$, $C_3 = (\{p_1, p_3\}, \{q_4\})$, $C_4 = (\{p_1, p_2, p_4\}, \{q_1 \, q_2\})$, $C_5 = (\{p_1, p_2, p_3, p_4\}, \{\})$

Thus, the concept-forming operators can be used to define formally the concept's extent as $\text{Ext}(P, Q, R) = \{B^\downarrow \mid B \in Q\}$ and concept's intent as $\text{Int}(P, Q, R) = \{A^\downarrow \mid A \in P\}$.

Definition 4 Subconcept-Superconcept. For the given formal context (P, Q, R), if (A_1, B_1) and (A_2, B_2) are the formal concepts then it holds a partial order relation $\leq$ such as: $(A_1, B_1) \leq (A_2, B_2)$ if and only if $A_1 \subseteq A_2$ and $B_2 \subseteq B_1$.

This partial order relation formally describes the subconcept - superconcept relationship which can be represented by drawing the line or Hasse diagram called concept lattice.

Definition 5 Concept Lattice. The concept lattice is defined as the hierarchical structure of partial-order relation $\leq$ denoted by ß(P, Q, R) such that $\{(A, B) \in 2^P \times 2^Q \mid A^\uparrow = B \text{ and } B^\downarrow = A\}$. The concept lattice for the corresponding formal context M is represented in the Fig. 2.

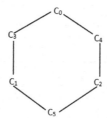

Fig. 2. Concept lattice

Thus, the FCA has been well explored in the following areas: text mining, web mining, software mining, bioinformatics, chemistry, medicine, ontology engineering, and so on [9]. In recent years, the application of FCA to recommender system has a massive attention and is still growing area in the research topics. In the next section, the paper discusses about the application of such FCA to recommender system which uses collaborative filtering technique.

3   Application of FCA with Collaborative Filtering-Based Recommender System

Collaborative filtering (CF) in recommender systems use the tabular data structure called as user-item rating matrix. The intuition behind working this algorithm is purely based on the ratings that are given by the active users when they bought or purchased the items. But in the real-world, it is rare to observe the ratings in the user-item rating matrix. Hence the nature of the user-item rating matrix becomes sparse which is the most challenge faced by the recommender system in today service. Generally, the CF technique is classified as Memory-based methods which predict the ratings of the active user's by matching the similar users with each other's [18] and Model-based methods which aim at predicting the ratings of the active users from the kind of pattern generated from the user-item rating matrix [19].

The novelty of this paper is applying a new and efficient mathematical approach called formal concept analysis into the field of recommender system which can effectively solve the most challenge faced by the recommender system called data sparsity and high-dimensional problem [20]. The general schema of user-based recommendation is used to build the presented system model [21, 27–30]. The input data to any recommender system is the user-item rating matrix where users are represented in the rows and items are represented in the columns and the values are represented in the corresponding cells of the matrix. Such a data representation is facilitated by the formal context in the FCA. The formal context $M = (P, Q, R)$ denotes that P containing the set of users = {Allen, Bob, Tom, Alice}, Q containing the set of items (movies) = {m_1, m_2, m_3, m_4, m_5} and R gives the relation between user and item (Fig. 3).

R	m_1	m_2	m_3	m_4	m_5
Allen	5	3		2	4
Bob	3	1	4		
Tom				5	
Alice	2	5	3		

Fig. 3. Formal context M representing user-item rating matrix

The paper proposes a new clustering algorithm based on the formal concept analysis known as User-based concept clustering recommendation algorithm (UBC-CRA). The idea behind this proposed algorithm is to cluster the similar or like-minded users based on the similar items purchased by these users. Based on the number of clusters formed, the similarity measure like most popularly used Pearson or cosine similarity measures can be induced to find the deepness of the similarity between each clusters [22–26]. Finally, the ranking method like Top-N Recommendation is used to recommend the items to the target users in the clusters. The User-based concept clustering recommendation algorithm (UBCCRA) is given below:

Algorithm 1 (User-based concept clustering recommendation algorithm (UBC-CRA))

Input: User-Item rating matrix
Output: Top-N Recommendation
Processing Steps:

  1. Take the user-item rating matrix M and transform it as formal context M' = (U,I,R) where U comprise of set of active users, I comprise of set of items and R stands for relation existing between user U and item I. If the user U has purchased an item I, (u, i) $\in$ R then mark it 1: (u, i) $\notin$ R else 0. Thus the dimension of the formal context M' is U X I.

  2. Generate the formal concepts from the formal context M' by using:
  $Tu^{\uparrow} = \{i \in I \mid$ for each $u \in Tu : (u,i) \in R\}$
  $Ti^{\downarrow} = \{u \in U \mid$ for each $i \in Ti : (u,i) \in R\}$

  3. Form the clusters of similar users purchased similar items by removing the redundant formal concepts (Tu,Ti): Tu $\subseteq$ U and Ti $\subseteq$ I where $Tu^{\uparrow} = $ Ti and $Ti^{\downarrow} = $ Tu

  4. Calculate the weighted concept cluster similarity $Sim_{\hat{w}}$ by applying the similarity measure Jaccard Index as shown below:

  $$Sim_{\hat{w}}(CC1, CC2) = \hat{w} * S(Tu1, Ti1) + (1 - \hat{w}) * S(Tu2, Ti2)$$

  where the weight $\hat{w}$ is from $0 \leq \hat{w} \leq 1$, concept clusters $CC1 = (Tu1, Ti1), CC2 = (Tu2, Ti2)$ and S is the Jaccard Similarity Index computed as:

  $$Jaccard\ Similarity\ Index, S = \frac{|Tu1 \cap Tu2|}{|Ti1 \cup Ti2|}$$

  5. Use the ranking method and select the top most concept cluster to perform the cluster-based recommendation.

The above presented algorithm performs the User-based concept clustering recommendation. The main contribution of this algorithm is to reduce the high dimensional data and simplify the complex data representation while analyzing the data. The above algorithm can be modified to perform Item-based concept clustering recommendation by transposing the user-item rating matrix where items are represented as rows and users are represented as columns. In the next section explains the User-based concept clustering recommendation algorithm (UBCCRA) by experimenting with a small dataset.

4 Experimental Results and Discussion

In this section, we have considered a small dataset which consist of 12 users and 8 movies in the movie recommendation system. The User-based concept clustering recommendation algorithm (UBCCRA) is applied to this small dataset to perform movie recommendation to the group-based users with the similar interest of preference. The user-item rating matrix M is converted to formal context M′ and represented as below (Figs. 4 and 5):

5	3	2	0	1	0	0	0
1	4	0	0	0	1	0	3
0	5	0	0	4	0	3	0
3	2	0	0	0	2	0	1
5	3	2	0	1	0	0	0
0	2	0	0	4	0	2	0
0	5	0	0	2	0	5	0
0	0	0	0	0	0	4	0
4	3	5	0	5	0	0	0
0	0	0	0	0	0	2	0
2	1	3	0	5	0	0	0
3	2	0	0	0	3	0	5

Fig. 4. User-Item rating matrix M

1	2	3	4	5	6	7	8
X	X	X		X			
X	X				X		X
	X			X		X	
X	X				X		X
X	X	X		X			
	X			X		X	
	X			X		X	
						X	
X	X	X		X			
						X	
X	X	X		X			
X	X				X		X

Fig. 5. Formal context M′ of User-Item rating matrix M

From the formal context M′, the clusters are formed by generating the formal concepts. The formal concepts are generated by matching the similar kind of items purchased by the similar kind of active users. From the generated formal concepts, the redundant formal concepts are obtained by applying the sub-super concept partial ordering relationship. Hence, the partial ordering gives the actual formal concepts which form the cluster with similar users and similar items without loss of data. Initially, there were 4096 formal concepts which are redundant in nature was constructed, of which only 9 formal concepts was considered as concept clusters after applying partial ordering. In the Fig. 6 the concept clusters are illustrated for the given dataset of size of 12×8 matrix.

CC_i	(Tu_i, Ti_j)
CC_0	({}, {1, 2, 3, 4, 5, 6, 7, 8})
CC_1	({1, 5, 9, 11}, {1, 2, 3, 5})
CC_2	({2, 4, 12}, {1, 2, 6, 8})
CC_3	({3, 6, 7}, {2, 5, 7})
CC_4	({3, 6, 7, 8, 10}, {7})
CC_5	({1, 3, 5, 6, 7, 9, 11}, {2, 5})
CC_6	({1, 2, 4, 5, 9, 11, 12}, {1, 2})
CC_7	({1, 2, 3, 4, 5, 6, 7, 9, 11, 12}, {2})
CC_8	({1, 2, 3, 4, 5, 6, 7, 8, 9, 10, 11, 12}, {})

Fig. 6. Concept clusters of formal context M′

For the concept clusters CC_i, the weighted concept cluster similarity $\text{Sim}_{\hat{w}}$ is applied which is used to find the deepness of similarity among the users and items between each clusters. Let the similarity between the concept clusters $CC1$ and $CC5$ be $\text{Sim}_{\hat{w}}(CC1, CC5) = 0.57$, where the weight is assumed to be 0.5 since the rating may be biased based on the feedback of recommendation. Finally the calculated similarities among the every cluster are ranked in the descending order and the top most concept with high similarity value is considered based on which the recommendation is generated to every of these clusters. Hence, the cluster-based recommendation is completed which might suitably fit the cluster users since the recommendation is generated based on the similar list of user preferences in the target cluster.

5 Conclusion

Collaborative filtering is the most popular recommender algorithm where there is an automatic generation of recommendation for the target users based on the similar taste of interest or preferences of the other active users. But the lack of user preferences or ratings boils down the accuracy of recommendation. In this paper, a new FCA-based concept clustering algorithm is proposed which is able to resolve the high dimensional data and thereby identifies the clusters of users with the similar user's interest or similar user's preference. The formal context is constructed for the given user-item rating matrix which has well addressed the high dimensional data. The method of generating the clusters is based on finding the non-redundant formal concept clusters. The deepness of similarity exhibited by each cluster is predicted by applying the weighted concept similarity and finally the top most similarity score is utilized to perform the recommendation for every cluster. In the future work, per-user based recommender algorithm can be developed using the FCA method.

References

1. Konstan, J.A., Riedl, J.: Recommender systems: from algorithms to user experience. User Model. User-Adapt. Interact. **22**, 101–123 (2012)
2. Pan, C., Li, W.: Research paper recommendation with topic analysis. In: Computer Design and Applications, pp. V4–V264. IEEE (2010)
3. Pu, P, Chen, L, Hu, R.: A user-centric evaluation framework for recommender systems. In: Proceedings of the Fifth ACM Conference on Recommender Systems, RecSys 2011, pp. 57–164. ACM, New York (2011)
4. Hu, R, Pu, P.: Potential acceptance issues of personality-ASED recommender systems. In: Proceedings of ACM Conference on Recommender Systems, RecSys 2009, New York City, NY, USA, p. 225, October 2009
5. Pathak, B., Garfinkel, R., Gopal, R., Venkatesan, R., Yin, F.: Empirical analysis of the impact of recommender systems on sales. J Manag. Inform. Syst. **27**(2), 159–188 (2010)
6. Pazzani, M.J., Billsus, D.: Content-based recommendation systems. In: Brusilovsky, P., Kobsa, A., Nejdl, W. (eds.) The Adaptive Web. LNCS, vol. 4321, pp. 325–341. Springer, Heidelberg (2007). https://doi.org/10.1007/978-3-540-72079-9_10

7. Su, X., Khoshgoftaar, T.M.: A survey of collaborative filtering techniques. In: Advances in Artificial Intelligence (2009)

8. Kilani, Y., Otoom, A.F., Alsarhan, A., Almaayah, M.: A genetic algorithms-based hybrid recommender system of matrix factorization and neighborhood-based techniques. J. Comput. Sci. **28**, 78–93 (2018)

9. Poelmans, J., Ignatov, D.I., Kuznetsov, S.O., Dedene, G.: Formal concept analysis in knowledge processing: a survey on applications. Expert Syst. Appl. **40**(16), 6538–6560 (2013)

10. Zhang, W., Du, Y.J., Song, W.: Recommender system with formal concept analysis (2015)

11. du Boucher-Ryan, P., Bridge, D.: Collaborative recommending using formal concept analysis. In: bramer, m, Coenen, F., Allen, T. (eds.) SGAI 2005, pp. 205–218. Springer, London (2006). https://doi.org/10.1007/978-1-84628-226-3_16

12. Ganter, B., Wille, R.: Formal Concept Analysis: Mathematical Foundations. Springer, Berlin (1999). https://doi.org/10.1007/978-3-642-59830-2

13. Doerfel, S., Jäschke, R., Stumme, G.: Publication analysis of the formal concept analysis community. In: Domenach, F., Ignatov, Dmitry I., Poelmans, J. (eds.) ICFCA 2012. LNCS (LNAI), vol. 7278, pp. 77–95. Springer, Heidelberg (2012). https://doi.org/10.1007/978-3-642-29892-9_12

14. Belohlavek, R., Vychodil, V.: Formal concept analysis and linguistic hedges. Int. J. Gen Syst. **41**(5), 503–532 (2012)

15. Ignatov D.I., Gnatyshak, D.V., Kuznetsov, S.O., Mirkin, B.G.: Triadic formal concept analysis and triclustering: searching for optimal patterns. Mach. Learn. (2015). https://doi.org/10.1007/s10994-015-5487-y

16. Yao, Y.: A comparative study of formal concept analysis and rough set theory in data analysis. In: Tsumoto, S., Słowiński, R., Komorowski, J., Grzymała-Busse, Jerzy W. (eds.) RSCTC 2004. LNCS (LNAI), vol. 3066, pp. 59–68. Springer, Heidelberg (2004). https://doi.org/10.1007/978-3-540-25929-9_6

17. Djouadi, Y.: Extended Galois derivation operators for information retrieval based on fuzzy formal concept lattice. In: Benferhat, S., Grant, J. (eds.) SUM 2011. LNCS (LNAI), vol. 6929, pp. 346–358. Springer, Heidelberg (2011). https://doi.org/10.1007/978-3-642-23963-2_27

18. Resnick, P., Iacovou, N., Suchak, M., Bergstrom, P., Riedl, J.: GroupLens: an open architecture for collaborative filtering of netnews. In: Proceedings of the 1994 ACM Conference on Computer Supported Cooperative Work, pp. 175–186. ACM, October 1994

19. Si, L., Jin, R.: Flexible mixture model for collaborative filtering. In: Proceedings of the 20th International Conference on Machine Learning, ICML 2003, pp. 704–711 (2003)

20. Bobadilla, J., Ortega, F., Hernando, A., Gutiérrez, A.: Recommender systems survey. Knowl.-Based Syst. **46**, 109–132 (2013)

21. Ignatov, D.I., Nenova, E., Konstantinova, N., Konstantinov, A.V.: Boolean matrix factorisation for collaborative filtering: an FCA-based approach. In: Agre, G., Hitzler, P., Krisnadhi, A.A., Kuznetsov, S.O. (eds.) AIMSA 2014, LNCS, vol. 8722, pp. 47–58. Springer, Cham (2014). https://doi.org/10.1007/978-3-319-10554-3_5

22. Formica, A.: Concept similarity in formal concept analysis: an information content approach. Knowl.-Based Syst. **21**(1), 80–87 (2008)

23. Tadrat, J., Boonjing, V., Pattaraintakorn, P.: A new similarity measure in formal concept analysis for case-based reasoning. Expert Syst. Appl. **39**(1), 967–972 (2012)

24. Wang, L., Liu, X.: A new model of evaluating concept similarity. Knowl.-Based Syst. **21**(8), 842–846 (2008)

25. He, H., Hai, H., Rujing, W.: FCA-based web user profile mining for topics of interest. In: 2007 IEEE International Conference on Integration Technology, pp. 778–782. IEEE, March 2007
26. Lin, Z.C., Zhu, G.J.: A concept similarity algorithm based on FCA. Comput. Technol. Dev. **9**, 112–114 (2008)
27. Sarwar, B.M., Karypis, G., Konstan, J.A., Riedl, J.: Item-based collaborative filtering recommendation algorithms. WWW **1**, 285–295 (2001)
28. Ma, H., King, I., Lyu, M.R.: Effective missing data prediction for collaborative filtering. In: Proceedings of the 30th Annual International ACM SIGIR Conference on Research and Development in Information Retrieval, pp. 39–46. ACM, July 2007
29. Wang, J., De Vries, A.P., Reinders, M.J.: Unifying user-based and item-based collaborative filtering approaches by similarity fusion. In: Proceedings of the 29th Annual International ACM SIGIR Conference on Research and Development in Information Retrieval, pp. 501–508. ACM, August 2006
30. Goldberg, D., Nichols, D., Oki, B.M., Terry, D.: Using collaborative filtering to weave an information tapestry. Commun. ACM **35**(12), 61–71 (1992)

Hedge Algebra Approach for Semantics-Based Algorithm to Improve Result of Time Series Forecasting

Loc Vuminh[1(✉)], Dung Vuhoang[2], Dung Quachanh[3], and Yen Phamthe[1,4]

[1] Giadinh University, Ho Chi Minh City, Vietnam
vuminhloc@gmail.com
[2] National University of Singapore, Singapore, Singapore
[3] Vanhien University, Ho Chi Minh City, Vietnam
[4] Graduate University of Science and Technology, Vietnam Academy of Science and Technology, Hanoi, Vietnam

Abstract. During the recent years, many different methods of using fuzzy time series for forecasting have been published. However, computation in the linguistic environment one term has two parallel semantics, one represented by fuzzy sets (computation-semantics) it human-imposed and the rest (context-semantic) is due to the context of the problem. If the latter semantics is not paid attention, despite the computation accomplished high level of exactly but it has been distorted about semantics. That means the result does not suitable the context of the problem. Hedge Algebras, an algebraic Approach to domains of linguistic variables, unifying the above two semantics of each term, is the basis of convenient calculation in the language environment and does not distort the semantics of terms. A new approach is proposed through a semantic-based algorithm, focus on two key steps: partitioning the universe of discourse of time series into a collection of intervals and mining fuzzy relationships from fuzzy time series, which outperforms accuracy and friendliness in computing.

The experimental results, forecasting enrollments at the University of Alabama and forecasting TAIEX Index, demonstrate that the proposed method significantly outperforms the published ones about accurate level, the ease and friendliness on computing.

Keywords: Hedge algebras · Fuzzy time series · Forecasting · Fuzziness intervals

1 Introduction

Fuzzy time series was originally proposed by Song and Chissom [1] and it has been applied to forecast the enrollments at University of Alabama [2, 3]. In Chen [4] opened a new study direction of using fuzzy time series to forecast time series source we have, the better forecasting values we get discourse such as [5] which is the first research confirmed the important role of partitioning the universe of discourse, this employed distribution and average based length as a way to solve the problem. In turn, Jilani et al.

© ICST Institute for Computer Sciences, Social Informatics and Telecommunications Engineering 2019
Published by Springer Nature Switzerland AG 2019. All Rights Reserved
P. C. Vinh and A. Rakib (Eds.): ICCASA 2019/ICTCC 2019, LNICST 298, pp. 188–202, 2019.
https://doi.org/10.1007/978-3-030-34365-1_15

[6] proposed frequency density, Huarng and Yu [7] suggested the ratios and Bas et al. [8] used modified genetic algorithm as basis to improve quality of interval.

The rest of this paper is organized as follows: Sect. 2 briefly introduces some basis concepts of HA; Sect. 3 presents the proposed method; Sect. 4 presents empirical results on forecasting enrollments at University of Alabama, Forecasting AITEX Index and comment; Sect. 5 concludes the paper.

2 Preliminaries

In this section, we briefly recall some concepts associated with fuzzy time series and hedge algebras.

2.1 Fuzzy Time Series

Fuzzy time series was first introduced by Song and Chissom [1], it is considered as this is fuzzy of time series. Formally, fuzzy time series are defined as following definition

Definition 1.
Let $Y(t)$ $(t = \ldots, 0, 1, 2, \ldots)$, a subset of R^1, be the universe of discourse on which $f_i(t)$ $(i = 1, 2, \ldots)$ are defined and $F(t)$ is the collection of $f_i(t)$ $(i = 1, 2, \ldots)$. Then $F(t)$ is called fuzzy time series on $Y(t)$ $(t = \ldots, 0, 1, 2, \ldots)$.

Song and Chissom employed fuzzy relational equations as model of fuzzy time series. Specifically, we have following definition:

Definition 2.
If for any $f_j(t) \in F(t)$, there exists an $f_i(t - 1) \circ F(t - 1)$ such that there exists a fuzzy relation $R_{ij}(t, t - 1)$ and $f_j(t) = f_i(t - 1) \circ R_{ij}(t, t - l)$ where 'o' is the max-min composition, then $F(t)$ is said to be caused by $F(t - 1)$ only. Denote this as $f_i(t - 1) \rightarrow f_j(t)$ Or equivalently $F(t - 1) \rightarrow F(t)$.

In [2, 3], Song and Chissom proposed the method which use fuzzy time series to forecast time series. Based upon their works, there are many studies focus on this field.

2.2 Some Basis Concepts of Hedge Algebras

"In the HA approach, it seems to be essential that the fuzziness measure of words of a variable, which is a quantitative characteristic expressing an essential and key semantic aspect of the fuzzy linguistic information, does play a centric role in the determination of other quantitative characteristics of words, such as the fuzziness intervals of words, the similarity intervals and the semantically quantifying mappings (or the numeric semantics of) words, when providing the values the fuzziness parameters of the variable. In summary, this approach is developed based on a convincing logical and mathematical foundation, as the inherent word semantics and its fuzziness are defined and formalized in an axiomatization manner" [14].

In this section, we briefly introduce some basis concepts in HA, these concepts are employed as basis to build our proposed method. HA are created by Ho Cat Nguyen et al. in 1990. This theory is a new approach to quantify the linguistic terms differing from the fuzzy set approach. The HA denoted by $AX = (X, G, C, H, \leq)$, where, $G = \{c^+, c^-\}$ is the set of primary generators, in which c^+ and c^- are, respectively, the negative primary term and the positive one of a linguistic variable X, C = {0, 1, W} a set of constants, which are distinguished with elements in X, H is the set of hedges, " $\leq$ " is a semantically ordering relation on X. For each $x \in$ X in HA, H(x) is the set of hedge u∈X that generated from x by applying the hedges of H and denoted $u = h_n \ldots h_1 x$, with $h_n, \ldots, h_1 \in$ H. $H = H^+ \cup H^-$, in which H^- is the set of all negative hedges and H^+ is the set of all positive ones of X. The positive hedges increase semantic tendency and vise versa with negative hedges. Without loss of generality, it can be assumed that

$$H^- = \{h_{-1} < h_{-2} < \ldots < h_{-q}\} \text{ and } H^+ = \{h_1 < h_2 < \ldots < h_p\}.$$

If X and H are linearly ordered sets, then $AX = (X, G, C, H, \leq)$ is called linear hedge algebra, furthermore, if AX is equipped with additional operations $\sum$ and Φ that are, respectively, infimum and supremum of H(x), then it is called complete linear hedge algebra (ClinHA) and denoted $AX = (X, G, C, H, \Sigma, \Phi, \leq)$.

Complete linear hedge algebra (ClinHA) There are also following important concepts and properties are present in [12].

- Fuzziness interval of terms in X and its properties.
- Semantically quantifying mapping $\upsilon: X \to [0, 1]$ of AX and its identification.
- Function Sign: $X \to \{-1, 0, 1\}$ is a mapping which is defined recursively.

It is user's Linguistic Frame of Cognitive and is basis of calculations on the word makes the calculation method are simple and accurate.

Here we just add two properties related to (ClinHA) which have two factors (one negative and one positive), i.e.

$$\mathbf{H = H - \cup H +}; \; \mathbf{H- = \{h - 1\}}, \; \mathbf{H+ = \{h + 1\}}.$$

Definition 1. [12] Given AX2 $k \geq 1$ the similar fuzzy space of set X (k) denoted $\zeta_{(k)}$ is a set of similar fuzzy space of all grades from $X_{(k)}$ for $\forall x \in X_{(k)}$, $\Im g(x) \in \zeta_{(k)}, g + l(x) = k$ unchanged i.e., $\forall x \in X_{(k)}$, $\Im g(x)$ made up of the same fuzzy space of level k* and $\zeta_{(k)}$ is a partition of [0, 1]. (See the Fig. 1).

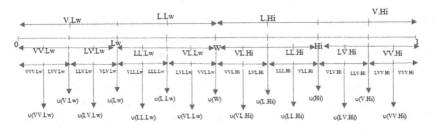

Partition [0,1] by the similar fuzziness iterval sets of the Hedge algebras
With G = {C⁻ = Low(Lw); C⁺ = Hight(Hi)}; H=H⁺∪H⁻ ; H⁻ = {Litle(L)}; H⁺ ={Very(V)}

Fig. 1. Shown partition [0, 1] by the similar fuzziness interval sets of the Hedge algebras)

Definition 2. [12] Give AX^2, 1, $k \geq 1$, $\forall x \in X_{(k)}$ identify the similar fuzzy space $\Im g(x) \in \zeta_{(k)}$ definition of the compatibility level $g = k + 2 - l(x)$ of quantitative value v for Grade x to be a mapping S_g: [0,1] x X $\rightarrow$[0,1]: determined based on the distance from v to $\upsilon(x)$ and two similar fuzzy space close to $\Im g(x)$ as follows

$$S_g(v, x) = max\left(min\left(\frac{v - \upsilon(x)}{\upsilon(x) - \upsilon(y)}, \frac{\upsilon(x) - v}{\upsilon(z) - \upsilon(x)} \right), 0 \right) \qquad (1)$$

Where y, z are two grades defining two similar fuzzy space neighbors left and right of $\Im g(x)$. (See the Fig. 2).

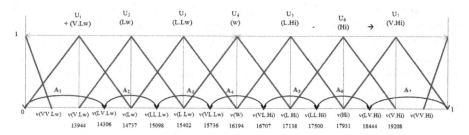

Fig. 2. Shown identify the similar fuzzy space $\Im g(x) \in \zeta_{(k)}$. Where Ai are similar fuzzy intervals and U_i are These are triangular fuzzy sets that represent their membership level function according to expression (1)

3 Proposed Method

3.1 Calculations on the Language Value Apply to the Forecast

In Fig. 2 we have triangular fuzzy sets: Here the set of 3 linguistic values for example the very little low-denominated (VL.Lw) are the vertices of the triangle.

$0\upsilon := (0, 0, \upsilon(VV.Lw))$; $1\upsilon := (\upsilon(VV.Hi), 1, 1)$.
$U1 := (0, \upsilon(V.Lw), \upsilon(Lw))$
$U2 := (\upsilon(V.Lw), \upsilon(Lw), \upsilon(L.Lw))$;
$U3 := (\upsilon(Lw), \upsilon(L, Lw), \upsilon(W))$;
$U4 := (\upsilon(L.Lw), \upsilon(W), \upsilon(L.Hi))$;
$U5 := (\upsilon(W), \upsilon(L.Hi), \upsilon(Hi))$;
$U6 := (\upsilon(L.Hi), \upsilon(Hi), \upsilon(V.Hi))$;
$U7 := (\upsilon(Hi), \upsilon(V.Hi), 1)$;

They are member functions representing the following similar fuzzy intervals, where in the order U1 corresponds to A1 and ...... U7 corresponds to A7 Here the set of 3 linguistic in order from left to right only the left end, the semantic core, and the right end of a similarity Interval for semantic.

$A1 := [0, \upsilon(V.Lw), \upsilon(LV.Lw)]$
$A2 := [\upsilon(LV.Lw), \upsilon(Lw), \upsilon(LL.Lw)];$
$A3 := [\upsilon(LL.Lw), \upsilon(L, Lw), \upsilon(VL.Lw)];$
$A4 := [\upsilon(VL.Lw), \upsilon(W), \upsilon(VL.Hi)];$
$A5 := [\upsilon(VL.Hi), \upsilon(L.Hi), \upsilon(LL.Hi)];$
$A6 := [\upsilon(LL.Hi), \upsilon(Hi), \upsilon(LV.Hi)];$
$A7 := [\upsilon(LV.Hi), \upsilon(V, Hi), 1];$

3.1.1 For Similar Fuzzy Space and Similar Fuzziness Interval

According to Definition 1. [12], Definition 2. [12] and on Fig. 2 Show: $0_U,, U_1,.......$
$U_7, 1_U$ are fuzzy triangular sets created Similar fuzzy space of elements {Very Low(V. Low), Low(Lw), LitleLow(L.Lw), W, LitleHigh(L.Hi), High(Hi), VeryHigh(V.Hi)}, It is also the membership function in the order of similar fuzziness interval $A_1, ... A_7$ In that $A_2 := ([\upsilon(LV.Lw), \upsilon(Lw), \upsilon(LL.Lw)]) \upsilon(LV.Lw), \upsilon(LL.Lw))$, are the left and right border of the linguistic value Low and $\upsilon(Lw)$ is semantically quantifying value. This means that all elements of this interval are similar to Low in the degree of acceptance. Mapping $S_g: [0,1] \times X \rightarrow [0,1]$ determined based on the distance from v to $\upsilon(x)$ and two similar fuzzy space close to $\Im g(x)$ as follows:

$$S_g(v, x) = max\left(min\left(\frac{v - \upsilon(x)}{\upsilon(x) - \upsilon(y)}, \frac{\upsilon(x) - v}{\upsilon(z) - \upsilon(x)}\right), 0\right) \quad (2)$$

Where y, z are two grades defining two similar fuzzy space neighbors left and right of x. This is membership function of similar fuzzy interval A_i (i = 1, ... 7). Easy to deduce that: if $v < \upsilon(x)$ then

$$S_g(v, x) = \frac{v - \upsilon()}{\upsilon(x) - \upsilon(y)}$$

if $v = \upsilon(x)$ then $S_g(v, x) = 1;$

if $v > \upsilon(x)$ then $S_g(v, x) = \frac{\upsilon(x)-}{\upsilon(z)-\upsilon(X)}$

In [15] we have clearly stated how to build a HA that matches the context of the problem. In this section we introduce additional expressions for calculating linguistic values according to two HA parameters. This works for problem solving. More importantly, it solves the problem by using the neural network method or the Ge.

3.1.2 Specifying Some Expressions

In Part F.2.1 have $\upsilon(W) = \theta = fm(\bar{c})$, $fm(c+) = 1 - \theta$, $\upsilon(c-) = \theta - \alpha fm(c-) = \beta fm(c-)$, $\upsilon(c+) = \theta + \alpha fm(c+)$, $fm(hx) = \mu(h)fm(x)$, $H+ = \{Very (V)\}$, $H- = \{Little(L)\}$, $\mu(V) = \beta$, $\mu(L) = \alpha$, $\alpha + \beta = 1 \rightarrow \alpha = 1 - \beta$ $fm(VL.Lw) = fm(LV.Lw) = \mu(V)\mu(L)fm(Lw)$, form $(Lw) = \theta\beta)$, $(W) = \theta$, $(Hi) = 1 - (1 - \theta)\beta$ and $fm(VL.Lw) = fm(LV.Lw) = \mu(V) \mu(L)fm(Lw)$, We calculate the number of fuzzy intervals fm(x) listed in the table below: if $\theta = 0.4563 = \mu(V) = 1 - \mu(L)$ add another lookup at Fig. 1 and results of the table above we have (Table 1):

Table 1. The value of the fuzzy spaces for the calculation.

fm(V. Lw)	fm(L. Lw)	fm(VL. Lw)	fm(LL. Lw)	fm(VV. Lw)	fm(V. Hi)	fm(L. Hi)	fm(VL. Hi)	fm(LL. Hi)	fm(VV. Hi)
0.20820	0.24801	0.13489	0.13488	0.09500	0.24801	0.29561	0.13489	0.16072	0.11320

$$\upsilon(\text{LL.Lw}) = \upsilon(\text{Lw}) + fm(\text{VLL.Lw}) = \beta * \theta + \mu(L) * fm(\text{LL.Lw})$$
$$= (0.4563)^2 + (1 - 0.4563) * 0.16072 = 0.26976$$

Similarly, for cases we have the numerical result in Fig. 2.

"There is an induced about the trend change in the forecasting in the discourse space into the space of [0, 1] where there is a trend change to the quantitative semantics value due to the impact on the terms of the hedges. That is the basic to we construct the mathematics model for forecasting time series by (HA) approach" [15]. We want to say about $\mu(h)$, the single operator impact on the operand (language value) generate new semantics for it - to create an upward or downward direction of the operand, corresponding to the change of time series at a time - is an important factor for the time series forecasting.

"According to the context, semantics of $\bar{F}(t)$ denotes number of the enrollment students at the medium level and W is the normalization value of $\bar{F}(t)$, they are calculated according formulas": [16]

$$\bar{F}(t) = \frac{1}{n} \sum_{i=1}^{n} x_i \qquad (3)$$

$$W = \frac{\bar{F}(t) - Min.F(t)}{Max.F(t) - Min.F(t)} \qquad (4)$$

Determining the two parameters of the HA through the analysis of the relationship of historical values in the properties:

- The average value - the boundary between the main semantic value: what is "high" and what is "low".
- Change of each value "Continue to increase or decrease" or "change in the opposite direction". As a bridge between the two semantics: "inherent" and "represented by fuzzy set imposed by the user" of each word.

On that basis, we propose the following new time series forecasting algorithm. The algorithm emphasizes semantics generated by the problematic context and focuses on two steps:

- Adjust spacing partitioning the universe of discourse.
- Set up a logical relationship group.

3.2   Forecasting Algorithm (Algorithm Based on Semantics)

- For convenience to present proposed method, we name the linguistic values of fuzzy time series as the variables A_i with $i \in N$. $Rev\upsilon(x)$ and $Rev\, f_m(x)$ are the reversed mapping of $\upsilon(x)$ and $f_m(x)$, respectively, from $[0, 1]$ to the universe of discourse of fuzzy time series U. Denote I_k, on U, is the interval corresponding to A_k.
- 7 basic language values: Very Low (V.Low), Low, L.Low, W, Little High(L.Hi), Hi, V.Hi.

Step 1: Constructing the Hedge Algebra (HA)

Constructing the Hedge algebra (HA) is consistent with the context of the forecasting problem by determining the fuzzy parameters set of HA based on the historical values relationship analysis of the time series. Specifically

- Determine the U, the universe of discourse of fuzzy time series $F(t)$.
   $U = [\min(F(t)) - D_1, \max(F(t)) + D_2]$, where D_1 and D_2 are proper positive numbers.

$$\bar{F}(t) = \frac{1}{n}\sum\nolimits_{i=1}^{n} x_i$$

$$W = \frac{\bar{F}(t) - Min.F(t)}{Max.F(t) - Min.F(t)}$$

with $x_i (1 \leq i \leq n)$ are historical values

$$\mu(h) = \frac{2\bar{S}}{(S^+ + S^-)}$$

If $S^+ \geq S^-$ then $h := h_{+1}$ else $h := h_{-1}$.

Step 2: Method for Partitioning the Universe of Discourse, Fuzzifying Historical Data of Time Series and Mining Fuzzy Relationships from Fuzzy Time Series

- Based on the explanation in Fig. 2, constructing 7 similar fuzzy intervals correspond to 7 basic language values to partitioning the universe of discourse
- Based upon the distribution of historical values, put them into the corresponding linguistic term fuzziness interval for fuzzifying historical data of time series.
- Adjust the position of the historical values near the boundaries of the divisors intervals to reach the optimal devise method.
- The logical relation group is established as follows for mining fuzzy relationships from fuzzy time series.

In $A_j \rightarrow A_i$ Who:

- if j > i then the group is forecasting down,
- if j = i then the group forecasting is equal,
- if j < i then the group is forecasting increase.

Step 3: Compute the Forecasting Values

Assume Set the group of fuzzy logical relationships is established in the Step 2 having the same left side:

$A_t \rightarrow A_u(m) \cdots A_v(n), m, \ldots, n$ are the number of iterations of fuzzy logical relationship $A_t \rightarrow A_u$ and $A_t \rightarrow A_v$.

- Suppose that the value of the time series at $(t-1)$ have known according to above logical relationship groups if $f(t)$ belong to $Revfm(At)$, then
- The forecasting value at t is

$$\frac{m * Rer\, \upsilon(Au) + \cdots n * Rer\, \upsilon(Av)}{m + \cdots.. n}$$

Table 2. Shown left, right and Rve. of A_i.

A_i	Left and right of A_i	Rve(A_i)
A_1	[0, 14096]	13665
A_2	[14096, 15832]	14888
A_3	[15832, 16194]	15832
A_4	[16194, 16625]	16194
A_5	[16625, 17750]	17138
A_6	[17750, 18694]	18263
A_7	[18694, 20000]	19208

4 Experiment Result and Comment

4.1 Enrollment Forecasting

The proposed approach is applied to forecast the enrollments at the University of Alabama from year 1971 to 1992 (n = 22). The result will then be compared with different published methods. To measure the accuracy of the forecasting methods, the following metrics are used for comparison that Defined in [15]

RMSE: The Root Mean Square Error;
NE(%): The Numerical Error (NE) percentage
NEE(%): The Normalized Numerical Error (NNE) percentage

According to [15] we have $\upsilon(W) = \theta = 0.4563$ and $\mu(V) = \beta = 0.4563$ are parameter values use to constructing 7 similar fuzzy intervals for partitioning the universe of discourse are illustrated in Fig. 2.

However, in this division at A4 there are two levels of value between the "low" and the "high" as the "elements of meaning" so that the semantic difference in this range is greater than the difference in numeric value. Therefore, these values must be adjusted accordingly. After adjusting the reasonable divisions we have (VL.Lw replace L.Low).

Table 3. Shown left, right and Rve. of A_i

A_i	Left and right of A_i	$Rve(A_i)$
A_1	[0, 14096]	13665
A_2	[14096, 15832]	14888
A_3	[15832, 16194]	15832
A_4	[16194,16625]	16194
A_5	[16625, 17750]	17138
A_6	[17750, 18694]	18263
A_7	[18694, 20000]	19208

The following is the result of our statistics together with the results of other authors for comparison. The details are shown in Table 4 below.

Table 4. Shown metrics of results of the methods

Metrics	Author			
	Wang et al. 14	Chen et al. 14	Lu et al. 15	Our approach
RMSE	506.0	486.3	445.2	39.6
NE (%)	2.68	2.52	2.30	1.79
NEE (%)	6.93	6.43	5.88	4.56

4.2 Forecasting AITEX Index

In this section, our proposed method is compared to [13]. Chen et al. [13] suggested a method consisting of 6 steps to calculate the forecast TAIEX Index, these steps are listed below:

Propose a method to fuzzify the historical training data of TAIEX into fuzzy sets to from fuzzy logical relationships.

Grouped the logical relationships into fuzzy logical relationship groups (FLRGs) based on the fuzzy variations of secondary factor.

Evaluate the leverage of the fuzzy variations between the main factor and the secondary factor to construct fuzzy variation groups.

Get the statistics of the fuzzy variations appearing in each fuzzy variation group.

Calculate the weight of the statistics of the fuzzy variations appearing in each fuzzy variation group, respectively.

Use the weights of the statistics of the fuzzy variations appearing in the fuzzy variation groups and the FLRGs to perform the forecasting the daily TAIEX.

Chen et al. [13] have applied their proposed method on the experimental data sets TAIEX Index of November and December 2004. The data set consists of 44 items. In the first step, the historical training data of TAIEX is fuzzified into 9 fuzzy sets (h = 9 form A1 to A9), the accuracy metrics of the result are

RSME = 56.86
NE(%) = 0.8
NNE(%) = 12.44.

Table 5. Shown the detailed results of the proposed method and the preceding results.

Year	With 7 split points (h = 7)							
	Actual enrollment	Chen et al. 96	Wang et al. 13	Wang et al. 14	Chen et al. 13	Lu15 et al. 15	Our approach	
							At. [15]	Proposed method
1972	13563	14000	13486	13944	14347	14279	14003	13665
1973	13867	14000	14156	13944	14347	14279	14003	13665
1974	14696	14000	15215	13944	14347	14279	14003	14888
1975	15460	15500	15906	15328	15550	15392	15510	14888
1976	15311	16000	15906	15753	15550	15392	15510	14888
1977	15603	16000	15906	15753	15550	15392	15510	14888
1978	15861	16000	15906	15753	15550	16467	15510	15832
1979	16807	16000	16559	16279	16290	16467	17138	17138
1980	16919	16833	16559	17270	17169	17161	17186	17138
1981	16388	16833	16559	17270	17169	17161	17186	16194
1982	15433	16833	16559	16279	16209	14916	15402	14888
1983	15497	16000	15906	15753	15550	15392	15510	14888
1984	15145	16000	15906	15753	15550	15392	15510	14888
1985	15163	16000	15906	15753	15550	15392	15510	14888
1986	15984	16000	15906	15753	15550	15470	15510	15832
1987	16859	16000	16559	16279	16290	16467	17138	17138
1988	18150	16833	16559	17270	17169	17161	17186	18263
1989	18970	19000	19451	19466	18907	19257	19207	19208
1990	19328	19000	18808	18933	18907	19257	19207	19208
1991	19337	19000	18808	18933	18907	19257	19207	19208
1992	18876	19000	18808	18933	18907	19257	19207	19208
	RMSE	638.4	578.3	506.0	486.3	445.2	400.4	339.6
	NE (%)	3.11	2.76	2.68	2.52	2.30	1.95	1.79
	NNE (%)	7.94	7.17	6.93	6.43	5.88	4.85	4.56

Our proposed method is applied to the same TAIEX datasets. The process is as follows According to Algorithm Based on semantics. According to [15] we have $\upsilon(W) = \theta = 0.52$ and $\mu(V) = \beta = 0.29$ are parameter values use to constructing 7 similar fuzzy intervals for partitioning the universe of discourse. Then perform the remaining steps of the algorithm. Forecast results according to the metrics as shown below with previous results for Compare. The details are shown in Table 6 below (Table 7).

Table 6. Shown Metrics of results of the methods

Metrics	Chen's	Our in [1, 6]	Proposed method
RMSE	56.86	48.02	26.88
NE(%)	0.80	0.5	0.37
NEE(%)	12.44	9.17	0.059

Table 7. Shown the detailed results of the proposed.

Date	Actual index	Chen' forecasted index	Our forecasted index at [15]	Our proposed method
		h = 9	h = 9	h = 7
2/11/2004	5759.61	5674.81	5743	
3/11/2004	5862.85	5768.14	5852	5886
4/11/2004	5860.73	5854.81	5876.04	5886
5/11/2004	5931.31	5908.26	5876.04	5934
8/11/2004	5937.46	5934.81	5912.05	5934
9/11/2004	5945.2	5943.81	5912.05	5934
10/11/2004	5948.49	5934.81	5912.05	5978
11/11/2004	5874.52	5937.12	5912.05	5886
12/11/2004	5917.16	5908.26	5919.27	5934
15/11/2004	5906.69	5934.81	5919.27	5934
16/12/2004	5910.85	5934.81	5919.27	5934
17/11/2004	6028.68	5937.12	5919.27	5978
18/11/2004	6049.49	6068.14	5979.18	5978
19/11/2004	6026.55	6068.14	5979.18	5978
22/11/2004	5838.42	5976.47	5979.18	5886
23/11/2004	5851.1	5854.81	5876.04	5886
24/11/2004	5911.31	5934.85	5876.04	5934
25/11/2004	5855.24	5934.81	5919.27	5886
26/11/2004	5778.65	5854.81	5876.04	5768
29/11/2004	5785.26	5762.12	5797.89	5768
30/11/2004	5844.76	5762.12	5852	5886
1/12/2004	5798.62	5834.85	5876.04	5768
2/12/2004	5867.95	5803.26	5797.89	5886
3/12/2004	5893.27	5854.81	5876.04	5886
6/12/2004	5919.17	5854.81	5919.27	5934
7/12/2004	5925.28	5937.12	5912.05	5934
8/12/2004	5892.51	5876.47	5912.05	5886
9/12/2004	5913.97	5854.81	5919.27	5934
10/12/2004	5911.63	5934.81	5919.27	5934
13/12/2004	5878.89	5937.12	5919.27	5886
14/12/2004	5909.65	5854.81	5919.27	5934

(*continued*)

Table 7. (*continued*)

Date	Actual index	Chen' forecasted index	Our forecasted index at [15]	Our proposed method
		h = 9	h = 9	h = 7
15/12/2004	6002.58	5934.81	5919.27	5978
16/12/2004	6019.23	6068.14	5979.18	5978
17/12/2004	6009.32	6062.12	5979.18	5978
20/12/2004	5985.94	6062.12	5979.18	5978
21/12/2004	5987.85	5937.12	5979.18	5978
22/12/2004	6001.52	5934.81	5979.18	5978
23/12/2004	5997.67	6068.14	5979.18	5978
24/12/2004	6019.42	5934.81	5979.18	5978
27/12/2004	5985.94	6068.14	5979.18	5978
28/12/2004	6000.57	5937.12	5979.18	5978
29/12/2004	6088.49	6068.14	5979.18	6087
30/12/2004	6100.86	6062.12	6119.36	6087
31/12/2004	6139.69	6137.12	6143.57	6144
RSME		56.86	48.02	26.88
NE (%)		0.80	0.59	0.37
NNE (%)		12.44	9.17	0.059

4.3 Comment

The First of all, this proposed method is an improvement of the method already in [15], so it has advantages over the methods of the previously published authors, we briefly recall: We compare our approach with the method Wei Lu et al. published in [11] to illustrate our superior efficiency. Conclusion of his methodological advantages of semantic assurance due to the context of Wei Lu stated "Interval information granules are always run through the whole process of finding optimal intervals, which make the partitioned intervals carry apparent semantics" [11]. As so, in the method of Wei Lu also pay attention to the balance between accuracy and semantics which is suitable with context in the calculation that is why we compare it with our approach. Our comparison focuses on two aspects: the calculation convenience and the forecasting accuracy.

- First, the convenience in calculations: only with the simple calculations using Method for partitioning the universe of discourse and Algorithm for forecasting, we have obtained results about group of logical relationship like the results from Lu [11]. However, our calculation is much simpler than theirs as shown in Table 2. [15]
- Second, the forecasting accuracy: Table 3. Shows our proposed method is about 10% better in term of accuracy (all metrics) compared to Lu et al. approach [11].

[15] The Second, As its name implies, semantic-based algorithms for performing two important steps are for partitioning the universe of discourse and data mining through logical relational grouping. Thus, a more convenient and efficient method of adjusting the divide interval and predicting more accurately than similar functional methods show in [15] (Table 5).

In terms of accuracy, the greater the number of divisions, the higher the accuracy. In both empirical problems forecasting enrollments at the University of Alabama forecasting (forecasting enrollments) and forecasting TAIEX Index (forecasting TAIEX) we used the divisor of 7 and compared the results of other methods with the number of divisions equal (7 for forecasting enrollments) and larger (9 for forecasting TAIEX). The accuracy of the method proposed (for metrics RMSE: The Root Mean Square Error) - for the forecasting enrollments problem was 20.23% higher than that of Lu and 15.25% higher than our results at [15] - for the forecasting TAIEX problem The accuracy of the proposed approach to the problem was 52.72% higher than that of Chen and 36.12% higher than our results at [15]. The numbers are very impressive and very convincing demonstrates the superiority of the accuracy of the proposed method! (Figs. 3 and 4).

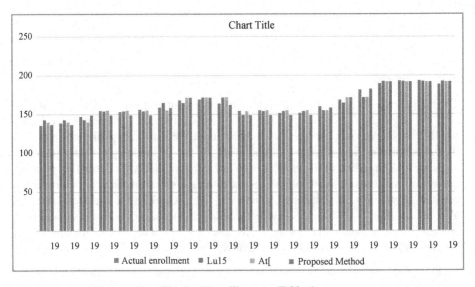

Fig. 3. Chart illustrates Table 4

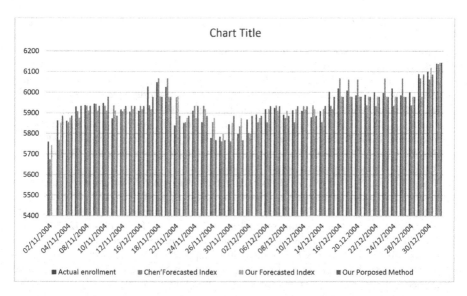

Fig. 4. Chart illustrates Table 6

5   Conclusion

In this approach, each linguistic domain can be considered as a hedge algebra (HA for short) and based on the structure of HAs, a notion of fuzziness measure of linguistic hedges and terms can be defined. It is highlights in proposed method:

Analyze the data of forecasting problem, special for historical values and their relationship to determine the fuzzy parameter set of hedge algebras.

Thereby the context-semantic of terms has preserved in the calculation. which concentrated on key steps: partitioning the universe of discourse of time series into a collection of intervals, mining fuzzy relationships from fuzzy time series,

Forecasting outputs it do not have to choose fuzzy sets for linguistics terms and defuzzifying output, which are the required steps in method based on fuzzy set theory.

This is subjective imposition and so it is the reason for separating the two types of semantics mentioned above. So this algorithm is the process of determining the parameters of hedge algebra. Naturally, the next research problem is to optimize the process. We continue to study this problem with Ge algorithm and Neuron network.

References

1. Song, Q., Chissom, B.S.: Fuzzy time series and its models. Fuzzy Sets Syst. **54**(3), 269–277 (1993)
2. Song, Q., Chissom, B.S.: Forecasting enrollments with fuzzy time series part I. Fuzzy Sets Syst. **54**(1), 1–9 (1993)
3. Song, Q., Chissom, B.S.: Forecasting enrollments with fuzzy time series part II. Fuzzy Sets Syst. **62**(1), 1–8 (1994)

4. Chen, S.-M.: Forecasting enrollments based on fuzzy time series. Fuzzy Sets Syst. **81**(3), 311–319 (1996)
5. Huarng, K.: Effective lengths of intervals to improve forecasting in fuzzy time series. Fuzzy Sets Syst. **123**(3), 387–394 (2001)
6. Jilani, T.A., Burney, S.M.A., Ardil, C.: Fuzzy metric approach for fuzzy time series forecasting based on frequency density based partitioning. World Acad. Sci. Eng. Technol. Int. J. Comput. Electr. Autom. Control Inf. Eng. **4**(7), 1194–1199 (2007)
7. Huarng, K., Yu, T.H.-K.: Ratio-based lengths of intervals to improve fuzzy time series forecasting. IEEE Trans. Syst. Man Cybern. Part B (Cybern.) **36**(2), 328–340 (2006)
8. Bas, E., Uslu, V.R., Yolcu, U., Egrioglu, E.: A modified genetic algorithm for forecasting fuzzy time series. Appl. Intell. **41**(2), 453–463 (2014)
9. Wang, L., Liu, X., Pedrycz, W.: Effective intervals determined by information granules to improve forecasting in fuzzy time series. Expert Syst. Appl. **40**(14), 5673–5679 (2013)
10. Wang, L., Liu, X., Pedrycz, W., Shao, Y.: Determination of temporal information granules to improve forecasting in fuzzy time series. Expert Syst. Appl. **41**(6), 3134–3142 (2014)
11. Wei, L., Chen, X., Pedrycz, W., Liu, X., Yang, J.: Using interval information granules to improve forecasting in fuzzy time series. Int. J. Approx. Reason. **57**, 1–18 (2015)
12. Ho, N.C., Son, T.T. and Long, D.T.: Hedge algebras with limited number of hedges and applied to fuzzy classification problems. J. Sci. Technol. **48**(5) (2012)
13. Chen, S.-M., Chen, C.-D.: Taiex forecasting based on fuzzy time series and fuzzy variation groups. IEEE Trans. Fuzzy Syst. **19**(1), 1–12 (2011)
14. Nguyen, C.H., Hoang, V.T., Nguyen, V.L.: A discussion on interpretability of linguistic rule based systems and its application to solve regression problems. Knowl.-Based Syst. **88**, 107–133 (2015)
15. Vu, M.L., Vu, H.D., Pham, T.Y.: The context-aware calculating method in language environment based on hedge algebras approach to improve result of forecasting time series. In: Cong Vinh, P., Ha Huy Cuong, N., Vassev, E. (eds.) ICCASA/ICTCC-2017. LNICST, vol. 217, pp. 110–123. Springer, Cham (2018). https://doi.org/10.1007/978-3-319-77818-1_11

ICTCC 2019

Post-quantum Commutative Encryption Algorithm

Dmitriy N. Moldovyan[1], Alexandr A. Moldovyan[1], Han Ngoc Phieu[2], and Minh Hieu Nguyen[2(✉)]

[1] Laboratory of Cybersecurity and Post-quantum Cryptosystems,
St. Petersburg Institute for Informatics and Automation of the
Russian Academy of Sciences (SPIIRAS), 39, 14 Liniya, St. Petersburg, Russia
mdn.spectr@mail.ru, maal305@yandex.ru
[2] Faculty of Electronics and Telecommunications,
Academy of Cryptography Techniques, 141 Chien Thang, Tan Trieu,
Thanh Tri, Hanoi, Vietnam
phieungochan@gmail.com, hieuminhmta@gmail.com

Abstract. It is considered an extended notion of the commutativity of the encryption. Using the computational difficulty of the hidden discrete logarithm problem, a new method and post-quantum probabilistic algorithm for commutative encryption are proposed. The finite non-commutative associative algebra containing a large set of the global left-sided unites is used as the algebraic carrier of the proposed method and probabilistic commutative cipher. The latter is secure to the known-plaintext attack and, therefore, efficient to implement on its base a post-quantum no-key encryption protocol. Main properties of the algebraic carrier, which are used in the commutative encryption method, are described.

Keywords: Post-quantum cryptography · Commutative probabilistic encryption · No-key protocol · Hidden logarithm problem · Finite non-commutative algebra · Associative algebra

1 Introduction

Currently the development of the practical post-quantum public-key cryptoschemes attracts significant attention of the cryptographic community [1, 2]. A cryptoscheme is called post-quantum, if it performs efficiently on ordinary computers and resists attacks with using hypothetic quantum computers (quantum attacks). Post-quantum public-key algorithms and protocols are to be based on some computationally difficult problems that are different from the factorization problem (FP) and discrete logarithm problem (DLP), since there are known polynomial in time algorithms for solving both the FP and the DLP [3, 4].

Many different post-quantum public-key algorithms and protocols have been designed and proposed as candidates for post-quantum public-key standards in frame of the world competition announced by NIST in the end of 2016 [2]. One should mention that the problem of providing post-quantum security relates also to the commutative

P. C. Vinh and A. Rakib (Eds.): ICCASA 2019/ICTCC 2019, LNICST 298, pp. 205–214, 2019.
https://doi.org/10.1007/978-3-030-34365-1_16

encryption algorithms possessing security to the known-plaintext attacks. Commutative ciphers possessing such property represent the base primitive of the no-key encryption protocols that are attractive for different practical applications. Development of the post-quantum commutative encryption algorithms is an open problem that is considered only in few papers. An interesting approach to the development of the post-quantum commutative cipher is the use of the computational difficulty of the hidden discrete logarithm problem (HDLP) [5]. However, the form of the HDLP defined in the finite algebra of quaternions and introduced in [5] can be reduced to the ordinary DLP in a finite field [6].

In the present paper it is introduced a new form of the HDLP that prevents the reductionist method developed in [6]. The paper is organized as follows. Section 2 presents the base notion connected with the HDLP. Section 3 introduces the 4-dimensional finite non-commutative associative algebra (FNAA) used as algebraic support of the proposed post-quantum commutative encryption method. Section 4 presents the novel interpretation of the notion of commutativity of the encryption and the proposed post-quantum commutative probabilistic encryption algorithm. Section 5 describes the post-quantum no-key encryption protocol based on the introduced commutative encryption algorithm. Final remarks are presented in the concluding Sect. 6.

2 Forms of the Hidden Discrete Logarithm Problem

The DLP consists in solving the equation $Y' = G'^x$ (where G' is the generator of the group and Y' is a group element) in a finite cyclic group relatively the unknown x. The HDLP is set in some m-dimensional FNAA, where $m \geq 4$ is an even number, which contains many different cyclic groups as subsets of the m-dimensional vectors (algebraic elements). The HDLP is defined as selection a base finite cyclic group with the generator G', generation a random integer x, performing the base exponentiation operation G'^x, and mapping one of the values G' and G'^x or both of them, using different map functions (operations) $\varphi(X)$ and $\psi(X)$. For example, (i) the values $Y = \varphi(G'^x)$ and G', (ii) $Y = \varphi(G'^x)$ and $G = \psi(G')$ are given and in each of the last two cases one should compute the value x.

The functions $\varphi(X)$ and $\psi(X)$ are called masking operations. To have possibility to design some public-key protocols and algorithms with the use of the values $Y = \varphi(G'^x)$ and $G = \psi(G')$ as parameters of the cryptoscheme, the masking operations should possess respective properties. The main requirement for the masking function is the mutual commutativity with the base exponentiation operation.

Finite non-commutative associative algebras of different types are very attractive for using them as algebraic supports of the HDLP. Automorphism-map functions and homomorphism-map function defined in some given FNAA can be used as masking operations.

The specific form of the HDLP is determined by the choice of a particular pair of the map functions $\varphi(X)$ and $\psi(X)$.

The known form [5, 7] of the HDLP can be characterized as the case $Y = \varphi(G'^x) = KG'^x K^{-1}$ and $G' = \psi(G')$, where the values K and x are elements of the private key; Y is the public key.

3 Algebraic Support of the Proposed Post-quantum Commutative Cipher

Let us consider a finite m-dimensional vector space defined over the ground finite field $GF(p)$. In the vector space there are defined two operations: (i) addition of vectors and (ii) multiplying a vector by a scalar. If one defines the additional operation (denoted as $\circ$) for multiplying arbitrary two vectors, which is distributive relatively the addition operation, then the considered vector space represents a new algebraic structure called finite m-dimensional algebra. Such complemented finite vector space is called finite algebra. If the multiplication operation is non-commutative and associative, then the algebra is FNAA. Suppose $\mathbf{e}_0, \mathbf{e}_1, \ldots, \mathbf{e}_{m-1}$ are the basis vectors. The vector A is denoted in the following two forms: $A = (a_0, a_1, \ldots, a_{m-1})$ and $A = a_0\mathbf{e}_0 + a_1\mathbf{e}_1 + \ldots + a_{m-1}\mathbf{e}_{m-1}$, where $a_0, a_1, \ldots, a_{m-1} \in GF(p)$.

Usually the multiplication operation of two vectors A and $B = \sum_{j=0}^{m-1} b_j\mathbf{e}_j$ is defined with the formula

$$A \circ B = \sum_{i}^{m-1}\sum_{j}^{m-1} a_ib_j(\mathbf{e}_i \circ \mathbf{e}_j),$$

where products of all pairs of basis vectors $\mathbf{e}_i \circ \mathbf{e}_j$ are to be substituted by a single-component vector $\lambda\mathbf{e}_k$, where $\lambda \in GF(p)$ is the structural constant, indicated in the so called basis vector multiplication table (BVMT). The intersection of the ith row and jth column defines the cell indicating the value of the product $\mathbf{e}_i \circ \mathbf{e}_j$.

For defining the HDLP of a new type we have set the BVMT describing the vector multiplication operation in the finite 4-dimensional vector space, which is presented as Table 1. This BVMT defines the 4-dimensional FNAA, containing p^2 different global left-sided units. To derive the formula describing the all such units one should solve the following vector equation:

$$X \circ A = A, \tag{1}$$

where $A = (a_0, a_1, a_2, a_3)$ is a fixed 4-dimensional vector and $X = (x_0, x_1, x_2, x_3)$ is the unknown. Using Table 1 one can reduce the vector Eq. (1) to the following two systems of two linear equations:

$$\begin{cases} (x_1 + x_2)a_0 + (x_0 + x_3)a_2 = a_0; \\ \lambda(x_0 + x_3)a_0 + (x_1 + x_2)a_2 = a_2; \end{cases} \tag{2}$$

$$\begin{cases} (x_1 + x_2)a_1 + \lambda(x_0 + x_3)a_3 = a_1; \\ (x_0 + x_3)a_1 + (x_1 + x_2)a_3 = a_3. \end{cases} \tag{3}$$

Table 1. Defining the multiplication operation in the 4-dimensional vector space (λ is quadratic non-residue in $GF(p)$)

$\circ$	e_0	e_1	e_2	e_3
e_0	λe_2	e_3	e_0	λe_1
e_1	e_0	e_1	e_2	e_3
e_2	e_0	e_1	e_2	e_3
e_3	λe_2	e_3	e_0	λe_1

Performing the variable substitution $u_1 = x_1 + x_2$ and $u_2 = x_0 + x_3$ one can establish that for all vectors A in the considered FNAA the set of the vectors L described with the formula

$$L = (l_0, l_1, l_2, l_3) = (x_0, x_1, 1 - x_1, -x_0), \tag{4}$$

where $x_0, x_1 = 0, 1, \dots p - 1$, represents solutions of the Eq. (1), i.e., each of the p^2 different values L is the global left-sided unit of the algebra (global means that the unit acts on each element of the algebra).

The right-sided units relating to some vector A can be computed from the vector equation

$$A \circ X = A \tag{5}$$

that can be reduced to the following two independent systems of two linear equations with the unknowns x_0, x_2 and x_1, x_3 correspondingly:

$$\begin{cases} (a_1 + a_2)x_0 + (a_0 + a_3)x_2 = a_0; \\ \lambda(a_0 + a_3)x_0 + (a_1 + a_2)x_2 = a_2; \end{cases} \tag{6}$$

$$\begin{cases} (a_1 + a_2)x_1 + \lambda(a_0 + a_3)x_3 = a_1; \\ (a_0 + a_3)x_1 + (a_1 + a_2)x_3 = a_3. \end{cases} \tag{7}$$

The systems (6) and (7) have the same main determinant that is equal to

$$\Delta_A = (a_1 + a_2)^2 - \lambda(a_0 + a_3)^2. \tag{8}$$

The value of the structural constant λ is selected from the set of non-residues modulo p (see Table 1), therefore only for p^2 different vectors A', namely, for vectors satisfying the conditions $a_1' = -a_2'$ and $a_1' = -a_3'$ we have $\Delta_{A'} \neq 0$. For all other vectors A we have $\Delta_A \neq 0$. Such vectors we call locally invertible, since for every of them Eq. (5) has one solution that defines unique local right-sided unit $R_A = (r_0, r_1, r_2,$

r_3) related to the vector A. Solving the systems (6) and (7) one can derive the following formulas describing the value R_A:

$$r_0 = \frac{a_0 a_1 - a_2 a_3}{\Delta_A}, \quad r_1 = \frac{a_1 (a_1 + a_2) - \lambda a_3 (a_0 + a_3)}{\Delta_A}, \tag{9}$$

$$r_2 = \frac{a_2 (a_1 + a_2) - \lambda a_0 (a_0 + a_3)}{\Delta_A}, \quad r_3 = \frac{a_2 a_3 - a_0 a_1}{\Delta_A}. \tag{10}$$

One can easily show that the formulas $r_2 = 1 - r_1$ and $r_3 = -r_0$ hold true, i.e., the vector R_A is contained in the set (4). Therefore, actually R_A is the local two-sided unit relating to the vector A. Evidently, the vector R_A is the local two-sided unit relating to the vectors A^i for all natural values i. Let us consider the sequence of the values A, A^2, ..., A^i, ... (generated by the vector A such that $\Delta_A \neq 0$). This sequence is periodic and do not contain the zero element $O = (0, 0, 0, 0)$. Indeed, assumption that for some minimum natural number j we have $A^{j-1} \neq O$ and $A^j = O$ leads to the following (due to the condition $\Delta_A \neq 0$):

$$A \circ A^{j-1} = O \Rightarrow A^{j-1} = O,$$

Proposition 1. Suppose for some vector A we have $\Delta_A \neq 0$. Then for some minimum natural number ω_A the condition $A^{\omega_A} = R_A$ holds true and the set of the vectors $\{A, A^2, \ldots, A^i, \ldots, A^{\omega_A}\}$ represents a finite cyclic group with the unit element R_A.

Proof. Since the sequence A, A^2, ..., A^i, ... is periodic, for some minimum natural $h > i$ we have $\{A^h = A^i\} \Rightarrow \{A^i \circ A^{h-i} = A^i\} \Rightarrow \{R_{A^i} = A^{h-i}\}$. For the right-sided unit R_A corresponding to the element A we have $\{A^i \circ R_A = A^{i-1} \circ (A \circ R_A) = A^i\} \Rightarrow \{R_{A^i} = R_A\} \Rightarrow \{R_A = A^{h-i}\}$. Thus, we have $R_A = A^{\omega_A}$, where $\omega_A = h - i$. Evidently, the vector R_A acts as two-sided unit on all elements of the set $\{A, A^2, \ldots, A^{\omega_A}\}$, therefore the element $A^{\omega-i}$ is inverses of the element A^i. Taking into account the associativity of the multiplication operation we conclude the set $\{A, A^2, \ldots, A^{\omega_A}\}$ is a finite cyclic group with the unit element equal to R_A. The Proposition 1 is proven.

Proposition 2. Suppose the vector L is a global left-sided unit. Then the map of the FNAA defined by the formula $\varphi_L(X) = X \circ L$, where the vector X takes on all values in the algebra, is a homomorphism.

Proof. For two arbitrary vectors X_1 and X_2 one can get the following:

$$\varphi_L(X_1 \circ X_2) = (X_1 \circ X_2) \circ L = (X_1 \circ L) \circ (X_2 \circ L)$$
$$= \varphi_L(X_1) \circ \varphi_L(X_2);$$
$$\varphi_L(X_1 + X_2) = (X_1 + X_2) \circ L = (X_1 \circ L) + (X_2 \circ L)$$
$$= \varphi_L(X_1) + \varphi_L(X_2).$$

The Proposition 2 is proven.

Proposition 3. Suppose $A \circ B = L$. Then for arbitrary natural number t the equality $A^t \circ B^t = L$ holds true.

Proof. $A^t \circ B^t = A^{t-1} \circ (A \circ B) \circ B^{t-1} = A^{t-1} \circ B^{t-1} = A^{t-2} \circ (A \circ B) \circ B^{t-2} = A^{t-2} \circ B^{t-2} = A \circ B = L'$. The Proposition 3 is proven.

Proposition 4. Suppose $A \circ B = L$. Then the formula $\psi_L = B \circ X \circ A$, where the vector X takes on all values in the considered 4-dimensional FNAA, sets the homomorphism map.

Proof. For two arbitrary 4-dimensional vectors X_1 and X_2 one can get the following:

$$\psi_L(X_1 \circ X_2) = B \circ (X_1 \circ X_2) \circ A = B \circ (X_1 \circ L' \circ X_2) \circ A$$
$$= (B \circ X_1 \circ A) \circ (B \circ X_2 \circ A) = \psi_{L'}(X_1) \circ \psi_{L'}(X_2);$$
$$\psi_L(X_1 + X_2) = B \circ (X_1 + X_2) \circ A = (B \circ X_1 \circ A)$$
$$+ (B \circ X_2 \circ A) = \psi_{L'}(X_1) + \psi_{L'}(X_2).$$

The Proposition 4 is proven.

We will use the homomorphism maps φ_L and ψ_L as masking operations in the post-quantum commutative encryption algorithm described in the next section. Evidently, each of these operations is mutually commutative with the exponentiation operation.

The algebra described in this section suits well as the algebraic support to implement an encryption algorithms based on the HDLP. The considered FNAA contains very large number of the finite cyclic groups having the same value of the order, that is equal to a divisor of the value $p^2 - 1$. Respectively, the order ω_A of some locally invertible vector A is a divisor of the value $p^2 - 1$.

4   Commutative Encryption Algorithm

Some message to be encrypted is represented in the form of the 4-dimensional vector $M = (m_0, m_1, m_2, m_3)$ coordinates of which are elements of the field $GF(p)$, where $p = 2q + 1$ and q is a 256-bit prime number. Probability that $\Delta_M = 0$ is negligible (is equal to p^{-2}), therefore we will consider that the vector M is locally invertible $(\Delta_M \neq 0)$. Like in the Pohlig-Hellman exponentiation cipher [8], the encryption/decryption key is generated as the triple of non-negative numbers (e, d, t) such that $ed \equiv 1 \mod p^2 - 1$. Besides the used FNAA, two vectors A and B such that $A \circ B = L_0$, where L_0 is some given global left-sided unit, are specified as common parameters of the proposed post-quantum cipher.

The encryption is performed as computation of two vectors R_M and C. The value R_M represents the right-sided unit related to the vector M and is computed using the formulas (9) and (10). To transform the message into the vector C, the single-use key in the form of randomly selected global left-sided unit is generated and then the value C is computed as follows:

$$C = B^t \circ M^e \circ A^t \circ L. \tag{11}$$

In the last formula the value L is the single-use subkey that is selected at random, i.e., the proposed encryption method relates to the probabilistic encryption procedures for which the value of the ciphertext is not predetermined even in the case, when the same source message is encrypted two times. The known interpretation of the commutativity of the encryption relates to the deterministic encryption procedures, namely, it is assumed that a cipher is commutative, if the double encryption of some fixed input message on two different fixed keys produces the same ciphertext independently of the order of using the keys [8, 9]. In the case of such definition of the commutativity of the encryption no probabilistic commutative ciphers are possible.

Thus, in this paper we use the extended interpretation of the commutative-encryption notion. We call an encryption algorithm commutative, if the double encryption of some fixed input message on two different fixed keys produces the ciphertext the can be correctly decrypted using the keys in each of two possible orders. below it is shown that the formula (11) defines the commutative encryption process.

Decryption of the ciphertext (R_M, C) is performed as computation of the vector M' with using the following formula:

$$M' = A^t \circ C^d \circ B^t \circ R_M. \tag{12}$$

Correctness proof of the proposed encryption method is as follows:

$$M' = A^t \circ C^d \circ B^t \circ R_M = A^t \circ (B^t \circ M^e \circ A^t \circ L)^d \circ B^t \circ R_M$$
$$= A^t \circ B^t \circ M^{ed} \circ A^t \circ B^t \circ R_M = L_0 \circ M \circ L_0 \circ R_M = M.$$

Let us show that the proposed encryption algorithm is commutative. Since the first encryption with the key (e, d, t) and the second encryption with the key $(\varepsilon, \delta, \tau)$ relates to the data having different size (because the ciphertext includes the vector R_M as the first part), we accept on definition that the value R_M is computed in frame of the first encryption and at the second encryption the value R_M is not transformed.

The double encryption with the key (e, d, t) and then with the key $(\varepsilon, \delta, \tau)$ produces the ciphertext (R_M, C'), where C' is computed as follows:

$$C' = B^{t+\tau} \circ M^{e\varepsilon} \circ A^{t+\tau} \circ L', \tag{13}$$

where L' is some random global left-sided unit used as the single-use key at the second encryption.

The double encryption with the key $(\varepsilon, \delta, \tau)$ and then with the key (e, d, t) produces the ciphertext (R_M, C''), where C'' is computed as follows:

$$C'' = B^{\tau+t} \circ M^{\varepsilon e} \circ A^{\tau+t} \circ L'', \tag{14}$$

where L'' is some random global left-sided unit used as the single-use key at the second encryption. The ciphertexts (R_M, C') and (R_M, C'') are different, however one can easily show that the double decryption of each of the ciphertexts (R_M, C') and (R_M, C'') outputs the source message M independently of the order of using the keys $(\varepsilon, \delta, \tau)$ and (e, d, t). For example, decryption of the ciphertext (R_M, C'') with the key $(\varepsilon, \delta, \tau)$ and then with the key (e, d, t) gives the following transformations:

$$
\begin{aligned}
C^* &= A^\tau \circ C''^\delta \circ B^\tau \circ R_M \\
&= A^\tau \circ \left(B^{\tau+t} \circ M^{\varepsilon e} \circ A^{\tau+t} \circ L''\right)^\delta \circ B^\tau \circ R_M \\
&= A^\tau \circ B^{\tau+t} \circ M^{\varepsilon e \delta} \circ A^{\tau+t} \circ L'' \circ B^\tau \circ R_M \\
&= A^\tau \circ B^t \circ B^\tau \circ M^e \circ A^t \circ A^\tau \circ B^\tau \circ R_M \\
&= L_0 \circ B^t \circ M^e \circ A^t \circ L_0 \circ R_M = B^t \circ M^e \circ A^t \circ R_M;
\end{aligned}
$$

$$
\begin{aligned}
M &= A^t \circ (C^*)^d \circ B^t \circ R_M \\
&= A^t \circ \left(B^t \circ M^e \circ A^t \circ R_M\right)^d \circ B^t \circ R_M \\
&= A^t \circ B^t \circ M^{ed} \circ A^t \circ R_M \circ B^t \circ R_M \\
&= L_0 \circ M^{ed} \circ L_0 \circ R_M = M.
\end{aligned}
$$

Thus, we have proposed the post-quantum commutative cipher suitable for implementing the no-key encryption protocol. However, we interpret the term "commutativity" in the extended sense. Namely, we call the encryption algorithm commutative, if the double encryption on two different keys produces the ciphertext that can be correctly decrypted using the keys in a different order.

From the formula (11) one can see that the known-plaintext attack on the described commutative cipher, which assumes finding the value e, represents the HDLP that is characterized in masking the vector M^e, i.e., the output of the base exponentiation operation, with two consecutive homomorphism maps ψ_{L0} and φ_L.

5 Post-quantum No-key Encryption Protocol

Notion "no-key encryption" relates to implementing a secure communication session without using some pre-agreed key. No-key protocol uses some commutative encryption function $E_K(M)$, where M is the input message and K is the encryption key, which is secure to the known plaintext attacks [9]. Usually the encryption function is called commutative, if the following equality holds:

$$
E_{K_A}(E_{K_B}(M)) = E_{K_B}(E_{K_A}(M))
$$

where K_A and K_B ($K_B \neq K_A$) are different encryption keys. Shamir's no-key protocol includes the following three steps [9]:

1. The sender (Alice) of the message M generates a random key K_A and calculates the ciphertext $C_1 = E_{K_A}(M)$. Then she sends C_1 to the receiver (Bob) via an open channel.

2. Bob generates a random key K_B, encrypts the ciphertext C_1 with the key K_B as follows: $C_2 = E_{K_B}(C_1) = E_{K_B}(E_{K_A}(M))$. Then he sends the ciphertext C_2 to Alice.
3. Alice, using decryption procedure $D = E^{-1}$, calculates the ciphertext

$$C_3 = D_{K_A}(C_2) = D_{K_A}(E_{K_B}(E_{K_A}(M))) = D_{K_A}(E_{K_A}(E_{K_B}(M))) = E_{K_B}(M)$$

and sends C_3 to Bob.

Bob discloses the message as follows: $M = E_{K_B}^{-1}(C_3)$.

If one uses the Pohlig-Hellman exponentiation cipher [8] as the function $E_K(M)$ in this protocol, then the protocol is as secure as the DLP is hard. However, security to quantum attacks is not provided.

Using the post-quantum commutative encryption algorithm described in Sect. 4 one can propose the following post-quantum version of the no-key protocol:

1. Alice generates a random key (e, d, t), the single-use key L and calculates the ciphertext (R_M, C_1), where $C_1 = B^t \circ M^e \circ A^t \circ L$. Then she sends (R_M, C_1) to Bob via a public channel.
2. Bob generates a random key $(\varepsilon, \delta, \tau)$, the single-use key L' and encrypts the ciphertext C_1 as follows: $C_2 = B^\tau \circ C_1^\varepsilon \circ A^\tau \circ L'$ and sends C_2 to Alice.
3. Alice generates the single-use key L'' and decrypts the ciphertext C_2 obtaining the ciphertext C_3: $C_3 = A^t \circ C_2^d \circ B^t \circ L''$. Then she sends C_3 to Bob.

Using the received ciphertext C_3 the receiver (i.e., Bob) recovers message M accordingly to the formula $M = A^{t_2} \circ C^{d_2} \circ B^{t_2} \circ R_M$.

The practical application of the no-key protocol relates to sending confidential messages via public (insecure) channels without using pre-agreed keys. Since security of the no-key protocol is based on the hardness of the underlying difficult problem (HDLP in the proposed version of the no-key protocol), only conditional (practical) security is provided. To provide unconditional (theoretical) security one should use secure communication channels and protocols of other types, for example, the quantum three-stage protocol [10] that is based on the quantum physics laws.

6 Conclusion

For the first time it is proposed a probabilistic commutative encryption method and a post-quantum commutative cipher based on the introduced method. Security of the proposed cipher is based on computational difficulty of the HDLP set in a new form using the 4-dimensional FNAA containing a large set of the global left-sided units as the algebraic support of the proposed encryption algorithm. The proposed commutative cipher have been used to design a post-quantum version of the no-key encryption protocol.

The proposed encryption method is very attractive to be combined with the pseudo-probabilistic method propose earlier in the papers [11, 12].

Acknowledgements. The reported study was partially funded by Russian Foundation for Basic Research (project #18-57-54002-Viet_a) and by VietNam Academy of Science and Technology (project # QTRU01.08/18-19).

References

1. Lange, T., Steinwandt, R. (eds.): PQCrypto 2018. LNCS, vol. 10786. Springer, Cham (2018). https://doi.org/10.1007/978-3-319-79063-3
2. First NIST Standardization Conference, 11–13 April 2018 (2018). http://prometheuscrypt. gforge.inria.fr/2018-04-18.pqc2018.html
3. Yan, S.Y.: Quantum Computational Number Theory, p. 252. Springer, Cham (2015). https:// doi.org/10.1007/978-3-319-25823-2
4. Yan, S.Y.: Quantum Attacks on Public-Key Cryptosystems, p. 207. Springer, Cham (2013). https://doi.org/10.1007/978-1-4419-7722-9
5. Moldovyan, D.N.: Non-commutative finite groups as primitive of public-key cryptoschemes. Quasigroups Relat. Syst. **18**(2), 165–176 (2010)
6. Kuzmin, A.S., Markov, V.T., Mikhalev, A.A., Mikhalev, A.V., Nechaev, A.A.: Cryptographic algorithms on groups and algebras. J. Math. Sci. **223**(5), 629–641 (2017)
7. Moldovyan, D.N., Moldovyan, N.A.: Cryptoschemes over hidden conjugacy search problem and attacks using homomorphisms. Quasigroups Relat. Syst. **18**(2), 177–186 (2010)
8. Hellman, M.E., Pohlig, S.C.: Exponentiation cryptographic apparatus and method. U.S. Patent # 4,424,414. (1984)
9. Menezes, A.J., Oorschot, P.C., Vanstone, S.A.: Applied Cryptography. CRC Press, New York (1996)
10. Nguyen, D.M., Kim, S.: Multi-bits transfer based on the quantum three-stage protocol with quantum error correction codes. Int. J. Theor. Phys. **58**(6), 2043–2053 (2019)
11. Moldovyan, N.A., Moldovyan, D.N., Le, Q.M., Nguyen, L.G., Ho, S.T., Nguyen, H.M.: Stream pseudo-probabilistic ciphers. In: Cong Vinh, P., Alagar, V. (eds.) ICCASA/ICTCC - 2018. LNICST, vol. 266, pp. 36–47. Springer, Cham (2019). https://doi.org/10.1007/978-3-030-06152-4_4
12. Moldovyan, N.A., Moldovyan, A.A., Nguyen, N.H., Tran, M.C., Nguyen, H.M.: Pseudo-probabilistic block ciphers and their randomization. J. Ambient Intell. Hum. Comput. **10**(5), 1977–1984 (2019)

Toward Aggregating Fuzzy Graphs
a Model Theory Approach

Nguyen Van Han[1,2]($\boxtimes$), Nguyen Cong Hao[3], and Phan Cong Vinh[4]

[1] Faculty of Information Technology, College of Science, Hue University,
77 Nguyen Hue street, Phu Nhuan ward, Hue city, Vietnam
nvhan@fit-hitu.edu.vn
[2] Ho Chi Minh City Industry and Trade College, 20 Tang Nhon Phu street,
Phuoc Long B Ward, District 9, Ho Chi Minh city, Vietnam
[3] Department of Inspection and Legislation, Hue University,
04 Le Loi street, Hue city, Vietnam
nchao@hueuni.edu.vn
[4] Faculty of Information Technology, Nguyen Tat Thanh University,
300A Nguyen Tat Thanh street, Ward 13 District 4, Ho Chi Minh city, Vietnam
pcvinh@ntt.edu.vn

Abstract. In this paper, we study fuzzy graph represents by using model theory. We use hedge algebra and linguistic variables for modeling and aggregating two graphs. We prove theorem of limiting in models state space. We also figure out preserved property of aggregation operator.

Keywords: Fuzzy logic · Linguistic variable · Hedge algebra · Aggregating fuzzy graphs

1 Introduction

In everyday life, people use natural language (NL) for analysing, reasoning, and finally, make their decisions. Computing with words (CWW) [5] is a mathematical solution of computational problems stated in an NL. CWW based on fuzzy set and fuzzy logic, introduced by Zadeh is an approximate method on interval $[0, 1]$. In linguistic domain, linguistic hedges play an important role for generating set of linguistic variables. A well known application of fuzzy logic (FL) is fuzzy cognitive map (FCM), introduced by Kosko [1], combined fuzzy logic with neural network. FCM has a lots of applications in both modeling and reasoning fuzzy knowledge [3,4] on interval $[0, 1]$ but not in linguistic values, However, many applications cannot model in numerical domain [5], for example, linguistic summarization problems [6]. To solve this problem, in the paper, we use an abstract algebra, called hedge algebra (HA) as a tool for computing with words.

© ICST Institute for Computer Sciences, Social Informatics and Telecommunications Engineering 2019
Published by Springer Nature Switzerland AG 2019. All Rights Reserved
P. C. Vinh and A. Rakib (Eds.): ICCASA 2019/ICTCC 2019, LNICST 298, pp. 215–222, 2019.
https://doi.org/10.1007/978-3-030-34365-1_17

The remainder of paper is organized as follows. Section 2 reviews some main concepts of computing with words based on HA in Subsect. 2.1 and describes several primary concepts for FCM in Subsect. 2.2. Section 3 reviews modeling with words using HA. Important Sect. 4 proves a new method to model fuzzy graph from model theory. Section 5 presents aggregation method to combine two fuzzy graphs. Section 6 outlines discussion and future work.

2 Preliminaries

This section presents basic concepts of HA and FCM used in the paper.

2.1 Hedge Algebra

In this section, we review some HA knowledges related to our research paper and give basic definitions. First definition of a HA is specified by 3-Tuple $HA = (X, H, \leq)$ in [7]. In [8] to easily simulate fuzzy knowledge, two terms G and C are inserted to 3-Tuple so $HA = (X, G, C, H, \leq)$ where $H \neq \emptyset$, $G = \{c^+, c^-\}$, $C = \{0, W, 1\}$. Domain of X is $\mathbb{L} = Dom(X) = \{\delta c | c \in G, \delta \in H^*(\text{hedge string over H})\}$, $\{\mathbb{L}, \leq\}$ is a POSET (partial order set) and $x = h_n h_{n-1} \dots h_1 c$ is said to be a canonical string of linguistic variable x.

Example 1. Fuzzy subset X *is Age*, $G = \{c^+ = young; c^- = old\}$, $H = \{less; more; very\}$ so term-set of linguistic variable Age X is $\mathbb{L}(X)$ or $\mathbb{L}$ for short:

$$\mathbb{L} = \{very\,less\,young; less\,young; young; more\,young; very\,young; very\,very\,young \dots\}$$

Fuzziness properties of elements in HA, specified by fm (fuzziness measure) [8] as follows:

Definition 2.1. A mapping $fm : \mathbb{L} \rightarrow [0, 1]$ is said to be the fuzziness measure of $\mathbb{L}$ if:

1. $\sum_{c \in \{c^+, c^-\}} fm(c) = 1$, $fm(0) = fm(w) = fm(1) = 0$.
2. $\sum_{h_i \in H} fm(h_i x) = fm(x)$, $x = h_n h_{n-1} \dots h_1 c$, the canonical form.
3. $fm(h_n h_{n-1} \dots h_1 c) = \prod_{i=1}^{n} fm(h_i) \times \mu(x)$.

2.2 Fuzzy Cognitive Map

Fuzzy cognitive map (FCM) is feedback dynamical system for modeling fuzzy causal knowledge, introduced by Kosko [1]. FCM is a set of nodes, which present concepts and a set of directed edges to link nodes. The edges represent the causal links between these concepts. Mathematically, a FCM bis defined by.

Definition 2.2. A FCM is a 4-Tuple:

$$\mathbb{FCM} = \{C, E, \mathcal{C}, f\} \tag{1}$$

In which:

1. $C = \{C_1, C_2, \ldots, C_n\}$ is the set of N concepts forming the nodes of a graph.
2. $E : (C_i, C_j) \longrightarrow e_{ij} \in \{-1, 0, 1\}$ is a function associating e_{ij} with a pair of concepts (C_i, C_j), so that e_{ij} = "weight of edge directed from C_i to C_j. The connection matrix $E(N \times N) = \{e_{ij}\}_{N \times N}$
3. The map: $\mathcal{C} : C_i \longrightarrow C_i(t) \in [0, 1], t \in N$
4. With $C(0) = [C_1(0, C_2(0), \ldots, C_n(0)] \in [0, 1]^N$ is the initial vector, recurring transformation function f defined as (Fig. 2):

$$C_j(t+1) = f(\sum_{i=1}^{N} e_{ij}C_i(t)) \tag{2}$$

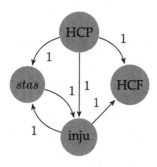

Example 2. Fig.1 shows a medical problem from expert domain of strokes and blood clotting involving. Concepts C={blood stasis (stas), endothelial injury (inju), hypercoagulation factors (HCP and HCF)} [2]. The conection matrix is:

$$E = (e_{ij})_{4 \times 4} = \begin{pmatrix} 0 & 1 & 1 & 1 \\ 0 & 0 & 1 & 0 \\ 0 & 1 & 0 & 1 \\ 0 & 0 & 0 & 0 \end{pmatrix}$$

Fig. 1. A simple FCM

FCMs have played a vital role in the applications of scientific areas, including expert system, robotics, medicine, education, information technology, prediction, etc. [3,4].

3   Modeling with Words

Fuzzy model, based on linguistic variables, is constructed from linguistic hedge of HA [10,11].

Definition 3.1 (Linguistic lattice). With $\mathbb{L}$ as in the Sect. 2.1, set $\{\wedge, \vee\}$ are logical operators, defined in [7,8], a linguistic lattice $\mathcal{L}$ is a tuple:

$$\mathcal{L} = (\mathbb{L}, \vee, \wedge, 0, 1) \tag{3}$$

Property 3.1. *The following are some properties for $\mathcal{L}$:*

1. $\mathcal{L}$ is a linguistic-bounded lattice.

2. $(\mathbb{L}, \vee)$ and $(\mathbb{L}, \wedge)$ are semigroups.

Definition 3.2. A linguistic cognitive map (LCM) is a 4-Tuple:

$$\text{LCM} = \{C, E, \mathcal{C}, f\} \tag{4}$$

In which:

1. $C = \{C_1, C_2, \ldots, C_n\}$ is the set of N concepts forming the nodes of a graph.
2. $E : (C_i, C_j) \longrightarrow e_{ij} \in \mathbb{L}$; $e_{ij} = $ "weight of edge directed from C_i to C_j. The connection matrix $E(N \times N) = \{e_{ij}\}_{N \times N} \in \mathbb{L}^{N \times N}$
3. The map: $\mathcal{C} : C_i \longrightarrow C_i^t \in \mathbb{L}, t \in N$
4. With $\mathcal{C}(0) = [C_1^0, C_2^0, \ldots, C_n^0] \in \mathbb{L}^N$ is the initial vector, recurring transformation function f defined as:

$$C_j^{t+1} = f(\sum_{i=1}^N e_{ij} C_i^t) \in \mathbb{L} \tag{5}$$

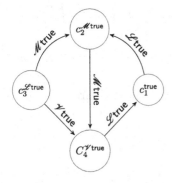

Example 3. Fig. 3 shows a simple LCM. Let

$$\mathbb{HA} = <\mathcal{X} = \text{truth}; c^+ = \text{true}; \mathcal{H} = \{\mathscr{L}, \mathscr{M}, \mathscr{V}\}> \tag{6}$$

be a $\mathbb{HA}$ with order as $\mathscr{L} < \mathscr{M} < \mathscr{V}$ ($\mathscr{L}$ for less, $\mathscr{M}$ for more and $\mathscr{V}$ for very are hedges). $C = \{c_1, c_2, c_3, c_4\}$ is the set of 4 concepts with corresponding values $\mathcal{C} = \{\text{true}, \mathscr{M}\text{true}, \mathscr{L}\text{true}, \mathscr{V}\text{true}\}$

Fig. 2. A simple LCM

Square matrix:

$$M = (m_{ij} \in \mathbb{L})_{4 \times 4} = \begin{vmatrix} 0 & \mathscr{L}\text{true} & 0 & 0 \\ 0 & 0 & 0 & \mathscr{M}\text{true} \\ 0 & \mathscr{M}\text{true} & 0 & \mathscr{V}\text{true} \\ \mathscr{L}\text{true} & 0 & 0 & 0 \end{vmatrix}.$$

is the adjacency matrix of $\mathbb{LCM}$. Causal relation between c_i and c_j is m_{ij}, for example if $i = 1, j = 2$ then causal relation between c_1 and c_2 is: *"if c_1 is true then c_2 is $\mathscr{M}$true is $\mathscr{L}$true"* or let $\mathcal{P} = $ "if c_1 is true then c_2 is $\mathscr{M}$true" be a fuzzy proposition $\mathcal{FP}$ [9] then $\mathsf{truth}(\mathcal{P}) = \mathscr{L}$true

Definition 3.3. A $\mathbb{LCM}$ is called complete if between any two nodes alway having a connected edge (without looping edges).

4   LCM Modeling with Binary Structure

We use logical structures with relational symbols to represent $\mathbb{LCM}$. For specifying vetex set and edge set, we utilize relations whose arity are whole number. A relational signature $\mathscr{G}$ is a set of relational symbols.

Definition 4.1. A binary relational signature $\mathscr{G}$ as:

$$\mathscr{G} = \{lab_\alpha, \; succ_\beta\} \tag{7}$$

In which $\alpha \in \mathbb{L}$ and $\beta \in \mathbb{L}$. $lab_\alpha, \; succ_\beta$ are relational symbols.

Structures are generated from $\mathscr{G}$ called $\mathsf{struct}[\mathscr{G}]$. By using $\mathsf{struct}[\mathscr{G}]$, vetex set C and edge set E of $\mathbb{LCM}$ can be formalized as follow:

Definition 4.2. A $\mathfrak{C}$ $\mathsf{struct}[\mathscr{G}]$ is a tuple:

$$\mathfrak{C} = \langle \mathbb{C}, \; lab_\alpha^\mathfrak{C}, \; succ_\beta^\mathfrak{C} \rangle \tag{8}$$

Where:

- Set $\mathbb{C}$ is domain of $\mathfrak{C}$
- $lab_\alpha^\mathfrak{C}$ is a unary relation: $\{\exists C \in \mathbb{C} \mid lab_\alpha^\mathfrak{C} C\}$, $\alpha \in \mathbb{L}$
- $succ_\beta^\mathfrak{C}$ is a binary relation: $\{C_1, \; C_2 \in \mathbb{C} \mid succ_\beta^\mathfrak{C}(C_1, \; C_2)\}$, $\beta \in \mathbb{L}$. C_2 is a *sucessor* of C_1 and $(C_1, \; C_2)$ is a directed edge.

We denote graphs on $\mathbb{HA}$ by $\mathcal{GR}[\mathbb{HA}]$ and represent $\mathbb{LCM}$ by using $\mathsf{struct}[\mathscr{G}]$.

Give a $\mathfrak{C}$ $\mathsf{struct}[\mathscr{G}]$ in (8), the complexity of $\mathfrak{C}$ is proportion to $\|\mathbb{C}\|$, $\|lab_\alpha\|$ and $\|succ_\beta\|$ - The sign $\|.\|$ is short for size of.

Example 4. Left figure shows a simple LCM on :

$$\mathcal{GR}[X = \text{truth}; c^+ = \text{true}; H = \{\mathcal{L}, \mathcal{M}, \mathcal{V}\}]$$

and $\mathfrak{C}$ struct$[\mathcal{G}]$ as:

$$\mathfrak{C} = \{\{C_1, C_2, C_3, C_4\}, lab_\alpha C_k, succ_\beta(C_i, C_j)\}$$

Values $i, j, k \in \{1, 2, 3, 4\}$, α, $\beta \in \mathbb{L}$.

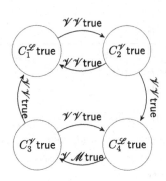

Fig. 3. A simple LCM on struct$[\mathcal{G}]$

Theorem 4.1. *There are:*

$$2^{2 \times \binom{\|C\| + 1}{2}} \tag{9}$$

different $\mathfrak{C}$ struct$[\mathcal{G}]$ *of size* $\|\mathbb{C}\|$.

We prove Theorem 4.1 by using combinatorial relations, symbol $\mathscr{P}(.)$ is power set.

Proof. Because a $n-ary$ relation on a set $\mathbb{C}$ is a subset of $\overbrace{\mathbb{C} \times \mathbb{C} \times \ldots \times \mathbb{C}}^{n\ times}$, therefore:

- Monadic relation lab_α has $\|lab_\alpha\| = \|\mathscr{P}(\mathbb{C})\| = 2^{\|\mathbb{C}\|}$
- Binary relation $succ_\beta$ has $\|succ_\beta\| = \|\mathscr{P}(\mathbb{C} \times \mathbb{C})\| = 2^{\|\mathbb{C}\|^2}$
- QED: $\|\mathscr{P}(\mathbb{C})\| \times \|\mathscr{P}(\mathbb{C} \times \mathbb{C})\| = 2^{2 \times \binom{\|\mathbb{C}\| + 1}{2}}$

$\square$

5   Aggregating Two LCMs

LCMs allow a aggregation of knowledge constructed from a few experts to form the final LCM which reduce potentially errors. We study a aggregation procedures for combining multiple LCMs preserved its properties.

Definition 5.1. Suppose $\mathfrak{A} = \langle \mathbb{A}, lab_\alpha^{\mathfrak{A}}, succ_\beta^{\mathfrak{A}} \rangle$ and $\mathfrak{B} = \langle \mathbb{B}, lab_\alpha^{\mathfrak{B}}, succ_\beta^{\mathfrak{B}} \rangle$ are struct$[\mathcal{G}]$.

$$\mathfrak{D} = \mathfrak{A} \bigcup \mathfrak{B} = \langle \mathbb{D}, lab_\alpha^{\mathfrak{D}}, succ_\beta^{\mathfrak{D}} \rangle \tag{10}$$

On the conditions that:

- $\mathbb{D} = \mathbb{A} \cup \mathbb{C}$
- $lab_\alpha^\mathbb{D} =$
$$\begin{cases} lab_\alpha^\mathfrak{A} = lab_\alpha^\mathfrak{B} & \text{if } lab_\alpha^\mathfrak{A} = lab_\alpha^\mathfrak{B} \\ lab_\alpha^\mathfrak{A} \vee lab_\alpha^\mathfrak{B} & \text{if } lab_\alpha^\mathfrak{A} \neq lab_\alpha^\mathfrak{B} \end{cases}$$

- $succ_\beta^\mathbb{D} =$
$$\begin{cases} succ_\beta^\mathfrak{A} = succ_\beta^\mathfrak{B} & \text{if } succ_\beta^\mathfrak{A} = succ_\beta^\mathfrak{B} \\ succ_\beta^\mathfrak{A} \vee succ_\beta^\mathfrak{B} & \text{if } succ_\beta^\mathfrak{A} \neq succ_\beta^\mathfrak{B} \end{cases}$$

Example 5. Using Eq. (10), graph in Fig. 3 is a aggregation of two graphs below:

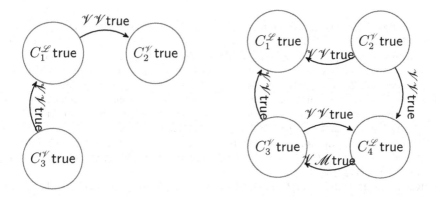

Property 5.1. *The aggregation operator defined in (10) preserved causal relation properties, that is:*

$$succ_\beta^\mathbb{D}(lab_\rho^\mathbb{D}, lab_\delta^\mathbb{D}) \models succ_\beta^\mathfrak{A}(lab_\rho^\mathfrak{A}, lab_\delta^\mathfrak{A}) \vee succ_\beta^\mathfrak{B}(lab_\rho^\mathfrak{B}, lab_\delta^\mathfrak{B}) \qquad (11)$$

6   Conclusions and Future Work

We have study a new method to present $\mathbb{LCM}$ using model theory. The impotant theorem in complexity of model space limited by expression $2^{2 \times \binom{\|\mathbb{C}\|+1}{2}}$.

We also introduce a method for aggregating fuzzy graphs. This aggregation operator preserves causal relation properties. Our next study is as follow:

Suppose $\mathbb{LCM}$s are fuzzy graphs on:

$$\mathcal{GR}[\{X, \mathcal{H}, \{c^+, c^-\}, \{0, W, 1\}, \leq\}] \qquad (12)$$

so that:

$$\mathbb{LCM} = \langle V^{\text{LCM}}, succ^{\text{LCM}}, lab^{\text{LCM}} \rangle \qquad (13)$$

Let $\mathcal{H}$ be all string generated from $\mathcal{GR}[.]$. V^{LCM} is the finite set of *vertices*; Relation $succ^{\text{LCM}} \subseteq V^{\text{LCM}} \times \mathcal{H} \times V^{\text{LCM}}$ saying that if two vertices are linked by an edge with label in $\mathcal{H}$. Total map $lab^{\mathrm{LCM}} : V^{\mathrm{LCM}} \to \mathcal{H}$ assigning a label in $\mathcal{H}$ to each vertex of $\mathbb{LCM}$.

The set of all $\mathbb{LCM}$ over $\mathcal{H}$ is denote $\mathbb{LCM}_{\mathcal{H}}$, and the set of all graphs isomorphic to $\mathbb{LCM}$ is denote $[\mathbb{LCM}_{\mathcal{H}}]$. A graph language $\mathscr{L}$ is a subset $\mathscr{L} \subset [\mathbb{LCM}_{\mathcal{H}}]$.

References

1. Kosko, B.: Fuzzy cognitive maps. Int. J. Man-Mach. Stud. **24**, 65–75 (1986)
2. Osoba, O.A., Kosko, B.: Fuzzy cognitive maps of public support for insurgency and terrorism. J. Def. Model. Simul. Appl. Methodol. **14**(1), 17–32 (2017)
3. Glykas, M.: Fuzzy Cognitive Maps: Advances in Theory, Tools and Applications. Springer, Heidelberg (2010). https://doi.org/10.1007/978-3-642-03220-2
4. Papageorgiou, E.I.: Fuzzy Cognitive Maps for Applied Science and Engineering: From Fundamentals to Extensions and Learning Algorithms. Springer, Heidelberg (2014). https://doi.org/10.1007/978-3-642-39739-4
5. Zadeh, L.A.: Computing with words: Principal Concepts and Ideas. Studies in Fuzziness and Soft Computing. Springer, Heidelberg (2012). https://doi.org/10.1007/978-3-642-27473-2
6. Kacprzyk, J., Wilbik, A., Zadrożny, S.: Linguistic summarization of trends: a fuzzy logic based approach. In: The 11th International Conference Information Processing and Management of Uncertainty in Knowledge-based Systems, pp. 2166–2172 (2006)
7. Ho, N.C., Wechler, W.: Hedge algebras: an algebraic approach to structure of sets of linguistic truth values. Fuzzy Sets Syst. **35**, 281–293 (1990)
8. Ho, N.C., Van Long, N.: Fuzziness measure on complete hedge algebras and quantifying semantics of terms in linear hedge algebras. Fuzzy Sets Syst. **158**(4), 452–471
9. Phuong, L.A., Khang, T.D.: Generalized if... then... else... inference rules with linguistic modifiers for approximate reasoning. Int. J. Comput. Sci. Issues (IJCSI) **9**(6), 184–190 (2012)
10. Van Han, N., Vinh, P.C.: Modeling with words based on hedge algebra. In: Cong Vinh, P., Alagar, V. (eds.) ICCASA/ICTCC -2018. LNICST, vol. 266, pp. 211–217. Springer, Cham (2019). https://doi.org/10.1007/978-3-030-06152-4_18
11. Van Han, N., Vinh, P.C.: Toward modeling and reasoning with words based on hedge algebra. EAI Endorsed Trans. Context-Aware Syst. Appl. **5**(15), e5 (2018)

An Android Business Card Reader Based on Google Vision: Design and Evaluation

Nguyen Hoang Thuan[1(✉)], Dinh Thanh Nhan[1], Lam Thanh Toan[1], Nguyen Xuan Ha Giang[1], and Quoc Bao Truong[2]

[1] Can Tho University of Technology,
256 Nguyen Van Cu Street, Can Tho City, Vietnam
{nhthuan,dtnhan,lttoan,nxhgiang}@ctuet.edu.vn
[2] College of Engineering Technology, Can Tho University,
3/2 Street, Can Tho City, Vietnam
tqbao@ctu.edu.vn

Abstract. Business cards have been widely used to greet business professionals and exchange contact information. However, the current paper-based way to manage business cards impedes their effective usage, leading to a need for digitalising and extracting business card information. This paper aims to design a business card reader (BCR) application for Android devices. Based on Google vision library, the application digitalises and extracts business card information. We evaluate the application on a dataset of 170 business cards. The results show that the application can digitalise business cards and extract contact information with 88.4% of accuracy. We then further conduct a comparative analysis of our application and other commercial BCR applications. Based on the results, the paper suggests several recommendations for future research.

Keywords: Business card reader · Android · Design science · Experiment

1 Introduction

Today, the exchange of business cards become a norm to start new business connections. Business cards help self introduction and provide contact information for future correspondence. In the current practice, business card receivers manage business cards manually, e.g. manually input contact information into a cell phone, which will take little effort to utilise business card information [1]. Further, managing the contact information manually leads to a risk of input errors. Thus, it will be more convenient to extract business card information automatically without any typing activities, which leads to the need of digitalising and extracting business card information [1–3].

From a user perspective, digitalising and extracting information from business cards brings the following benefits. First, it saves time and efforts to transfer paper-based business cards into contact information [2, 4]. Second, it supports business card receivers to manage and search particular contacts since information are stored in digitalised form. The searching capability is especially important in cases where too many business cards are received. Third, it is easier to access and back up business card information in digitalised form than a paper-based form. Finally, when users are on

© ICST Institute for Computer Sciences, Social Informatics and Telecommunications Engineering 2019
Published by Springer Nature Switzerland AG 2019. All Rights Reserved
P. C. Vinh and A. Rakib (Eds.): ICCASA 2019/ICTCC 2019, LNICST 298, pp. 223–236, 2019.
https://doi.org/10.1007/978-3-030-34365-1_18

movement (e.g. business travel), digitalised business cards provide flexibility and convenience in comparison to a bunch of paper-based business cards.

These benefits have motivated an increased research interest in business card reader (BCR) applications. By and large, the literature related to BCR applications can be classified into two research streams, which focus on problems related to computer science (CS) and information systems (IS). In the computer science domain, researchers focus on optical character recognition (OCR) to identify business cards' texts at the technical levels [3, 5, 6]. They proposed techniques and algorithms to process business card images [7], find text blocks [8], and extract texts [3, 4]. These algorithms and techniques provide a foundation supporting the development of BCR applications.

From a different perspective, the IS domain focuses on the design, adoption, use of BCR applications at the business levels. Examples of IS problems include design BCR applications on certain mobile platforms [1, 2, 6], management of semantics, and evaluation of the designed BCR applications [9, 10]. Consequently, several BCR applications have been designed and evaluated. They are based on several computer vision libraries, including Mobile Vision, OpenCV and Tesseract [2, 9, 10]. However, other computer vision libraries like Google Vision exist, which have not been used to design BCR applications. Further, the evaluation so far is limited in terms of sample size, e.g. experimenting on less than 55 business cards [2, 6, 10].

This paper adopting an IS perspective concerns the design and evaluation of BCR applications. In particular, we are interested in designing an Android BCR application based on Google Vision [11] and Image Cropper [12], developing algorithms to extract business card information, and then evaluating the application on a sample of 170 business cards. This problem is challenging: while Google Vision can detect and extract texts from business card images with high accuracy, the extracted texts have no semantics. Thus, our design needs to add meaning to the extracted texts and transfer them to useful contact information (i.e. name, phone number, and email address). This problem is relevant because the proposed solution creates opportunities for further evaluating BCR applications.

In particular, we aim to address the following goals:

- Enable users to digitalise business cards and extract contact information from business card pictures. For the purpose, we develop an Android BCR application that extracts business card texts, adds semantics to the extracted data and transfers them to useful information;
- Evaluate the developed application to measure the accuracy of extracted information. Here, we aim to evaluate the application using a reasonable sample size, which fulfils the current research gap where the related research is limited in its sample size in evaluating BCR applications [2, 6, 10].

The current study adopts a design science research (DSR) paradigm to design and evaluate an Android BCR application. DSR focuses on identification of a relevant problem, design artefacts to address the problem, evaluation to assess the artefact's utility [13–15]. Translating into the current research, we address the problem of digitalising business cards, design an Android BCR application, and evaluate the application through the sample size of 170 business cards. We further conduct a comparative analysis to assess the capabilities of our application against other commercial BCR applications (e.g. ABBYY and CamCard).

This research contributes to explore the design and adoption of BCR applications. It contributes to fulfill the need to digitalise and extract business card information. The research designs a BCR application that allows end users to extract and manage business card information. The design extends the research stream of BCR development [2, 6, 10] by using alternative computer vision libraries, i.e. Google Vision and Image Cropper. Further, the research also addresses the problem of the evaluation using a reasonable sample size of 170 business cards and using comparative analysis, which illustrates the usefulness of the BCR application.

2 Literature Review

Business card readers (BCR) aim to transfer business card pictures into useful information using optical character recognition (OCR). At the early time, BCR were researched as long as the development of OCR technology, and thus belong to the research stream of computer science. Saiga et al. [16] proposed an OCR system for reading business cards based on line segmentation and linguistic processing. In the same vein, Luo et al. [17] developed an OCR method based on multi-resolution analysis of document images to implement a BCR application. To improve the accuracy of optical character recognition, several algorithms have been developed. For instance, Lin [3] used neural network to extract texts from business card pictures while Mollah et al. [7] used fuzzy-based algorithms to improve OCR accuracy. All in all, this research stream contributes to the improvement of OCR capabilities to recognise texts from business card pictures, which, to some extent, founds the development of BCR applications.

Recently, the BCR research area has gained momentum with the availability of several computer vision libraries. Examples of qualified computer vision libraries include Tesseract OCR, Mobile Vision, OpenCV, and Google Vision. This availability has shifted the BCR research focus from CS domain into the IS domain, where research concerns how to utilise the computer vision libraries to develop BCR applications and assess their usage in practice.

In the IS domain, researchers have developed and evaluated many BCR applications based on available computer vision libraries. Dangiwa and Kumar [2] based on Tesseract library built a BCR application that extracted names, phone numbers, and email addresses for iOS devices. They evaluated the application using a sample of 55 business cards with the accuracy of 74%. Also using available libraries, Dat [10] combined OpenCV and Tesseract to develop an Android BCR application. The application was tested on a sample of 50 business cards with the accuracy of 81.1%. Other BCR applications have been developed based on Tesseract and Mobile Vision [6, 9].

Table 1 summarises the related research using available computer vision libraries for developing BCR applications.

Table 1. Summary of related research

Related research	Library	Experimental sample size	Accuracy
[9]	Mobile Vision	4	Name: 100% Phone number: 100% Email address: 50%
[10]	OpenCV & Tesseract	50	Name: 80.32% Phone number: 83% Email address: 80.04%
[2]	Tesseract	55	Name: 53.8% Phone number: 100% Email address: 83.3%
Current research	Google Vision & Image Cropper	>100	To improve accuracy level

We further position the current research into Table 1 in order to show how it extends the related literature. In the current research, we adopt an alternative library using a combination of Google Vision and Image Cropper to construct an Android BCR application, namely CTUT_NameCard. We further note that the related research is limited in the sample size of evaluating BCR applications (less than 55 business cards), which impedes an overall assessment of the BCR applications. The current research addresses this research gap by increasing the sample size for evaluating the CTUT_NameCard application. Further, our research also aims to improve the accuracy level of extracting business card information.

The paper proceeds as follows. In Sect. 3, we propose an architecture backing the development of CTUT_NameCard application. Section 4 introduces the design of CTUT_NameCard application, while Sect. 5 experiments the application on a dataset of 170 business cards and then compares it with other commercial BCR applications. In Sect. 6, we discuss the findings, their implications, and outline future work.

3 Architecture

In this section, we propose an architecture for building CTUT_NameCard application. The architecture is based on the work by Holsapple [18], which seems to clearly separate the major application components [19]. Figure 1 shows the architecture which relies on three components: GUI, library, and semantic.

The GUI component manages the interaction between the CTUT_NameCard application and its users, i.e. business card receivers who want to digitalise business cards. This component accepts business card pictures as its inputs through two means. The component allows users to take pictures of business cards by cell phone cameras. Alternatively, users may want to load business card pictures that are stored in the cell phone library. These inputs are processed by the library component.

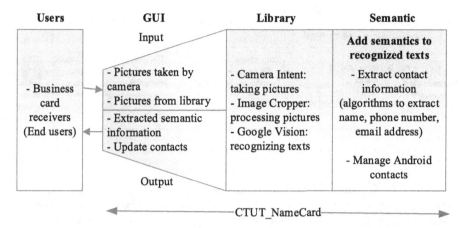

Users	GUI	Library	Semantic
	Input		**Add semantics to recognized texts**
- Business card receivers (End users)	- Pictures taken by camera - Pictures from library - Extracted semantic information - Update contacts	- Camera Intent: taking pictures - Image Cropper: processing pictures - Google Vision: recognizing texts	- Extract contact information (algorithms to extract name, phone number, email address) - Manage Android contacts
	Output		

CTUT_NameCard

Fig. 1. Architecture for CTUT_NameCard (adapted from [18])

The Library component consists of three libraries founding the development of the CTUT_NameCard application: Android camera intent, Image Cropper, and Google Vision. Android camera intent provides functionalities for cell phones to capture pictures. In CTUT_NameCard, the component takes pictures of business cards and thus uses mainly back camera. The component then calls Image Cropper library to process the captured pictures. Image Cropper allows users to choose, flip, rotate, and crop business card images for eliminating noise background and focusing the areas that include business card information. Then, Google Vision is used to recognise texts from the business card images. This library returns a bunch of texts, which are normally high accuracy yet have no semantics. This bunch of texts feed the semantic component.

The Semantic component adds meaning to the extracted texts. In CTUT_NameCard, this component develops algorithms to classify business card information (e.g. name, phone number, and email address). After classifying business card information, this component enables users to update their contacts. As a result, it provides semantics for the extracted texts and manage Android contacts, which are presented as GUI's outputs.

4   Design and Implementation

This section presents the design and implementation of CTUT_NameCard application. We start with an overview on the workflow of the application that involves five main activities. Figure 2 shows the application workflow.

First, business card receivers (users) access the application and select how to load business card images. They can either use cell phone's camera to take a picture of business cards or load an existing business card image from Gallery. As a result, the business card image is loaded. Second, users can crop the loaded image for focusing on the main content of the picture, which removes noise background. If the image is vertical, users can choose to rotate it in order to support the text recognition in the next activity.

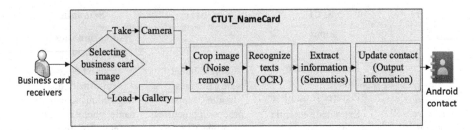

Fig. 2. Workflow of CTUT_NameCard

Third, CTUT_NameCard recognises texts on the pictures. It calls Google Vision for identifying and recognising texts, which return a bunch of texts without semantics. Fourth, we add semantics to the recognised texts. More precisely, we develop three algorithms to extract contact information regarding name, phone number, and email address from the recognised texts. Finally, the extracted information is used to update the users' contact list.

4.1 Implementation

The CTUT_NameCard application was developed using Java and Android Studio. The graphical user interface of the application is shown in Figs. 3, 4, and 5.

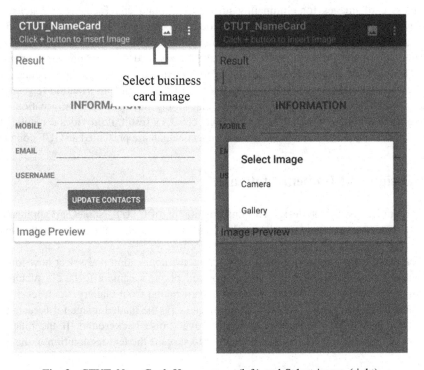

Fig. 3. CTUT_NameCard: Home screen (left) and Select image (right)

In particular, Fig. 3 (left-hand side) shows the home screen of the application, where users can select business card images in order to digitalise and extract information. In the right-hand side of Fig. 3, users can choose taking pictures of business cards or loading pictures from gallery. As a result, business card images are loaded into the application, ready for the next processing functions.

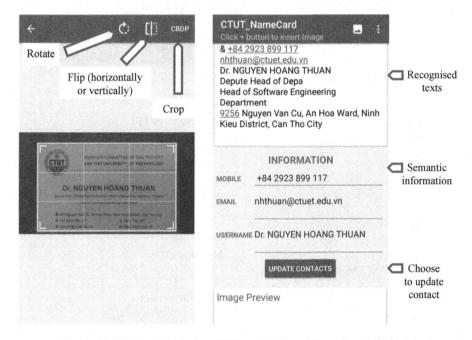

Fig. 4. CTUT_NameCard: Crop (left) and OCR and Sematic screen (right)

Figure 4 (left-hand side) shows the Crop screen. The application auto-detects the focus of the business card image and shows a cropping grid surrounding the image. Users may adjust this grid to remove noise background. They may also rotate, flip, and crop images, which will increase the accuracy of recognising texts.

With the cropped business card image, the OCR and semantic functions are operated, and their outcomes are displayed on the right-hand side of Fig. 4. The top part shows the OCR outcome that recognises texts from the business card image. The recognised texts are presented line by line without semantics. The bottom part shows the semantic outcome that adds meaning to the recognised texts. More precisely, the recognised texts are extracted and classified into useful information, i.e. phone number, email address, and name, which are ready for updating Android contacts.

Figure 5 shows the update contact screen where the extracted information is transferred into Android contacts. Here, the user can check and modify the extracted contact information before updating (left-hand side of Fig. 5). The updated outcome is shown in the right-hand side of Fig. 5.

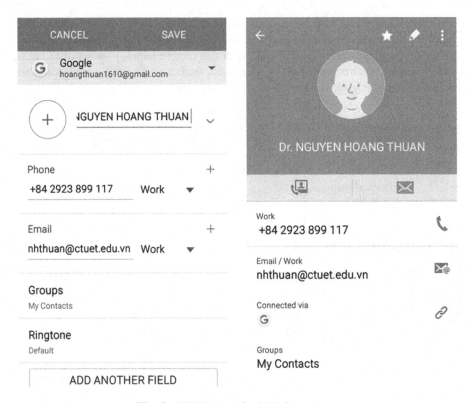

Fig. 5. CTUT_NameCard: Update contact

5   Evaluation

Experiments were arranged to evaluate the CTUT_NameCard application for its accuracy. The evaluation was conducted in two different phases: analytical assessment and comparative assessment.

5.1   Analytical Assessment

In the analytical assessment, we analysed how the application meets its designed target of extracting business card information. For the purpose, we tested the application using a sample of 170 business cards. The sample was collected through a convenient approach, where the business cards were collected through the authors' relationships. For each business card, we used the application to digitalise it and then consider whether the application correctly extracts its contact information: name, phone number, and email address.

Table 2 presents an example of the assessment results. In this table, the first column shows a picture of the business card, digitalised by the application. The second column shows the application's screen that extracts business card information. The third column shows the evaluation results of extracting name, phone number, and email address. If the extracted information is correct, the column value is 'T'. Otherwise, it is 'F'.

Table 2. An example of the assessment results

Business cards	Information digitalised and extracted by CTUT_NameCard	Evaluation results (True/False)		
		Name	Phone number	Email address
	CANTHO UNIVERSITY OF TECHNOLOGY 256 Nguyen Van Cu Street, An Hoa Ward, Ninh Kieu District, Can Tho City, Viet Nam ms CTUT Tel: +84 292 3514 555 Mobile: +84 919 209 555 Fax:+84 292 3894 103 Meritorious Teacher, Senior Lecturer Assoc.Prof.PhD. HUYNH THANH NHA Rector Website: w.ctuet.edu.vn E-mail: htnha@ctuet.edu.vn htnha@ctec.edu.vn	T	T	T

After testing the application on the sample of 170 business cards, we calculated the positive rate and negative rate. The positive rate is defined as proportion of correctly digitalising and extracting contact information. The negative rate is defined as proportion of falsely digitalising and extracting contact information. Table 3 presents the evaluation results of CTUT_NameCard.

Table 3. Evaluation results of CTUT_NameCard

Assessment		Number of business card (n = 170)	Percentage
Name	Positive rate	131	77.1%
	Negative rate	39	22.9%
Phone number	Positive rate	159	93.5%
	Negative rate	11	6.5%
Email address	Positive rate	161	94.7%
	Negative rate	9	5.3%

As seen via Table 3, CTUT_NameCard identified and extracted business cards' name, phone number, and email address with the positive rate of 77.1%, 93.5%, and 94.7% respectively. On average, the accuracy of digitalising and extracting contact information is 88.4%. We note that the positive rates of extracting phone numbers and email addresses are higher than the positive rate of extracting names. This is because phone numbers and email addresses have clear semantic patterns. For instance, if recognised texts include the character '@', they are mostly identified as email addresses. On the other hand, names do not have clear semantic patterns, which can be used to differentiate them and other information on the business cards like company's names and addresses.

To further interpret the evaluation results, Table 4 presents the evaluation results of the current study with the evaluation of the related studies. Table 4 also adds the average levels of accuracy regarding each research, which shows that the current research yields highly reasonable level of accuracy in digitalising and extracting contact information (88.4%).

Table 4. Evaluation results of CTUT_NameCard and related research

Related research	Library	Experimental sample size	Accuracy
[9]	Mobile Vision	4	Name: 100% Phone number: 100% Email address: 50% **Average: 83.0%**
[10]	OpenCV & Tesseract	50	Name: 80.3% Phone number: 83.0% Email address: 80.0% **Average: 81.1%**
[2]	Tesseract	55	Name: 53.8% Phone number: 100% Email address: 83.3% **Average: 79.0%**
CTUT_NameCard	Google Vision & Image Cropper	170	Name: 77.1% Phone number: 93.5% Email address: 94.7% **Average: 88.4%**

To provide another view on the evaluation results, Table 5 shows the number of business cards that CTUT_NameCard correctly identified three, two, one, zero fields of contact information. Out of 170 business cards, the application correctly identified all three information fields in 122 cards (72%), two information fields in 38 cards (22%), one information field in 10 cards (6%). There is no case that the application could not identify any information field.

Table 5. Evaluation results: three, two, one fields of contact information

Assessment	Number of business card (n = 170)	Percentage
All three fields of contact information	122	72%
Two fields of contact information	38	22%
One field of contact information	10	6%
No field of contact information	0	0%

From these results, we suggest the application has met its designed goals for digitalising and extracting business card information with high level of accuracy.

5.2 Comparative Assessment

While the above assessment has showed utility of the CTUT_NameCard, we note that the evaluation results may be biased, given that it used a convenient sample approach. To overcome this limitation, we now evaluate the application using a sample provided by a third party.

For the purpose, we conducted a comparative assessment. We used a dataset provided by a third party in order to compare our application with two commerce BCR applications, i.e. CamCard and ABBYY. We installed CamCard, ABBYY, and CTUT_NameCard in the same smartphone, and used them to digitalised 50 business cards from the Stanford mobile visual search dataset [20]. We checked the accuracy of digitalising and extracting contact information regarding each application on the given dataset. Table 6 shows the comparative assessment results.

Table 6. Comparative results: CamCard, ABBYY, and CTUT_NameCard

BCR applications	Information field	Number of business card (n = 50)	Positive rate
CamCard	Name:	36	72%
	Phone number:	41	82%
	Email address:	36	72%
	Average:		**75.3%**
ABBYY	Name:	38	76%
	Phone number:	42	84%
	Email address:	35	70%
	Average:		**76.7%**
CTUT_NameCard	Name:	26	52%
	Phone number:	43	86%
	Email address:	42	84%
	Average:		**74%**

From this table, we suggest that on average CTUT_NameCard performs as well as other commerce BCR applications. In particular, it achieves the positive rate of 74%, while CamCard and ABBYY achieve a little higher positive rate of 75.3% and 76.7%

respectively. The results show that CTUT_NameCard extracts phone numbers and email addresses with higher levels of accuracy than the other applications. However, it extracts names with lower levels of accuracy, which suggests us to improve this feature in the future.

6 Conclusion

BCR applications are developed to allow the business card receivers digitalising and extracting contact information from the paper-based business cards. This study designed and evaluated CTUT_NameCard to digitalise and extract contact information with ease of use and accuracy. We designed the application based on Google Vision and Image Cropper. Inheriting the strength of Google Vision to recognise texts, we integrate several semantic algorithms to extract useful information, i.e. phone number, email address, and name. The application was evaluated in two experiments. The first experiment used the application to digitalise 170 business cards, while the second experiment analytically compared the applications with CamCard and ABBYY. The evaluation results have showed that the application met its design goals of digitalising and extracting contact information with high level of accuracy.

This study fulfils the need to digitalise and extract business card information. As seen via Table 1, the related research has addressed this need by designing BCR applications based on Mobile Vision, OpenCV and Tesseract [2, 9, 10]. We extend this stream of research by designing an BCR application based on Google Vision. Our work suggests that Google Vision is an important library for digitalising and extracting business card information.

Another contribution of the current study is its empirical evaluation. The evaluation on the dataset of 170 business cards has showed that the application has achieved high level of accuracy in digitalising and extracting contact information (88.4%). When positioning the empirical results within the related research, we note that the domain has a shortage of sample size in evaluating BCR applications (e.g. evaluating with less than 55 business cards [2, 6, 10]). This research addresses the above shortage and shows the evaluation results on a larger sample of 170 business cards.

From a practical viewpoint, the paper provides an Android BCR application for digitalising and extracting business card information. This BCR application has been starting used in practice. The comparative assessment has showed that the application performs as well as other commercial BCR applications (Table 6).

Our work presents several opportunities for future work. First, future work can improve our semantic algorithms in order to increase the levels of accuracy for extracting contact information, e.g. extracting names. Second, during our work, we note that many business cards use symbols for presenting information. For instance, the symbol ☎ indicates information of phone number. Consequently, our next version of the application targets to identify these symbols for increasing the ability of recognising and extracting information. Third, future work should also develop BCR application for multiple languages, like both English and Vietnamese [6]. Finally, while two experiments were conducted to test the application, they were conducted in the lab environment. Thus, future work should bring actual users into the experiments. Their feedbacks are really important to improve the application.

Acknowledgement. We would like to thank Phi Thi Ngoc Minh for helping us taking business card pictures and compare business card data and data extracted by the application.

References

1. Hing, V., Khoo, H.K.: Business card reader with augmented reality engine integration. In: Ibrahim, H., Iqbal, S., Teoh, S.S., Mustaffa, M.T. (eds.) 9th International Conference on Robotic, Vision, Signal Processing and Power Applications. LNEE, vol. 398, pp. 219–227. Springer, Singapore (2017). https://doi.org/10.1007/978-981-10-1721-6_24
2. Dangiwa, B.A., Kumar, S.S.: A business card reader application for iOS devices based on Tesseract. In: 2018 International Conference on Signal Processing and Information Security (ICSPIS). IEEE (2018)
3. Lin, L., Tan, C.L.: Text extraction from name cards using neural network. In: Proceedings of 2005 IEEE International Joint Conference on Neural Networks. IEEE (2005)
4. Madan Kumar, C., Brindha, M.: Text extraction from business cards and classification of extracted text into predefined classes. Int. J. Comput. Intell. IoT **2**(3), 595–602 (2019)
5. Mollah, A.F., et al.: Text/graphics separation for business card images for mobile devices. In: IAPR International Workshop on Graphics Recognition, pp. 263–270 (2009)
6. Hung, P.D., Linh, D.Q.: Implementing an android application for automatic Vietnamese business card recognition. Pattern Recogn. Image Anal. **29**(1), 156–166 (2019)
7. Mollah, A.F., Basu, S., Nasipuri, M.: Text detection from camera captured images using a novel fuzzy-based technique. In: 2012 Third International Conference on Emerging Applications of Information Technology. IEEE (2012)
8. Mollah, A.F., et al.: Text region extraction from business card images for mobile devices. In: Information Technology and Business Intelligence (2009)
9. Duy, N.: Xây dựng ứng dụng nhật diện danh thiếp trên Android. Can Tho University: in Vietnamese, Bachelor thesis (2017)
10. Đat, N.T.: Ứng dụng nhật diện danh thiếp tiếng Việt trên Android. Da Lat University: in Vietnamese (2018)
11. Google. Google Vision, 2017 Jun 2019. https://developers.google.com/android/reference/com/google/android/gms/vision/text/package-summary
12. Arthur. Android Image Cropper, 2016 June 2019. https://github.com/ArthurHub/Android-Image-Cropper
13. Hevner, A., Chatterjee, S.: Design Research in Information Systems: Theory and Practice. Integrated Series in Information Systems, vol. 22. Springer, Heidelberg (2010). https://doi.org/10.1007/978-1-4419-5653-8. Ed. R. Sharda and S. Voß
14. Hevner, A., et al.: Design science in information systems research. MIS Q. **28**(1), 75–105 (2004)
15. Thuan, N.H., Drechsler, A., Antunes, P.: Construction of design science research questions. Commun. Assoc. Inf. Syst. **44**(1), 332–363 (2019)
16. Saiga, H., et al.: An OCR system for business cards. In: Proceedings of 2nd International Conference on Document Analysis and Recognition (ICDAR 1993). IEEE (1993)
17. Luo, X.-P., Li, J., Zhen, L.-X.: Design and implementation of a card reader based on build-in camera. In: Proceedings of the 17th International Conference on Pattern Recognition (ICPR). IEEE (2004)

18. Holsapple, C.W.: DSS architecture and types. In: Burstein, F., Holsapple, C.W. (eds.) Handbook on Decision Support Systems 1, pp. 163–189. Springer, Heidelberg (2008). https://doi.org/10.1007/978-3-540-48713-5_9
19. Thuan, N.H.: Business Process Crowdsourcing: Concept, Ontology and Decision Support. Progress in IS. Springer, Heidelberg (2019). https://doi.org/10.1007/978-3-319-91391-9. Ed. C. Rauscher
20. Chandrasekhar, V., et al.: Dataset: Stanford Mobile Visual Search Dataset, V. Research Datasets for Image, and Multimedia Systems Group at Stanford, Editor. Stanford (2013)

Predicted Concentration TSS (Total Suspended Solids) Pollution for Water Quality at the Time: A Case Study of Tan Hiep Station in Dong Nai River

Cong Nhut Nguyen[(⊠)] [iD]

Faculty of Information Technology, Nguyen Tat Thanh University,
Ho Chi Minh City, Vietnam
ncnhut@ntt.edu.vn

Abstract. Water is essential for human life and socio-economic development. Water pollution is a concern for all mankind. In Vietnam, due to the development of factories and factories, water pollution has become more severe, including the Dong Nai River. In this article, the author uses the concentration of TSS at the Tan Hiep control station in Dong Nai River, using the Kriging interpolation method to find the appropriate model and give the results of water pollution prediction. Dong Nai river area over time with high reliability. TSS data were monitored continuously for three months (from the beginning of February 2018 to the end of April 2018), the predicted results using Kriging interpolation with high accuracy with regression coefficient equal to 1,005, the coefficient is 0.859 (the best value is 1), the forecast error is 2.258, the standard error is 0.044. It shows that using the Kriging interpolation method is an effective and suitable solution in mathematical problems with time information.

Keywords: Water pollution · Geostatistics · Kriging · Semivariogram

1 Introduction

Water pollution is an issue of social concern both in Vietnam in particular and the world in general. Water pollution caused by industrial factories increasingly degrades environments quality, leads to severe problems in health for local inhabitants. The building of water quality monitoring stations is also essential, but also difficult because of expensive installation costs, no good information of selected areas for installation in order to achieve precise results. According to the Center for Monitoring and Analysis Environment (Department of Natural Resources and Environment Binh Duong), automatic water quality monitoring network of Binh Duong province has 4 stations observation including Tan Hiep, Vinh Nguyen, Thu Dau Mot and Tan Uyen. The system continuously monitors daily with monitoring parameters such as TSS, pH, Nitrate, temperature and salinity. With a large area, the province needs to install more new monitoring stations. However, with the rapid development of industrial parks, the problem of environmental pollution, especially water pollution is a hot issue, the scarcity of clean water and polluted water leads to many diseases danger. Therefore, it is necessary to have a

© ICST Institute for Computer Sciences, Social Informatics and Telecommunications Engineering 2019
Published by Springer Nature Switzerland AG 2019. All Rights Reserved
P. C. Vinh and A. Rakib (Eds.): ICCASA 2019/ICTCC 2019, LNICST 298, pp. 237–246, 2019.
https://doi.org/10.1007/978-3-030-34365-1_19

mathematical model to predict whether the quality of water in a certain area is safe to use in the future? By using continuous monitoring data for 3 consecutive months (from February to April 2018, at Tan Hiep station), the author provides an appropriate mathematical model to predict water pollution in the following months.

Currently, there are a number of models predicting water pollution such as models QUAL2K, IPC model, ... Many water quality models were developed over the past years for various types of water bodies. QUAL2E water quality model developed during the earlier stages had many limitations. To overcome those limitations, QUAL2K was developed by Park and Lee in 2002 [1]. Model QUAL2K is a version of the model QUAL2E [2]. This model was developed due to the cooperation between Tufts University and the US Environmental Environment Center (US.EPA). The model is widely used to predict river water quality developments and predict the load of waste into rivers. IPC model developed by the World Bank, the World Health Organization and the US health organization. IPC model assesses river water quality, forecast changes in river water quality, calculates the amount to be cut by each source.

2   Materials and Methods

Dong Nai River is the longest inland river in Vietnam, the second largest in the South to the basin, just behind the Mekong River. The Dong Nai river flows through Lam Dong, Dak Nong, Binh Phuoc, Dong Nai, Binh Duong and Ho Chi Minh cities with a length of 586 km (364 miles) and a basin of 38,600 km^2 (14,910 mi2). If calculating from the beginning of the Da Dang river source, it is long 586 km. If calculating from the confluence point with Da Nhim river under Pongour waterfall, it is long 487 km. Dong Nai river flows into the East Sea in Can Gio district. 89 data were collected from Tan Hiep automatic water monitoring station on Dong Nai river, continuously monitored daily from February 1st, 2018 to April 31, 2018 (see Table 1).

Table 1. Pollution data of TSS water at Tan Hiep station.

Time	TSS (mg/l)	Time	TSS (mg/l)	Time	TSS (mg/l)
2/1/2018	21	3/1/2018	19	4/1/2018	24
2/2/2018	19	3/2/22018	16	4/2/2018	26
......	......	......	......	......	......
2/28/2018	15	3/28/2018	23	4/28/2018	30
		3/29/2018	19	4/29/2018	31
		3/30/2018	15	4/30/2018	37
		3/31/2018	20		

TSS parameters (turbidity and suspendid solids) are total suspended solids. Usually, it is measured with a turbidity meter (turbidimeter). Turbidity is caused by the interaction between light and suspended solids in water such as sand, clay, algae, microorganisms and organic matter in water. Suspended solids disperse light or absorb them and re-emit them in the manner depending on the size, shape and composition of suspended particles and thus allow application turbidity measuring devices to reflect the change in the type, size and concentration of the particles in the sample, etc. The author uses a geostatistical method to predict the concentration of TSS water pollution in the next time.

The main tool in geostatistics is the variogram which expresses the spatial dependence between neighbouring observations. The variogram $\gamma(h)$ can be defined as one-half the variance of the difference between the attribute values at all points separated by has followed [3, 8]

$$\gamma(h) = \frac{1}{2N(h)} \sum_{i=1}^{N(h)} [Z(s_i) - Z(s_i + h)]^2 \tag{1}$$

where $Z(s)$ indicates the magnitude of the variable, and $N(h)$ is the total number of pairs of attributes that are separated by a distance h.

Under the second-order stationary conditions [4, 9] one obtains

$$E[Z(s)] = \mu$$

and the covariance

$$Cov[Z(s), Z(s+h)] = E[(Z(s) - \mu)(Z(s+h) - \mu)] = E[Z(s)Z(s+h) - \mu^2] = C(h) \tag{2}$$

Then $\gamma(h) = \frac{1}{2}E[Z(s) - Z(s+h)]^2 = C(0) - C(h)$

The most commonly used models are spherical, exponential, Gaussian, and pure nugget effect [5, 8]. The adequacy and validity of the developed variogram model is tested satisfactorily by a technique called cross-validation.

Crossing plot of the estimate and the true value shows the correlation coefficient r^2. The most appropriate variogram was chosen based on the highest correlation coefficient by trial and error procedure.

Kriging technique is an exact interpolation estimator used to find the best linear unbiased estimate. The best linear unbiased estimator must have a minimum variance of estimation error. We used ordinary kriging for spatial and temporal analysis. Ordinary kriging method is mainly applied for datasets without and with a trend.

The general equation of linear kriging estimator is

$$\hat{Z}(s_0) = \sum_{i=1}^{n} w_i Z(s_i) \tag{3}$$

In order to achieve unbiased estimations in ordinary kriging the following set of equations should be solved simultaneously.

$$\begin{cases} \sum_{i=1}^{n} w_i \gamma(s_i, s_j) - \lambda = \gamma(s_0, s_i) \\ \sum_{i=1}^{n} w_i = 1 \end{cases} \tag{4}$$

where $\hat{Z}(s_0)$ is the kriged value at location s_0, $Z(s_i)$ is the known value at location s_i, w_i is the weight associated with the data, λ is the Lagrange multiplier, and $\gamma(s_i, s_j)$ is the value of variogram corresponding to a vector with origin in s_i and extremity in s_j.

Kriging minimizes the mean squared error of prediction

$$\min \sigma_e^2 = \mathbb{E}[Z(s_0) - \hat{Z}(s_0)]^2$$

For second order stationary process the last equation can be written as

$$\sigma_e^2 = C(0) - 2 \sum_{i=1}^n w_i C(s_0, s_i) + \sum_{i=1}^n \sum_{j=1}^n w_i w_j C(s_i, s_j) \text{ subject to } \sum_{i=1}^n w_i = 1 \quad (5)$$

Therefore the minimization problem can be written as

$$\min \left\{ C(0) - 2 \sum_{i=1}^n w_i C(s_0, s_i) + \sum_{i=1}^n \sum_{j=1}^n w_i w_j C(s_i, s_j) - 2\lambda \left(\sum_{i=1}^n w_i - 1 \right) \right\} \quad (6)$$

where λ is the Lagrange multiplier. After differentiating (6) with respect to w_1, w_2, ..., w_n, and λ and set the derivatives equal to zero we find that

$$\sum_{j=1}^n w_j C(s_i, s_j) - C(s_0, s_i) - \lambda = 0, \ i = 1, 2, \ldots, n \text{ and } \sum_{i=1}^n w_i = 1$$

Using matrix notation the previous system of equations can be written as

$$\begin{pmatrix} C(s_1, s_1) & C(s_1, s_2) & \cdots & C(s_1, s_n) & 1 \\ C(s_2, s_1) & C(s_2, s_2) & \cdots & C(s_2, s_n) & 1 \\ \vdots & \vdots & \ddots & \vdots & \vdots \\ C(s_n, s_1) & C(s_n, s_2) & \cdots & C(s_n, s_n) & 1 \\ 1 & 1 & \cdots & 1 & 0 \end{pmatrix} \begin{pmatrix} w_1 \\ w_2 \\ \vdots \\ w_n \\ -\lambda \end{pmatrix} = \begin{pmatrix} C(s_0, s_1) \\ C(s_0, s_2) \\ \vdots \\ C(s_0, s_n) \\ 1 \end{pmatrix}$$

Therefore the weights w_1, w_2, ..., w_n and the Lagrange multiplier λ can be obtained by

$$W = C^{-1} c$$

where $W = (w_1, w_2, \ldots, w_n, -\lambda)$

$$c = (C(s_0, s_1), C(s_0, s_2), \ldots, C(s_0, s_n), 1)'$$

$$
C = \begin{cases} C(s_i, s_j), & i = 1, 2, \ldots, n, \quad j = 1, 2, \ldots, n, \\ 1, & i = n+1, \qquad\ j = 1, 2, \ldots, n, \\ 1, & i = 1, 2, \ldots, n, \quad j = n+1, \\ 0, & i = n+1, \qquad\ j = n+1. \end{cases}
$$

The GS+ software (version 5.1.1) was used for geostatistical analysis in this study [6].

3   Results and Discussions

In order to check the anisotropy of TSS, the conventional approach is to compare variograms in several directions [7]. In this study major angles of $0°$, $45°$, $90°$, and $135°$ with an angle tolerance of $\pm45°$ were used for detecting anisotropy.

Figure 1 shows fitted variogram for spatial analysis of TSS. Gaussian model [Nugget = 6.5 (mg/l); Sill = 64 (mg/l); Range = 95 (mg/l); r^2 = 0.969, and RSS = 101]. It shows the best fitted omnidirectional variogram of water pollution obtained based on cross-validation. Through variogram map of parameter TSS, the model of isotropic is suitable. The variogram values are presented in Table 2.

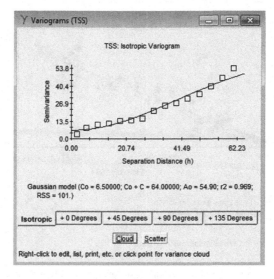

Fig. 1. Model of isotropic variogram for TSS parameters.

Table 2. Variogram values of TSS.

	Nugget	Sill	Range	r^2	RSS
Linear	0	46.75	60.79	0.951	152
Gaussian	6.5	64	95	0.969	101
Spherical	0.2	61.4	114	0.932	215
Exponetial	0.1	61.2	169.2	0.882	410

Residual Sums of Squares (RSS) provides an exact measure of how well the model fits the variogram data; the lower the reduced sums of squares, the better the model fits. When GS+ autofits the model, it uses RSS to choose parameters for each of the variogram models by determining the combination of parameter values that minimizes RSS for any given model. The Residual SS displayed in the This Fit box is calculated for the currently defined model.

r^2 provides an indication of how well the model fits the variogram data; this value is not as sensitive or robust as the Residual SS value for best-fit calculations; use RSS to judge the effect of changes in model parameters.

Model Testing: The reliable result of model selection using appropriate interpolation is expressed in Table 3 by coefficient of regression, coefficient of correlation and interpolated values, in addition to the error values as the standard error (SE) and the standard error prediction (SE Prediction) [10, 11].

Table 3. Testing the model parameters.

Coefficient regression	Coefficient correlation	SE	SE Prediction
1.005	0.859	0.044	2.258

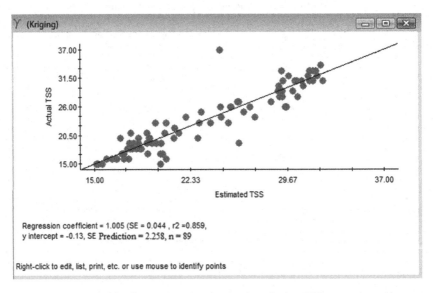

Fig. 2. Error testing result of prediction TSS.

Figure 2 shows the results of testing the error between the estimated value and the actual value by interpolation method kriging with isotropic TSS. The regression coefficient is 1.005, the correlation coefficient is close to 0.859 (the best result is 1), the standard error is 0.044 (close to 0) and the forecast error of 2.258 shows the choice of Kriging interpolation model in accordance with the set data in Fig. 3.

Cross Validation (Kriging) a)

Record	X-Coordinate	Y-Coordinate	Actual Z	Estimated Z	Error (E-A)
1	1.00	1.00	24.00	27.18	3.18
2	2.00	2.00	26.00	26.78	0.78
3	3.00	3.00	28.00	29.05	1.05
4	4.00	4.00	33.00	29.21	-3.79
5	5.00	5.00	31.00	31.32	0.32
6	6.00	6.00	32.00	29.71	-2.29
7	7.00	7.00	28.00	30.44	2.44
8	8.00	8.00	29.00	29.23	0.23
9	9.00	9.00	29.00	30.03	1.03
10	10.00	10.00	31.00	30.19	-0.81
11	11.00	11.00	31.00	31.58	0.58
12	12.00	12.00	33.00	31.35	-1.65
13	13.00	13.00	32.00	31.92	-0.08
14	14.00	14.00	31.00	32.35	1.35
15	15.00	15.00	33.00	31.36	-1.64
16	16.00	16.00	32.00	31.22	-0.78
17	17.00	17.00	31.00	29.29	-1.71
18	18.00	18.00	26.00	29.46	3.46
19	19.00	19.00	27.00	28.39	1.39
20	20.00	20.00	29.00	28.95	-0.05
21	21.00	21.00	30.00	30.83	0.83
22	22.00	22.00	33.00	31.61	-1.39
23	23.00	23.00	34.00	32.20	-1.80
24	24.00	24.00	33.00	31.81	-1.19
25	25.00	25.00	31.00	30.39	-0.61
26	26.00	26.00	28.00	29.24	1.24
27	27.00	27.00	26.00	29.55	3.55
28	28.00	28.00	30.00	28.99	-1.01
29	29.00	29.00	31.00	30.74	-0.26
30	30.00	30.00	37.00	24.48	-12.52
31	31.00	31.00	19.00	25.93	6.93
32	32.00	32.00	16.00	20.48	4.48
33	33.00	33.00	17.00	19.07	2.07

Cross Validation (Kriging) b)

Record	X-Coordinate	Y-Coordinate	Actual Z	Estimated Z	Error (E-A)
34	34.00	34.00	20.00	19.18	-0.82
35	35.00	35.00	21.00	20.33	-0.67
36	36.00	36.00	21.00	21.44	0.44
37	37.00	37.00	23.00	20.43	-2.57
38	38.00	38.00	20.00	21.02	1.02
39	39.00	39.00	20.00	19.22	-0.78
40	40.00	40.00	17.00	20.18	3.18
41	41.00	41.00	21.00	17.79	-3.21
42	42.00	42.00	17.00	20.05	3.05
43	43.00	43.00	19.00	20.11	1.11
44	44.00	44.00	22.00	21.09	-0.91
45	45.00	45.00	23.00	22.94	-0.06
46	46.00	46.00	25.00	23.13	-1.87
47	47.00	47.00	23.00	25.14	2.14
48	48.00	48.00	26.00	24.57	-1.43
49	49.00	49.00	26.00	25.36	-0.64
50	50.00	50.00	25.00	26.31	1.31
51	51.00	51.00	27.00	25.86	-1.14
52	52.00	52.00	27.00	25.94	-1.06
53	53.00	53.00	26.00	25.28	-0.72
54	54.00	54.00	24.00	24.60	0.60
55	55.00	55.00	23.00	23.81	0.81
56	56.00	56.00	24.00	21.93	-2.07
57	57.00	57.00	20.00	22.84	2.84
58	58.00	58.00	23.00	19.66	-3.34
59	59.00	59.00	19.00	19.41	0.41
60	60.00	60.00	15.00	20.01	5.01
61	61.00	61.00	20.00	18.38	-1.62
62	62.00	62.00	21.00	19.03	-1.97
63	63.00	63.00	19.00	19.72	0.72
64	64.00	64.00	19.00	19.03	0.03
65	65.00	65.00	19.00	18.40	-0.60
66	66.00	66.00	18.00	17.91	-0.09

Cross Validation (Kriging) c)

Record	X-Coordinate	Y-Coordinate	Actual Z	Estimated Z	Error (E-A)
67	67.00	67.00	17.00	17.15	0.15
68	68.00	68.00	16.00	16.70	0.70
69	69.00	69.00	16.00	16.34	0.34
70	70.00	70.00	16.00	16.71	0.71
71	71.00	71.00	17.00	17.11	0.11
72	72.00	72.00	18.00	17.73	-0.27
73	73.00	73.00	19.00	17.71	-1.29
74	74.00	74.00	18.00	17.75	-0.25
75	75.00	75.00	17.00	17.25	0.25
76	76.00	76.00	16.00	17.27	1.27
77	77.00	77.00	17.00	17.18	0.18
78	78.00	78.00	18.00	17.50	-0.50
79	79.00	79.00	18.00	18.22	0.22
80	80.00	80.00	19.00	17.98	-1.02
81	81.00	81.00	18.00	18.47	0.47
82	82.00	82.00	18.00	18.57	0.57
83	83.00	83.00	20.00	16.99	-3.01
84	84.00	84.00	16.00	17.63	1.63
85	85.00	85.00	16.00	15.95	-0.05
86	86.00	86.00	15.00	15.63	0.63
87	87.00	87.00	15.00	15.18	0.18
88	88.00	88.00	15.00	15.10	0.10
89	89.00	89.00	15.00	15.29	0.29

Fig. 3. Cross-Validation (Kriging) (a), (b) và (c) của TSS.

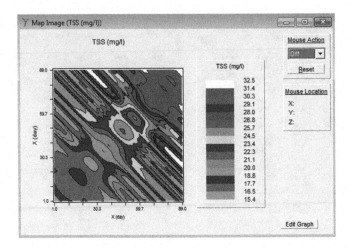

Fig. 4. Kriging interpolation for TSS parameters in 2 dimensions.

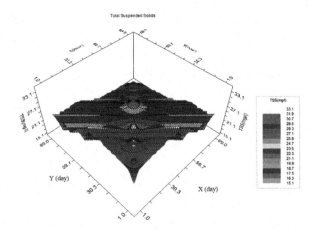

Fig. 5. Kriging interpolation for TSS parameters in 3 dimensions.

From Figs. 4 and 5 we see that from February to April (from 1 to 89 days), in February there is the lowest concentration of TSS and gradually increases to April this is also consistent with the fact because February is the dry season and April is the beginning of the rainy season, so TSS increases. The X-axis and Y-axis represent the number of days (starting from February 1st, 2018 to April 30, 2018, which means 89 days. Based on Figs. 4 and 5, we can predict the TSS contamination concentration in next month (May) and offer remedial solutions.

The application of geotechnical methods mentioned to predict the concentration of TSS pollution at Tan Hiep station shows that the forecast results are small errors as shown in Fig. 2. Through this forecast study, methods and tissues are used. Based on interpolation, we can predict the level of TSS pollution levels for the following months without monitoring data, thus suggesting measures to improve and protect the environment.

From the forecast map, we find that the forecast gives the best results in the 89 days period, outside of this time the forecast results may be inaccurate. The more time the pollutant observes, the easier it is to select interpolation models, with higher interpolation results and vice versa. Different colors show different levels of pollution. The lowest level of pollution is blue and the highest is white. Areas of the same color have the same level of pollution. The results of the model still have this error, which may be due to many other factors affecting TSS parameters such as salinity, temperature, nitrate content, water flow ... This is the first article the author uses the method. Kriging interpolation to predict water pollution over time.

4   Results and Discussions

The statistical applications for predicting TSS concentrations in rivers at the Tan Hiep monitoring station have resulted in small errors between estimated values and real values (standard errors equal to 0.044 and projected errors reported by 2.258). Since then, the study has shown the effectiveness and rationality with the high reliability of geostatistics to build appropriate predictive models. When building the model, author should pay attention to the error values of the model, the data characteristics of the object. Author also consider the results of the model selection in order to select the most suitable model for the actual data, because separate models provide different accuracy. Therefore, the experience of selecting models also plays a very important role in interpolation results. Finally a comparison of the proposed method with several other methods can be made as follows. Polygon (nearest neighbor) method has advantages such as easy to use, quick calculation in 2D; but also possesses many disadvantages as discontinuous estimates; edge effects/sensitive to boundaries; difficult to realize in 3D. The Triangulation method has advantages as easy to understand, fast calculations in 2D; can be done manually, but few disadvantages are triangulation network is not unique. The use of Delaunay triangles is an effort to work with a "standard" set of triangles, not useful for extrapolation and difficult to implement in 3D. Local sample mean has advantages are easy to understand; easy to calculate in both 2D and 3D and fast; but disadvantages possibly are local neighborhood definition is not unique, location of sample is not used except to define local neighborhood, sensitive to data clustering at data locations. This method does not always return answer valuable. This method is rarely used. Similarly, the inverse distance method are easy to understand and implement, allow changing exponent adds some flexibility to method's adaptation to different estimation problems. This method can handle anisotropy; but disadvantages are difficulties encountered when point to estimate coincides with data point ($d = 0$, weight is undefined), susceptible to clustering.

This paper, QUAL2K is not suitable, because QUAL2K has been used to predict pollution on the river section and it has not been applied to the forecast of pollution over time.

Acknowledgment. The paper's author expresses his sincere thank to Dr. Man N.V. Minh Department of Mathematics, Faculty of Science, Mahidol University, Thai Lan and Dr. Dung Ta Quoc Faculty of Geology and Petroleum Engineering, Vietnam. Furthermore, author greatly appreciate the anonymous reviewer whose valuable and helpful comments led to significant improvements from the original to the final version of the article.

References

1. Park, S.S., Lee, Y.S.: A water quality modeling study of the Nakdong River, Korea. Ecol. Model. **152**(1), 65–75 (2002)
2. Ashwani, S., Vivek, B., Ratnoji, S., Jayakumar, P., Jainet, P.J.: Application of Qual2K model for prediction of water quality in a selected stretch of Pamba River. Int. J. Civil Eng. Technol. (IJCIET) **8**(6), 75–84 (2017)
3. Ahmadi, S.H., Sedghamiz, A.: Geostatistical analysis of spatial and temporal variations of groundwater level. Environ. Monit. Assess. **129**, 277–294 (2007)
4. Webster, R., Oliver, M.A.: Geostatistics for Enviromental Scientists, 2nd edn, pp. 6–8. Wiley, Chichester (2007)
5. Isaaks, E., Srivastava, M.R.: An Introduction to Applied Geostatistics. Oxford University Press, New York (1989)
6. Gamma Design Software: GS+ Geostatistics for the Environmental Science. Gamma Design Software, LLC, Plainwell (2001). version 5.1.1
7. Goovaerts, P.: Geostatistics for Natural Resources Evaluation. Oxford University Press, New York (1997)
8. Kitadinis, P.K.: Introduction to Geostatistics: Applications to Hydrogeology. Cambridge University Press, Cambridge (2003)
9. Gentile, M., Courbin, F., Meylan, G.: Interpolating point spread function anisotropy. Astron. Astrophys. **549**, A1 (2012). manuscript no. psf'interpolation
10. Nhut, N.C., Nguyen, M.V.M.: Analyzing incomplete spatial data in air pollution prediction. J. SE-Asian J. Sci. **6**(2), 111–133 (2018). ISSN 2286–7724
11. Nhut, N.C.: Metropolitan air pollution prediction: A case study using PM10 data observed in Ho Chi Minh City. Báo cáo tại Hội nghị Khoa học Công Nghệ, Đại học Hoa Sen (2016)

Applying Geostatistics to Predict Dissolvent Oxygen (DO) in Water on the Rivers in Ho Chi Minh City

Cong Nhut Nguyen[✉] [iD]

Faculty of Information Technology, Nguyen Tat Thanh University,
Ho Chi Minh City, Vietnam
ncnhut@ntt.edu.vn

Abstract. Geostatistics is briefly concerned with estimation and prediction for spatially continuous phenomena, using data measured at a finite number of spatial locations to estimate values of interest at unmeasured locations. In practice, the costs of installing new observational stations to observe metropolitan water pollution sources, as DO (Dissolvent Oxygen), COD (Chemical Oxygen Demand) and BOD (Biochemical oxygen Demand) concentrations are economically high. In this study, spatial analysis of water pollution of 32 stations monitored during 3 years was carried out. Geostatistics which has been introduced as a management and decision tool by many researchers has been applied to reveal the spatial structure of water pollution fluctuation. In this article, author use the recorded DO concentrations (is the amount of dissolvent oxygen in water required for the respiration of aquatic organisms) at several observational stations on the rivers in Ho Chi Minh City (HCMC), employ the Kriging interpolation method to find suitable models, then predict DO concentrations at some unmeasured stations in the city. Our key contribution is finding good statistical models by several criteria, then fitting those models with high precision. From the data set, author found the best forecast model with the smallest forecast error to predict DO concentration on rivers in Ho Chi Minh City. From there we propose to the authorities to improve areas where DO concentrations exceed permissible levels.

Keywords: Geostatistics · Interpolation · Kriging · Spatial · Variogram

1 Introduction

Water pollution is an issue of social concern both in Vietnam in particular and the world in general. Water pollution caused by industrial factories increasingly degrades environments quality, leads to severe problems in health for local inhabitants. The building of water quality monitoring stations is also essential, but also difficult because of expensive installation costs, no good information of selected areas for installation in order to achieve precise results. According to the Center for Monitoring and Analysis Environment (Department of Natural Resources and Environment HCMC), network quality monitoring water environment of HCMC has 32 stations observation on water in the rivers in HCMC. However, with a large area, the city needs to install more new monitoring stations. The cost to install a new machine costs tens of billions VND, and

© ICST Institute for Computer Sciences, Social Informatics and Telecommunications Engineering 2019
Published by Springer Nature Switzerland AG 2019. All Rights Reserved
P. C. Vinh and A. Rakib (Eds.): ICCASA 2019/ICTCC 2019, LNICST 298, pp. 247–257, 2019.
https://doi.org/10.1007/978-3-030-34365-1_20

the maintenance is also difficult. Therefore, the requirements are based on the remaining monitoring stations using mathematical models based to predict air pollution concentration at some unmeasured stations in the city.

Sources of water pollution are diverse. Many industrial zones, industrial plants and urban areas have discharged untreated wastewater to rivers and lakes which has polluted water sources severely. As a result, water sources in many areas cannot be used. Socio-economic development in each river basin is different and the contribution of pollutants to the environment from different sectors also varies. However, the pressure of waste water mainly comes from industrial and domestic activities. Waste water discharged from industrial establishments and industrial zones exerts the greatest pressure on the surface water environment in the country. Agriculture is the largest user of water, mainly for the irrigation of rice and other water intensive crops. Consequently, waste water discharged by agricultural activities into surface water makes up the largest proportion. Quantity of pollutants from untreated urban waste water. There is an increasing demand for running water in urban areas to meet the need of population growth and the development of urban services. Currently, most cities do not have a treatment system for domestic waste water. In those cities which have this system, the rate of treated waste water is much lower than required. Untreated domestic waste water from residential and tourism areas and discharged by small industrial and handicraft establishments are the major cause of pollution to water sources within cities and their outskirts.

The study area is HCMC in South of Vietnam. It is located between $10°10'$–$10°38'$ northing and $106°22'$–$106°54'$ easting and the area has more than 2096 km^2 (2018). HCMC has more than 9 million people (2018). Figure 1 shows the study area. The city has a tropical climate, specifically a tropical wet and dry climate, with an average humidity of 78–82%. The average temperature is 28 °C (82 °F) (degrees Fahrenheit).

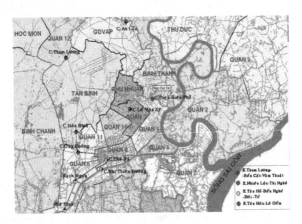

Fig. 1. Location of the study area[a]. a. Department of natural resources and environment HCMC.

With the rapid population growth rate, the infrastructure has not yet been fully upgraded, and some people are too aware of environmental protection. So, HCMC is currently facing a huge environmental pollution problem. The status of untreated wastewater flowing directly into the river system is very common. Many production facilities, hospitals and health facilities that do not have a wastewater treatment system are alarming. Figure 2 shows the geographical location of the monitoring stations. The coordinates system used in Fig. 2 is Universal Transverse Mercator (UTM).

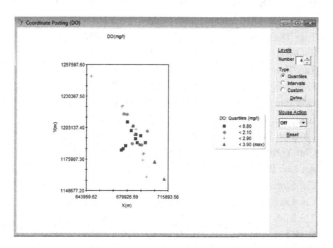

Fig. 2. Map of water quality monitoring stations in HCMC.

2 Materials and Methods

Dissolved oxygen (DO) refers to the level of free, non-compound oxygen present in water or other liquids. It is an important parameter in assessing water quality because of its influence on the organisms living within a body of water. In limnology (the study of lakes), dissolved oxygen is an essential factor second only to water itself. A dissolved oxygen level that is too high or too low can harm aquatic life and affect water quality. The dataset is obtained from monitoring stations in the rivers HCMC with these parameter DO. Figure 2 shows map of water quality monitoring stations in HCMC. DO data of water environment measures 32 stations from 2015 to 2017, (see Table 1). Author applied a geostatistical method to predict concentrations of air pollution at unobserved areas surrounding observed ones.

The main tool in geostatistics is the variogram which expresses the spatial dependence between neighbouring observations. The variogram $\gamma(h)$ can be defined as one-half the variance of the difference between the attribute values at all points separated by has followed [1, 6]

Table 1. DO data of water quality monitoring stations in HCMC.

Station	x(m)	y(m)	DO (mg/l)
Ba Son	687020.74	1193517.41	0.60
Den Do Apex	692372.50	1188205.59	2.10
Cat Lai Pier	695674.23	1190158.06	3.40
Rach Chiec-Sai Gon	691502.97	1196219.97	0.80
Phu Dinh Port	676558.28	1184762.57	0.20
Binh Khanh Ferry	693943.68	1180318.17	2.80
VCD-Binh Dien Bridge	674736.35	1183824.89	0.20
Tam Thon Hiep	704119.33	1173806.02	3.10
Soai Rap River	693691.06	1175042.20	2.30
Tan Thuan Port	688506.94	1190249.21	0.80
Phu Long Bridge	685004.43	1204724.99	1.50
Hoa Phu Pump station	676867.55	1215207.46	1.80
Bridge Binh Trieu	687447.50	1197076.03	0.70
Lo Gom Bridge	678772.16	1187429.76	0.70
Chu Y Bridge	684059.70	1189290.14	0.90
An Loc Bridge	683576.38	1200370.94	0.70
Cai Stream	697408.50	1200142.76	1.10
Cat Lai	695671.18	1190161.11	0.70
Thi Tinh River	675253.16	1221229.09	2.20
Binh Loi Bridge	686955.30	1197608.09	3.70
Phu My	690858.99	1188710.28	3.00
Rach Tra	680156.73	1207934.77	0.70
Trung An	676079.87	1222198.63	2.20
Phu Cuong	679609.36	1214736.71	1.70
Hao Phu	677250.67	1215117.32	1.30
Phu Long	685004.36	1204737.28	3.20
Tam Thon Hiep	704291.61	1173475.08	3.70
Vam Co	712393.56	1158677.20	3.90
Binh Phuoc	687747.10	1201605.25	2.90
Vam Sat	696879.34	1160493.97	2.50
Nha Be	694496.87	1180871.54	2.20

$$\gamma(h) = \frac{1}{2N(h)} \sum_{i=1}^{N(h)} [Z(s_i) - Z(s_i + h)]^2 \qquad (1)$$

where $Z(s)$ indicates the magnitude of the variable, and $N(h)$ is the total number of pairs of attributes that are separated by a distance h.

Under the second-order stationary conditions [2, 7] one obtains

$$E[Z(s)] = \mu$$

and the covariance

$$Cov[Z(s), Z(s+h)] = E[(Z(s) - \mu)(Z(s+h) - \mu)] = E[Z(s)Z(s+h) - \mu^2] = C(h) \tag{2}$$

Then $\gamma(h) = \frac{1}{2}E[Z(s) - Z(s+h)]^2 = C(0) - C(h)$

The most commonly used models are spherical, exponential, Gaussian, and pure nugget effect [3, 6]. The adequacy and validity of the developed variogram model is tested satisfactorily by a technique called cross-validation.

Crossing plot of the estimate and the true value shows the correlation coefficient r^2. The most appropriate variogram was chosen based on the highest correlation coefficient by trial and error procedure.

Kriging technique is an exact interpolation estimator used to find the best linear unbiased estimate. The best linear unbiased estimator must have a minimum variance of estimation error. Author used ordinary kriging for spatial and temporal analysis. Ordinary kriging method is mainly applied for datasets without and with a trend.

The general equation of linear kriging estimator is

$$\hat{Z}(s_0) = \sum_{i=1}^{n} w_i Z(s_i) \tag{3}$$

In order to achieve unbiased estimations in ordinary kriging the following set of equations should be solved simultaneously.

$$\begin{cases} \sum_{i=1}^{n} w_i \gamma(s_i, s_j) - \lambda = \gamma(s_0, s_i) \\ \sum_{i=1}^{n} w_i = 1 \end{cases} \tag{4}$$

where $\hat{Z}(s_0)$ is the kriged value at location s_0, $Z(s_i)$ is the known value at location s_i, w_i is the weight associated with the data, λ is the Lagrange multiplier, and $\gamma(s_i, s_j)$ is the value of variogram corresponding to a vector with origin in s_i and extremity in s_j.

Kriging minimizes the mean squared error of prediction

$$\min \sigma_e^2 = \mathbb{E}[Z(s_0) - \hat{Z}(s_0)]^2$$

For second order stationary process the last equation can be written as

$$\sigma_e^2 = C(0) - 2 \sum_{i=1}^{n} w_i C(s_0, s_i) + \sum_{i=1}^{n} \sum_{j=1}^{n} w_i w_j C(s_i, s_j) \text{ subject to } \sum_{i=1}^{n} w_i = 1 \tag{5}$$

Therefore the minimization problem can be written as

$$\min\left\{C(0) - 2\sum_{i=1}^{n} w_i C(s_0, s_i) + \sum_{i=1}^{n}\sum_{j=1}^{n} w_i w_j C(s_i, s_j) - 2\lambda(\sum_{i=1}^{n} w_i - 1)\right\} \quad (6)$$

where λ is the Lagrange multiplier. After differentiating (6) with respect to $w_1, w_2, \ldots, w_n$, and λ and set the derivatives equal to zero we find that

$$\sum_{j=1}^{n} w_j C(s_i, s_j) - C(s_0, s_i) - \lambda = 0, \ i = 1, 2, \ldots, n \text{ and } \sum_{i=1}^{n} w_i = 1$$

Using matrix notation the previous system of equations can be written as

$$\begin{pmatrix} C(s_1, s_1) & C(s_1, s_2) & \cdots & C(s_1, s_n) & 1 \\ C(s_2, s_1) & C(s_2, s_2) & \cdots & C(s_2, s_n) & 1 \\ \vdots & \vdots & \ddots & \vdots & \vdots \\ C(s_n, s_1) & C(s_n, s_2) & \cdots & C(s_n, s_n) & 1 \\ 1 & 1 & \cdots & 1 & 0 \end{pmatrix} \begin{pmatrix} w_1 \\ w_2 \\ \vdots \\ w_n \\ -\lambda \end{pmatrix} = \begin{pmatrix} C(s_0, s_1) \\ C(s_0, s_2) \\ \vdots \\ C(s_0, s_n) \\ 1 \end{pmatrix}$$

Therefore the weights $w_1, w_2, \ldots, w_n$ and the Lagrange multiplier λ can be obtained by

$$W = C^{-1}c$$

where $W = (w_1, w_2, \ldots, w_n, -\lambda)$

$$c = (C(s_0, s_1), C(s_0, s_2), \ldots, C(s_0, s_n), 1)'$$

$$C = \begin{cases} C(s_i, s_j), & i = 1, 2, \ldots, n, \quad j = 1, 2, \ldots, n, \\ 1, & i = n+1, \quad\quad\ j = 1, 2, \ldots, n, \\ 1, & i = 1, 2, \ldots, n, \quad j = n+1, \\ 0, & i = n+1, \quad\quad\ j = n+1. \end{cases}$$

The GS+ software (version 5.1.1) was used for geostatistical analysis in this study [4].

3   Results and Discussions

In order to check the anisotropy of TSS, the conventional approach is to compare variograms in several directions [5]. In this study major angles of $0°$, $45°$, $90°$, and $135°$ with an angle tolerance of $\pm 45°$ were used for detecting anisotropy.

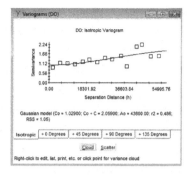

Fig. 3. Fitted variogram for the spatial analysis of parameter DO.

Figure 3 shows fitted variogram for spatial analysis of DO. Gaussian model [Nugget = 0.1 (mg/l); Sill = 2 (mg/l); Range = 75864 (mg/l); r^2 = 0.486]. It shows the best fitted omnidirectional variogram of water pollution obtained based on cross-validation. Through variogram map of parameter DO, the model of isotropic is suitable. The variogram values are presented in Table 2.

Table 2. Isotropic variogram values of DO.

	Nugget	Sill	Range	r^2	RSS
Linear	0.9	1.8	53583	0.485	1.05
Gaussian	1	2	75864	0.486	1.05
Spherical	0.22	1.421	4500	0.136	1.77
Exponential	0.883	2.471	201600	0.484	1.06

Residual Sums of Squares (RSS) provides an exact measure of how well the model fits the variogram data; the lower the reduced sums of squares, the better the model fits. When GS+ autofits the model, it uses RSS to choose parameters for each of the variogram models by determining the combination of parameter values that minimizes RSS for any given model. The Residual SS displayed in the This Fit box is calculated for the currently defined model.

r^2 provides an indication of how well the model fits the variogram data; this value is not as sensitive or robust as the Residual SS value for best-fit calculations; use RSS to judge the effect of changes in model parameters.

Model Testing: The reliable result of model selection using appropriate interpolation is expressed in Table 3 by coefficient of regression, coefficient of correlation and interpolated values, in addition to the error values as the standard error (SE) and the standard error prediction (SE Prediction).

Table 3. Testing the model parameters.

Coefficient regression	Coefficient correlation	SE	SE Prediction
0.936	0.205	0.336	1.001

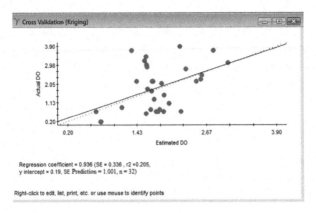

Fig. 4. Error testing result of prediction DO.

Figure 4 shows results of testing of error between real values and the estimated values by the model by cokriging method with isotropic DO. Coefficients of regression are close to 1, where the error values is small (close to 0) indicates that the selected model is a suitable interpolation in Fig. 5.

Record	X-Coordinate	Y-Coordinate	Actual Z	Estimated Z	Error (E-A)
1	687020.74	1193517.41	0.60	1.59	0.99
2	692372.50	1188205.59	2.10	1.87	-0.23
3	695674.23	1190158.06	3.40	1.59	-1.81
4	691502.97	1196219.97	0.80	1.82	1.02
5	676558.26	1184762.57	0.20	0.77	0.57
6	683943.68	1160318.17	2.80	2.29	-0.51
7	674736.35	1183824.89	0.20	0.79	0.59
8	704119.33	1173806.02	3.10	3.04	-0.06
9	693691.06	1175042.20	2.30	2.56	0.26
10	688506.94	1190249.21	0.80	1.67	0.87
11	685004.43	1204724.99	1.50	1.91	0.41
12	676887.55	1215207.46	1.80	1.61	-0.19
13	687447.50	1197076.03	0.70	1.78	1.08
14	878772.16	1187429.76	0.70	0.70	-0.00
15	884059.70	1189290.14	0.90	1.16	0.26
16	683576.38	1200370.94	0.70	1.80	1.10
17	697408.50	1200142.76	1.10	1.99	0.89
18	695671.18	1190161.11	0.70	2.21	1.51
19	675253.16	1221229.09	2.20	1.70	-0.50
20	686955.30	1197608.09	3.70	1.33	-2.37
21	690858.99	1168710.28	3.00	1.60	-1.40
22	680156.73	1207934.77	0.70	1.90	1.20
23	676079.87	1222198.63	2.20	1.72	-0.48
24	679609.36	1214736.71	1.70	1.69	-0.01
25	677250.67	1215117.32	1.30	1.73	0.43
26	685004.36	1204737.28	3.20	1.56	-1.64
27	704291.61	1173475.08	3.70	2.78	-0.92
28	712393.56	1158677.20	3.90	2.19	-1.71
29	687747.10	1201605.25	2.90	1.61	-1.29
30	698879.34	1160493.97	2.50	2.58	0.08
31	694496.87	1180871.54	2.20	2.48	0.28
32	647959.62	1247597.60	2.20	1.43	-0.77

Fig. 5. Cross-Validation (Kriging) of DO.

From Figs. 6 and 7, we see that, from 2015 to 2017 at Phu Dinh Port and Vam Co Dong - Binh Dien Bridge neighborhood has low pollution levels. Neighborhood of Vam Co have high pollution levels. The Sai Gon river basin extends through many provinces and is strongly impacted by different pollution sources. The major pollution sources derive from industrial activities. The surface water in sections which run through provinces in the southern key socio-economic area where many industrial zones and towns are located is badly polluted. Saigon River begins to be polluted by organic matter and microorganisms from the Thi Tinh river estuary and the pollution increases in its lower section. The section crossing Ho Chi Minh City is particularly affected by organic matter. The content of BOD_5, COD and bioorganisms all fail to meet the standards set for surface water as a source to supply drinking water.

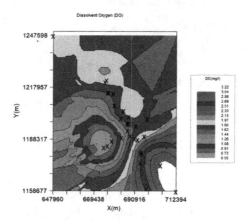

Fig. 6. 2D Cokriging Interpolation Map of DO.

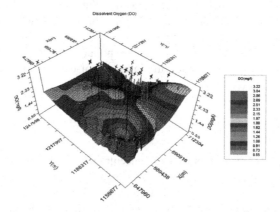

Fig. 7. 3D Cokriging Interpolation Map of DO.

Based on the map, we can also predict the water pollution concentration in the city near the air monitoring locations and to offer solutions to overcome. The mentioned method of applied geostatistics to predict the water pollution concentrations DO on the rivers in HCMC showed that the forecast regions closer together have the forecast deviations as small Fig. 8, meanwhile further areas contribute the higher deviation. Through this forecast case study using spatial interpolation based methods and models, we can predict air pollution levels for regions that have not been installed air monitoring sites, from which proposed measures to improve the air quality can be taken into account. If the density of monitoring stations is high and the selection of interpolation models is easier, interpolation results have higher reliability and vice versa.

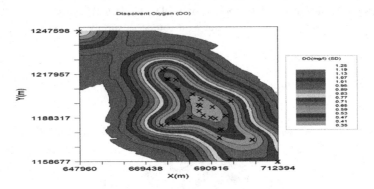

Fig. 8. Estimated error by Cokriging method of DO.

From the forecast maps, we see that, forecast for the region's best results in areas affected 88921 m, located outside the affected region on the forecast results can be inaccurate. If the density of monitoring stations is high and the selection of interpolation models is easier, interpolation results have higher reliability and vice versa. The middle area represents key outcomes of computation on data. The different colors represent different levels of pollution. The lowest pollution level is blue and the highest is white. Regions having the same color likely are in the same levels of pollution.

Limitations of the article: The forecast results of the model also have errors due to other DO pollutants in the water also have other pollutants such as BOD_5, COD, TSS, ... So in the future, author will study the influence of other pollutants on the DO to reduce the error in the forecast.

4   Conclusion

Geostatistical applications to predict DO concentrations on the rivers in HCMC gave the result with almost no error difference between the estimated values and the real values. Therefrom, the study showed that efficacy and rationality with high reliability of theoretical Geostatistical to building spatial prediction models are suitable. When building the model we should pay attention to the values of the model error, data characteristic of the object. We also looked at the result of the model selection which aimed to choose the most suitable model for real facts, since distinct models provide different accuracies. Therefore, experiencing the selected model also plays a very important role in the interpolation results.

Finally a comparison of the proposed method with several other methods can be made as follows. Polygon (nearest neighbor) method has advantages such as easy to use, quick calculation in 2D; but also possesses many disadvantages as discontinuous estimates; edge effects/sensitive to boundaries; difficult to realize in 3D. The Triangulation method has advantages as easy to understand, fast calculations in 2D; can be done manually, but few disadvantages are triangulation network is not unique. The use of Delaunay triangles is an effort to work with a "standard" set of triangles, not useful for extrapolation and difficult to implement in 3D. Local sample mean has advantages are easy to understand; easy to calculate in both 2D and 3D and fast; but disadvantages possibly are local neighborhood definition is not unique, location of sample is not used except to define local neighborhood, sensitive to data clustering at data locations. This method does not always return answer valuable. This method is rarely used. Similarly, the inverse distance method are easy to understand and implement, allow changing exponent adds some flexibility to method's adaptation to different estimation problems. This method can handle anisotropy; but disadvantages are difficulties encountered when point to estimate coincides with data point ($d = 0$, weight is undefined), susceptible to clustering.

In Vietnam, the modelling methods used the more common, especially in the current conditions of our country. The tangled diffusion model of Berliand and Sutton was used by Anh Pham Thi Viet to assess the environmental status of the atmosphere of Hanoi in 2001 by industrial discharges [8]. In 2014, Yen Doan Thi Hai has used models Meti-lis to calculate the emission of air pollutants from traffic and industrial activities in Thai Nguyen city [9].

Acknowledgment. The paper's author expresses his sincere thank to Dr. Man N.V. Minh Department of Mathematics, Faculty of Science, Mahidol University, Thai Lan and Dr. Dung Ta Quoc Faculty of Geology and Petroleum Engineering, Vietnam. Furthermore, author greatly appreciate the anonymous reviewer whose valuable and helpful comments led to significant improvements from the original to the final version of the article.

References

1. Ahmadi, S.H., Sedghamiz, A.: Geostatistical analysis of spatial and temporal variations of groundwater level. Environ. Monit. Assess. **129**, 277–294 (2007)
2. Webster, R., Oliver, M.A.: Geostatistics for Enviromental Scientists, 2nd edn, pp. 6–8. Wiley, Chichester (2007)
3. Isaaks, E., Srivastava, M.R.: An Introduction to Applied Geostatistics. Oxford University Press, New York (1989)
4. Gamma Design Software: GS+ Geostatistics for the Environmental Science. Gamma Design Software, LLC, Plainwell (2001)
5. Goovaerts, P.: Geostatistics for Natural Resources Evaluation. Oxford University Press, New York (1997)
6. Kitadinis, P.K.: Introduction to Geostatistics: Applications to Hydrogeology. Cambridge University Press, Cambridge (2003)
7. Gentile, M., Courbin, F., Meylan, G.: Interpolating point spread function anisotropy. Astron. Astrophys. **549**, A1 (2012). manuscript no. psf interpolation
8. Anh, P.T.V.: Application of airborne pollutant emission models in assessing the current state of the air environment in Hanoi area caused by industrial sources. In: 6th Women's Science Conference, Ha Noi national university, pp. 8–17 (2001)
9. Yen, D.T.H.: Applying the Meti-lis model to calculate the emission of air pollutants from traffic and industrial activities in Thai Nguyen city, orienting to 2020. J. Sci. Technol. **106**(6) (2013).Thai Nguyen university

Author Index

Printed in the United States
By Bookmasters